A Theatre *for* Women's Voices

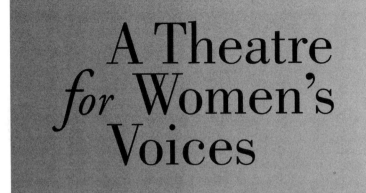

A Theatre *for* Women's Voices

Plays & History from the Women's Project at *25*

Edited by
Julia Miles

Introduction by
Alexis Greene

Assistant Editors
Suzanne Bennett and
Karen Keagle

Photographs by Martha Holmes
(unless otherwise noted)

HEINEMANN
Portsmouth, NH

Heinemann
A division of Reed Elsevier Inc.
361 Hanover Street, Portsmouth, NH 03801–3912
www.heinemanndrama.com

Offices and agents throughout the world

Library of Congress Cataloging-in-Publication Data
A theatre for women's voices : plays and history from the Women's
Project at 25 / edited by Julia Miles; assistant editors, Suzanne Bennett and Karen
Keagle ; photographs by Martha Holmes unless otherwise noted.
    p. cm.
  Includes bibliographical references.
  ISBN 0-325-00557-5 (alk. paper)
    1. American drama—Women authors. 2. American drama—20th century.
3. Feminist drama. 4. Women—Drama. I. Miles, Julia. II. Women's Project
(New York, N.Y.).

  PS628.W6 T49 2003
  812'.540809287—dc21   2002153292

Editor: Lisa Barnett
Production: Lynne Reed
Cover design: Joni Doherty
Typesetter: Drawing Board Studios
Manufacturing: Steve Bernier

Printed in the United States of America on acid-free paper
07 06 05 04 03 DA 1 2 3 4 5

Dedicated to
María Irene Fornés and all the women in the Women's Project

Contents

Julia Miles, Women's Project & Productions Founder and
Artistic Director, 2002. Photo © by Martha Holmes.

Preface:
A Sampler of Twenty-Five Years

With the six plays in this volume and Alexis Greene's history, we offer a sampling of work from our twenty-five years of producing plays written by women. The plays were chosen from some anthologies that are no longer in print and from our more recently produced plays.

In *Little Victories*, Lavonne Mueller places Susan B. Anthony and Joan of Arc together on stage because they both lived, died, and triumphed in a world of men without knowing their fame. Caroline Kava and Linda Hunt found the individuality of Susan and Joan while finding their commonality in their characters' passion and commitment.

A . . . My Name Is Alice is a musical compiled by Joan Micklin Silver and Julianne Boyd with over twenty-five women and men writers. One of the lyrics written by David Zippel for the "All-Girl Band" spoke to many of us: "I was trapped in the doubt of my life." We gave up trying to be perfect at everything in our lives and became not perfect, but good at many things. The wonderfully talented cast—Mary Gordon Murray, Alaina Reed, Charlaine Woodard, Randy Graff, and Roo Brown—all went on to have illustrious careers in the theatre.

For me, María Irene Fornés, as in the children's game, "stands alone." She's "The Cheese!" My association with Irene began at the American Place Theatre when Wynn Handman and I produced *Fefu and Her Friends*. *Abingdon Square* was a Women's Project production on the American Place stage and featured the talented actors Madeleine Potter and John Seitz, who created the complex relationship between the older man and his discontent younger wife.

Etta Jenks by Marlane Gomard Meyer is one of those scripts that you read and want to produce immediately because of its gutsiness. The play exposes those women who get lost in Hollywood mythology. As portrayed by Deirdre O'Connell in our co-production here and in L.A., Etta survives in a hard-core male industry and manages to retain some humanity. With an edgy, compelling production directed by Roberta Levitow, the play launched the career of Marlene Meyer.

The Exact Center of the Universe by Joan Vail Thorne was directed by John Tillinger with the estimable Frances Sternhagen in the lead. Set in Joan's Louisiana home territory, which she knows well, the play tells the story of a

Southern mother who learns, with a little help from her friends, to accept and finally love her adored only son's wife.

Saint Lucy's Eyes by Bridgette Wimberly takes place in Memphis in 1968 against a backdrop of the garbage worker strikes and King's assassination. A young girl "in trouble" has to go to "Grandma" to have an abortion. Years later the young woman, now a lawyer, repays the favor to "Grandma" by defending her. Bridgette captures an historical moment with the story of a very particular woman powerfully portrayed by Ruby Dee.

All of these plays received memorable productions that, of course, were expensive and I am deeply grateful to the Ford Foundation who gave us our first grant in 1978. They have continued to support us over the years, including helping to finance this book.

As I think about the work of our theatre over these twenty-five years, I know it could not have flourished without an excellent and supportive Board of Trustees, initially chaired by Pat Schoenfeld for two long terms, and now by Tina Chen, and a hardworking, devoted staff. Our many talented playwrights are the foundation of the theatre and one of them, Sallie Bingham, put her financial support where her heart is, and gave generously over the years. In our twenty-fifth season, we are pleased to name our theatre for her.

Julia Miles, Artistic Director
January 2003

Introduction: Making a Theatre for Women's Voices

by Alexis Greene

IT BEGAN WITH A WOMAN.

Julia Hinson grew up in Pelham, Georgia, a one-street town in the southwestern corner of the state, not far from the Florida line. Her parents, John Cornelius and Saro Priscilla Jones Hinson, owned a tobacco and cotton farm, and Julia was the second of their three children.

She left Pelham to spend the last two years of high school at Brenau Academy in Gainesville, Georgia. She wanted to act and her beloved Aunt Grace, who had gone to New York City years earlier to be in musical theatre, encouraged Julia to study at Northwestern University in Evanston, Illinois. The day she was graduated, she married a writer and actor named William Miles, and they came to New York.

Like many young actors who came to New York in the 1950s, Julia Miles took classes with Lee Strasberg of the Actors Studio. Strasberg did not mind that the petite, black-haired woman with the strong profile brought her infant daughter, Stacey, to the audition. There was no one else to look after the baby, and in that era before day care centers, no place to leave her. Ultimately Strasberg only cared about the work. "I remember her doing Desdemona," said Billie Allen, an actor and director who later became a stalwart member of the Women's Project board. "She did the Willow Song like a Southern Baptist hymn, and it was very deep and very moving. I think she would have gone on to be an extraordinary actor if she had stuck with it."

But Miles hated the business of acting: cattle calls, auditions, slogging from one agent's office to another with résumés and eight-by-ten glossy photographs in hand. "I found it so discouraging and frightening and horrifying," she told Nadine Honigberg during an interview for the Winter 1985 issue of *Theater*. "You were just the least important person in the world, and even when you had a job nobody cared what you thought. . . . You really had no control over anything."

"Acting is first about selling," she said years later. "And I'm not good at that."

1

In 1956, Miles gave birth to a second daughter, Lisa, but in 1958 her marriage ended. About that time she banded together with three women who, like herself, were tending young children, looking for work, and preferred to work for themselves if they could. Miles did not give up performing, but she delved into a side of theatre that gave her more autonomy and control: producing.

An actor and close friend named Sally Weeks lived in Brooklyn Heights near St. Ann's Church. There Miles, Weeks, Terry Trilling, and Jan Henry formed Theatre Current: Brooklyn's Only Professional Resident Company, presenting everything from Irish author Edna O'Brien to the Wakefield Mystery Plays of fifteenth-century England. Then around 1961, a friend of Miles', a lawyer and producer named Samuel C. Cohn, brought her what she considered "a wild and marvelous" play by an innovative dramatist and teacher, Arnold Weinstein. Titled *Red Eye of Love*, this irreverent satire mingled a love triangle with the history of the United States, symbolized by a department store that sells only meat and rises fifty stories. Budgeting stringently, Theatre Current produced it for $1,207.72.

Theatre critics were intrigued, and Cohn and his friend John Wulp, a designer, photographer, and self-proclaimed director, brought the play into Manhattan. Miles acted a small role, understudied the lead, was associate producer, and managed the production, which opened in June at the Living Theatre's space on Sixth Avenue and 14th Street. "I never knew about managing," Miles said, "but once you decide to do something, you just do it." Suffering from migraines, she would lie on a mattress in the theatre until she felt able to work again. "She had a hard time of it," recalled Wulp, who became a good friend. The acclaimed production soon moved to the more visible Provincetown Playhouse.

Miles warmed to producing as she never had to acting. In late 1961, Wulp, Cohn, Weinstein, and the composer Frances Thorne leased the Maidman Playhouse on West 42nd Street for a year to produce new writers in general and Weinstein in particular, and Miles became their associate producer. Unfortunately, the group was less successful this time out. In January 1962, the critics loathed Weinstein's musical *Fortuna*. In March, they had little praise for *Three by Three*—an evening of brief comedies that included Weinstein's *The Twenty-Five Cent White Cap*, *George Washington Crossing the Delaware* by the poet Kenneth Koch, and Elaine May's *Not Enough Rope* about a woman who tries to hang herself to attract her male neighbor's attention. Reviewers thought *Rope* the best of the trio by far. Richard Watts Jr. of the *New York Post* wrote condescendingly that "the distaff member of the brilliant satirical team of Nichols and May revealed a promising gift for humorous writing."

That August, Miles and Cohn were married.

Off Broadway was thriving at the beginning of the 1960s. Still, productions were largely commercial. Not-for-profit stages were few and often specialized in the European avant-garde or revivals of classics.

But in the early sixties, a director and acting teacher named Wynn Handman and an actor named Michael Tolan conceived of a not-for-profit theatre devoted to cultivating and producing new American plays. With help from the Reverend Sidney Lanier, they obtained free space at St. Clement's Church on 46th Street between 9th and 10th Avenues, and started the American Place Theatre with Handman as artistic director. Spurred by a generous grant from the Ford Foundation, in 1964 the American Place opened its first production: poet Robert Lowell's lyrical trilogy, *The Old Glory*.

Jonathan Miller was rehearsing *The Old Glory* on the day Miles walked up the dark wood stairs to St. Clement's scruffy proscenium theatre. By now, Miles and Cohn, who was becoming an influential agent, were living on the Upper West Side with their new baby, Marya, and Miles' two daughters. For the first time since coming to New York, Miles was not looking for a paying job, nor did she have to stay at home with her children, and she wanted to reconnect with theatre. She had attended services at St. Clement's on occasion and knew Lanier, and he suggested volunteering at the American Place.

She watched the rehearsal of *Old Glory*, and when Miller took a break, he walked back to where she was sitting and asked what she thought. Surprised and delighted, she complimented the production and in that moment decided to work there. When Handman first saw Miles, as he liked to tell for years afterward, she was "sitting in a corner" collating sheets for a brochure and "hardly said anything."

Miles did not remain in the corner. She became the assistant to the general manager, then general manager, and by 1971 when the American Place moved to new housing in an office building at 46th Street and Sixth Avenue, Miles was the associate director.

"Julia was a very capable manager," said Handman. "I felt that she was a really wonderful partner. For one thing, her aesthetic judgments and taste were very harmonious with mine. She was fully involved in the work and supportive of it. I thought we were an excellent team."

Miles evaluated her progress at the American Place straightforwardly. "I guess this is a woman's thing," she said, "but I've always been ready to do the work. That's probably been the secret of my success. Which is not very admirable. I see something and want to get it accomplished. I just do it."

Miles arrived at the American Place shortly before the 1960s exploded into cultural, political, and sexual rebellion. Out of that contention and change arose a largely white, middle-class, women's movement, which yearned to correct the inequities and throw off the restraints that had saddled American women at least since the end of World War II.

In the American theatre, women began to notice the nationwide scarcity of female playwrights and directors. An organization called Action for Women in Theatre, which had been started by two young directors named

Nancy Rhodes and Carole Rothman, surveyed employment for female playwrights and directors in the professional not-for-profit theatre from 1969 to 1976. The results were disturbing: only 7 percent of the plays produced were written by women, only 6 percent were directed by women. Despite a spurt in women writing for off-off Broadway during the 1960s and early 1970s, few women had breached the walls of mainstream not-for-profit theatres. Few had written plays for the militant—and sexist—Black Arts Movement of the 1960s.

During the late 1970s, the situation seemed to improve. In New York, a handful of prominent theatres dipped into the pool of women who were writing plays. At the New York Shakespeare Festival in 1976, Joseph Papp produced Ntozake Shange's riveting choreopoem, *for colored girls who have considered suicide/when the rainbow is enuf*. The following year, the Phoenix Theatre staged Wendy Wasserstein's bittersweet look at women's attitudes about success and failure, *Uncommon Women and Others*, and in 1978, the American Place plucked *Fefu and Her Friends*, María Irene Fornés' groundbreaking feminist drama, from off-off Broadway and produced it.

But overall, the list was short. Indeed at the American Place, male playwrights considerably outnumbered female playwrights. From 1964 through 1977, the American Place presented fifty-seven main-stage productions; five were of plays by women. "It's not that the American Place was prejudiced against women," Miles said around the time she started the Women's Project. "We weren't getting the scripts."

A vision is born of many sources.

The Women's Movement heightened Miles' awareness that the American theatre was not paying attention to its women. As she later explained to Honigberg at *Theater*, "So many women were becoming lawyers and doctors and everything else, that I thought: what is this—the theatre is behind."

Action for Women's (un)employment survey landed on Miles' desk. She saw *Fefu and Her Friends* at New York Theatre Strategy in 1977 and responded viscerally to a truly woman-centered piece.

"Julia started to talk about how we ought to do something about getting plays from women," Handman recalled. "I said, 'We do get plays from women. We've done plays by women.' She said, 'Yes, but those are established and known playwrights. We're not getting plays written by women no one's ever heard of. If we had something here that women knew was for them, then we'd get more plays.'"

"I wanted to start something that would address the problem," she said simply.

Around that time, the Ford Foundation was funding initiatives that focused on women in the arts. Miles and Handman met with Gayle Counts, an assistant program officer at Ford, and Miles floated her idea for a women's project at the American Place. On April 8, 1978, she and Handman sent a two-page letter to Counts, describing a plan to develop "American women playwrights and directors." Quoting the poet Anne Sexton, they cited a need for " . . . a community, a family for my art." On July 1, with $80,000 for one year, Ford funded what became known as the Women's Project.

Miles' instinct had been as true as an arrow homing on its target: When women had their own theatre, they sent plays. "Once we got the word out that there was a place—a home—for women playwrights," she said, "we began to get five to six hundred scripts."

Gayle Austin, who had been Handman's assistant, became a co-administrator of the Project, with a director named Caymichael Patten and a young actor named Kathleen Chalfant. The three women got the word out, read scripts, set up readings. There was no time for philosophizing about feminism or even for mulling the Project's aims. "It wasn't really about grand thoughts," remembered Austin, who later became a theatre professor and feminist critic. With Miles, action was paramount. "It was very much a pragmatic, get the next play up kind of thing," said Austin.

Get plays up they did. There were twenty rehearsed readings and seven staged readings during 1978–79, a schedule that energized the Project's enthusiastic staff and stretched the limits of the American Place. Handman's theatre had three below-ground performance spaces, and the Project's readings generally took place in the one called the Subplot—an open area that resembled an extended hallway more than a room. If the American Place was using the Subplot, the Project held its Monday night readings in a basement room under the main stage, or anyplace else that no one was using for about three hours.

"We were making it up as we went along," Kathleen Chalfant remembered, "trying to have two organizations fit into the time and space of one."

"We knew we were doing a spring festival," said Austin. "That's why there were so many readings—to look for plays for production. We knew what readings were; we didn't know what doing twenty of them in one year would be like. I poured a lot of wine."

Audiences, largely women, crowded to hear the plays and voice their thoughts during the discussions, which Miles led with the playwright and director. Playwrights hung around afterward, talking and networking. "There really hadn't been a place where women playwrights could come together in any numbers and be acknowledged," said Austin. "The gratitude, the water-on-the-desert-flower thing, was amazing."

At the American Place, Miles would give her opinion about a play, but Handman decided whether to produce. Now Miles herself was choosing plays. "The search is to find the script that, in some elusive way, interests one," she

Kathleen Chalfant at the Women's Project & Productions 24th Women of Achievement Awards Gala, 2002. Photo © by Martha Holmes.

told Honigberg. "It's like falling in love. How do you fall in love? One person picks another person; it's a process which is almost indescribable."

That first year, Miles selected four studio productions: *Choices*, a one-woman vehicle created by journalist Patricia Bosworth, Caymichael Patten, and the actor Lily Lodge; *Signs of Life* by Joan Schenkar; Lavonne Mueller's *Warriors From a Long Childhood*; and *Letters Home* by Rose Leiman Goldemberg. The Project mounted *Choices* in November and December of 1978, and the other three between late May and the end of June 1979.

The plays embraced a gamut of forms and subjects. They were realistic and metaphorical, about private themes and public issues, involving both men and women, lesbian love, and the love between a mother and her inspired but suicidal daughter. *Choices* was a compilation of the thoughts and memories of female poets, essayists, and novelists. *Warriors From a Long Childhood* dramatized the physical and psychological strain of four soldiers in a prison camp at the end of the Korean War. Lavonne Mueller recalled worrying that, "This was an unusual play for the Women's Project. But Julia was not scared away. She called me in DeKalb, Illinois, where I was living, and offered me a reading. Critics said they thought the play was written by a man. Many people were surprised that a woman could write a play with an all-male cast; even women would come up to me and say, `How did you write that?' I could only respond: We are married to men, we have brothers and fathers. Why wouldn't a woman be able to write about men!"

The plays had sprung from their authors violently and tenderly and personally. Schenkar described *Signs of Life*, which starred a brilliant Kathleen Chalfant as Alice James, "as an extremely urgent play." Writing about its emergence, she recalled:

> "An actor . . . had given me Frederick Treves' account of the Elephant Man, and I had already been enthralled by a gorgeous book on American male attitudes toward women in the nineteenth century, *The Horrors of the Half-Known Life*, which introduced me to that master medical criminal Dr. J. Marion Simms, America's first gynecologist. I began to imagine what would happen if an Elephant *Woman* were introduced to a Dr. Simms-like character—a character who became the suave and sinister Dr. Sloper of *Signs of Life*. Henry James very soon joined the cast, along with his complicated sister Alice, her lover Katherine Loring and an alcoholic P.T. Barnum, and I gleefully abandoned a Ph.D. dissertation on fathers and daughters in the works of Henry James to write the play. In retrospect, I think *Signs of Life* was a kind of dramatic history of the nineteenth-century American mind, written by a twentieth-century playwright with a very metaphorical imagination. The play was released in me the moment I found its form: that menacing and repetitive recurrence to a tea table with Dr. Sloper and Henry James toasting the health of each other and their "victims" in increasingly suspicious liquids.

One summer in the mid-1970s, Rose Leiman Goldemberg read the poet Sylvia Plath's autobiographical collection of correspondence, *Letters Home*. "I was a mother and a daughter," Goldemberg said, "and this was about a mother and daughter who were very famous, and I had always related to them. It was a tragedy that both women had tried to avoid. I saw a play in it."

In 1978, Goldemberg met with Miles to discuss a play about immigrants and ended up talking about *Letters Home* instead. "Julia asked, `What are you doing, what are you writing, and would you like to develop it here at the Women's Project?' I was very pleased; it was good to have a home." To play Sylvia Plath, Miles suggested Mary McDonnell, whose acting she greatly admired; Goldemberg recommended Doris Belack for Plath's mother, Aurelia.

Miles offered space, time, little money. "We went into rehearsal, which was trial and error," said Goldemberg. "I would bring stuff in, and the actors would perform it, and sometimes it would work and sometimes it wouldn't. From what they did, I carved the play, but all the material came from the book. It was in a sense editing, but I was trying to tell the story that I believed was true, of what had really happened."

Staged by Dorothy Silver in the Subplot, *Letters Home* provoked such intense feeling in audiences, and so much attention in the press, that Handman decided to open the main stage with it in the fall of 1979. Eventually the play would be produced all over the world. The Women's Project had already fulfilled one of its aims: to bring the plays of women into the mainstream.

There were contentious moments that first year. Directors and playwrights chafed under the lean budgets, unaware, it seems certain, that Miles was budgeting tightly to pay them even for readings. For Joan Schenkar, the political stance of the Women's Project was too cautious. "It seemed to be dipping only its little finger into the daintier droplets of the great radical wave that was the Women's Movement in 1979," she said. But Schenkar added, "There was the incontrovertible fact that Julia Miles was almost the only producer in New York City who actually recognized the need for a place where women's work could be developed."

The birth of the Women's Project (WP) had been spontaneous and joyous. Its first decade would be both creative and frustrating.

Doris Belack and Mary McDonnell in *Letters Home* by Rose Leiman Goldemberg, 1978. Photo © by Martha Holmes.

*—The problem with playwriting, which makes it one of the
most difficult forms, is that the entire performance value of the story must
live so entirely on the stage of the writer's mind. Conversation imagined is
one thing, conversation dramatized is another. I call this the conceptual
loneliness of playwriting—that vacuum between imagination and performance that must be filled again and again if the playwright is to come to
grips with the nature of [her] craft.*

—Kathleen Collins

Over the next three years, the Ford Foundation gave the Women's Project
$137,000, which Miles supplemented by raising money from other sources.
The WP continued to present a gargantuan number of rehearsed readings. As
in the first season, WP taped the readings and audience discussions for the
playwright, then about a week later Miles and Gayle Austin, who in effect became WP's first literary manager, met with the writer to talk about the script.
Each season, Miles continued to select two or three of these scripts to produce.

To develop writers and plays charged Miles' spirit. "New plays. The first
time. It's like other first times," she said twenty-five years after founding the
Women's Project. "It's the most interesting. It gives you the most possibilities
of fulfilling the script. It also challenges you. No matter how many plays
you've produced, the first time is always a new time, because the play is different and the actors are different and the director is different, and your hopes
are high."

Miles often felt particularly drawn to a writer's first effort. "Sometimes
the first plays are the best, from both men and women, because it's the thing
they are most bursting to share with the world," she said.

First plays and productions, themes not usually associated in the public
mind with female writers, fresh perspectives on women's rights in the contemporary world—all this became part of WP's theatrical vocabulary. In 1980,
Miles invited Emily Mann to direct the New York premiere of *Still Life*, Mann's
ruthlessly honest drama of the Vietnam War based on private testimonies
from a soldier and two women in his life. During the 1981–82 season, in a co-
production with Maine's Portland Stage Company, the Woman's Project presented Paula Cizmar's *The Death of a Miner*—a cinematic drama that explored
the life and death of a woman striving to exist in coal mining's male-
dominated culture. And in the early 1980s, Billie Allen introduced Miles to the
work of Kathleen Collins, a filmmaker and teacher whom Allen had met at the
Frank Silvera Writers Workshop.

"Kathleen wrote informed, sensitive black women," said Allen, "and
wrote from the upper-middle-class black perspective. I hate to use that phrase,
but up until that time, we usually had plays about poverty, ghetto, living, and
kill whitey—what white men had done to us and look how badly off we are.

Then this young woman comes along and she's writing about these very different people."

Collins, who died of breast cancer in 1988 at 46, had written a play about four brothers, most of whom are disappointed in their lives. The twist to *The Brothers* is that the audience never meets the men, but learns about them through their funny, stylish, angry wives, a mother-in-law, and one adoring sister. To the public, the Edwards men may be dignified and capable, but to the women who have wasted their own lives taking care of them, they are weak, overbearing, and often cruel.

"Kathleen was lyrical in her writing," said Allen. "She paints it. You feel colors when you read Kathleen: violets and yellows. You feel textures."

Miles produced *The Brothers* in the Subplot in March 1982. This was only Collins' second play, and the first to be staged professionally. She would sit in on rehearsals, writing furiously. "The writing would create so much noise on the paper," said Allen, "and I'd say, `Kathleen, you can't do that, because the actors become very intimidated.' She'd say, `I'm just writing notes.' And I'd say, `But you must write gently.' We got through that."

Collins wrote Miles a letter later that spring:

> In a sense, when I think of you, and of the Theatre, it is with a great feeling of comfort. Its presence, the fact that I can take a play to you at a stage when I can no longer bear to have it dead-end in my mind, then hear it read, and *feel* it from a performance perspective, brings me a level of comfort, a way of distancing myself that bridges some of the loneliness. It also makes me bolder. I say to myself, well, let's try this, then when I hear it read I'll see if it works. And finally, it has allowed me to recognize and accept that the writing of a play is only one stage, but that its shaping, its editing, its final form, is a collaborative process.

The collaborative process reached its zenith in 1983 with *A . . . My Name Is Alice*, a jaunty revue conceived and directed by Joan Micklin Silver and Julianne Boyd, which both celebrated and satirized the Women's Movement.

Miles, ever the magician when it came to securing grants, raised money to support a workshop. In the fall of 1983, Boyd, Silver, five actors—Roo Brown, Randy Graff, Mary Gordon Murray, Charlaine Woodard, and Alaina Reed—and twenty-eight writers found themselves toiling in the American Place basement, where, said Boyd, there was "no air, fluorescent lights. But the excitement was unbelievable."

Reviewers were invited for the second workshop in February 1984 (also in the cellar). The material and the performers overcame their surroundings, and all but the most die-hard feminist critics adored the show. A producer transferred the revue to the Top of the Gate in Greenwich Village, making *Alice* the first production in WP's history to move directly to a commercial venue.

In the early 1980s, the Women's Project started to focus more intently on women who wanted to direct.

From the beginning, Miles knew that female directors had a difficult time finding jobs in America's male-run professional theatre. "We interviewed a million directors for *Letters Home*," said Rose Leiman Goldemberg, "and every woman we talked to hardly had any experience except what she had created for herself."

In 1980, the director Susan Lehman prepared a report for the Women's Project, "Women Directing in Theatre: A Study to Investigate the Hiring Patterns of Women Directors." She found the situation abysmal. "Enough women haven't achieved a great deal of success directing," said Miles at the time, "for people to want to give women that traditional male role of leader of the whole shebang, which a director is."

Julianne Boyd was one woman who had led the whole shebang, for in 1978 she had staged the Broadway musical *Eubie!* "I was the only woman directing on Broadway," said Boyd. "There were no role models. Women directors did not have a place to try out their work. So over the years, one of the things that I and others encouraged Julia to do was match up women directors with women playwrights."

Miles was planning a festival of one-act plays for the end of the 1983–84 season and, realizing that it might be difficult to find enough skilled female directors, and that "the more women helping playwrights get their work on, the better," she asked the Ford Foundation to support a training program for directors, which was to start in December 1983. Ford gave $60,000 over a seven-month period, and the Directors Forum emerged.

Elinor Renfield, who had directed at notable off-Broadway and regional theatres, ran the program. Monday-night sessions got the thirty-five directors on their feet, working on scenes and conceptual presentations. At other times, the meetings simply allowed them to ventilate. "It was an opportunity," said Renfield, "for women who were beginning to make their mark or aspiring to, to talk about ideas, politics, about what theatres seemed more accepting of women than others. But more importantly, to try to learn about what in each of our sensibilities was motivating us to direct." The Forum's inaugural year ended with "Special Family Things: A Festival of Six One-Act Plays."

Ford continued to support the Forum during the springs of 1985 and 1986. In 1985, JoAnne Akalaitis and Emily Mann joined Renfield to give four-session workshops. Akalaitis concentrated on the avant-garde ("The thing I'm least interested in is couple psychology," she announced). Mann focused on classics ("Works that work," as she put it), and Renfield on psychological realism. The third year culminated in a spring series of one-acts that brought the Forum's directors and the Women's Project playwrights together to create plays on the theme "Women Heroes." By that time, Renfield had left—among other things, she was directing Shirley Lauro's *Open Admissions* on Broadway. Miles and Suzanne Bennett, a professor of theatre who had joined the

Women's Project as literary manager in the fall of 1984, shepherded *Women Heroes: In Praise of Exceptional Women* to production.

As Bennett noted in the spring 1986 issue of *Dialogues,* the WP newsletter that she started and edited, one might have expected the playwrights to dramatize the lives of such legendary females as Florence Nightingale, Marie Curie, and Harriet Tubman. But the playwrights proved more inventive.

Fueled perhaps by the desire to bring to light women whom historians had neglected, the dramatists emerged with less familiar names. *Parallax*, written and directed by Denise Hamilton, focused on Daisy Bates, a civil rights activist in Little Rock, Arkansas. In *How She Played the Game*, Cindy Cooper told the stories of the athletes Gertrude Ederle, Babe Didrickson, Althea Gibson, and Gretel Bergmann. "I didn't know much about women sports figures of the past," said Cooper; "Women athletes weren't hailed in the feminist writings, and they weren't included in sports writing either. But I didn't want to tell about one woman, I wanted a mosaic that showed women who were willing to pursue their abilities even in the face of disapproval and discouragement." The play later received more than a hundred productions in the United States and Europe.

Over the years the Directors Forum evolved and changed. After a hiatus while the Women's Project separated from the American Place, the Forum resumed in 1988 under the direction of Melanie Joseph. In 1991–92, Liz Diamond ran the program, and in 1992–93, Susanna Tubert. Bennett took over in 1994. Each woman left the imprint of her personality and style, but in general the program became smaller; members remained for several years and they received more guidance with practical skills.

"We have sessions on pitching a project," explained Bennett. "Sessions on fund-raising. A fight director does a workshop on staging fights. Actors come in, and the directors have open rehearsals. People share rehearsal techniques." In 1999, Bennett and Lisa McNulty, who was literary manager from 1997 to 2000, initiated a day-long retreat for the directors and the members of the Playwrights Lab so that these artists could meet and work together.

"I think that directing is a very impossible role," said Elinor Renfield. "When you have the idea in your heart that it's something you can do and when you are in your late twenties and there hasn't been a map, it's very helpful to create the map together. And that is what the Women's Project did."

✦ ✦ ✦

—We are now in the midst of a strange place in the Women's Movement.
"Is the Movement dead?" asks a fund-raising appeal for the Women's
Campaign fund. Should there be an art museum for women artists only?
Clearly, for some, the Women's Movement is on hold in the late 1980s . . .

—Julia Miles, *Dialogues*, Spring 1987

Change was palpable. The Women's Movement, so vibrant in the 1970s, had suffered real and philosophical set-backs. The combined impact of conservative Republican administrations; the new political power of the religious right; and, ironically, women's own achievements in the marketplace had undercut feminism. Political and cultural reactionaries derided feminists for wanting to emasculate men and masculinize themselves, while many women, riding a wave of economic attainment, seemed to have forgotten how they got there. In 1979, Joan Schenkar was concerned that the Women's Project was not politically radical; in 1984, women sat in the Directors Forum and questioned whether they should even belong to an organization that specialized in women's art for fear the connection would prevent them from being hired by male (and female) producers. Miles found herself saying that she really wanted the Women's Project to become extinct one day because everyone would have found jobs.

As change occurred in the outside world, the Women's Project reevaluated its place in the universe of theatre. Among the situations to be reassessed was whether it should remain at the American Place.

Miles had told Honigberg that, "the best thing about having the Women's Project at the American Place Theatre is that it adds weight and credibility. Most women's theatres are regarded as fringe or experimental. The American Place gives validity to the plays by placing them within the mainstream of an Off-Broadway establishment."

But what had seemed like a good marriage was showing strain. Miles was doing two jobs. She was associate director of the American Place and director of the Women's Project, and there was no question which role she preferred.

If being a program of the American Place gave the Women's Project a roof, in Miles' view it also restricted the WP's artistic independence. "We haven't been able to create as unique an organization as I might have liked since we are part of an established Off-Broadway theatre," she said. "It was a trade-off. You buy respectability and you trade the opportunity to be more experimental."

And then there was money. Like a wife who depends on her husband for income, the Women's Project was largely tethered by the funds the American Place allotted her. The American Place's budget was around $900,000 in the mid-1980s, of which only 15 to 20 percent, or about $135,000, went to the Women's Project. Miles did a great deal of the fund-raising. When it opened in

1964, the American Place largely stood alone as a not-for-profit theatre developing new American plays. Since then, it had received lively competition from The Public Theater/New York Shakespeare Festival, Playwrights Horizons and Manhattan Theatre Club, among others, and grants and audience subscriptions had fallen drastically.

The solution to the Project's dilemma came from a writer and arts patron named Sallie Bingham. A member of the family that had owned and published the *Louisville Courier* for several generations, Bingham was mainly writing short stories when, in the mid-1970s, she turned to theatre. The result was *Milk of Paradise*, a delicate memory play about a Southern girl who essentially is raised by her rich parents' African American servants. The Women's Project gave the play a rehearsed reading during its first season and produced the drama the following year.

Since then, Bingham and Miles had become friends, and Miles was always the first person to whom Bingham sent her plays. "I really trust her instinct," said Bingham. "And she's tough. She has no problem telling me this is just not working. I remember during *Paducah*, in the spring of 1985, the director and I were getting frantic about this actress who could not learn her lines, and I asked Julia to sit down and talk to me. I said, 'You know, she's destroying the production.' And Julia said to me in a steely voice, 'You mean there's nothing wrong with this play?' I was horribly taken aback, but I really valued her for that. She's very courageous and she wasn't going to let me off the hook. I went home and cried probably."

Around the time that the Project was getting restless, the Bingham family was selling its newspaper company, and Sallie Bingham decided to use the money she received from the sale to support women in the arts. "Over the generations that the family had owned this company," said Bingham, "many women had toiled there, usually in the lower ranks, and it made sense to me to put that money back into women's work."

"It seemed natural," she added, "that if I was going to have this windfall, that she in whom I had so much faith would get an amount of money that would allow her to cut loose from the American Place, because I was aware that she was pinched there. She couldn't really expand and do what she wanted to do."

In September 1986, Bingham's Kentucky Foundation for Women gave the Women's Project $1 million over five years on the condition that the Project incorporate separately from the American Place.

Miles quietly contemplated this gift of longed-for independence for some time. Finally, with encouragement from her friend Pat Schoenfeld, she formed a seventeen-member board with Schoenfeld as chairperson and called the new organization Women's Project & Productions (WPP). Schoenfeld, a ceramicist and a founder of the International Center of Photography whom Miles said "could talk anybody into anything," would head the board for ten years.

But if Miles thought that the American Place would easily accept this new, well-funded entity in its midst, she was being disingenuous. At first, she did not want WPP to separate physically from the American Place. After all, it had been home to the Women's Project for nearly a decade, and Miles' theatrical home for longer than that. Emotional meetings took place, but Handman and Miles could not agree on how to allocate financial resources and space. In October 1987, when WPP produced María Irene Fornés' fine new play *Abingdon Square* on the main stage—a production that the American Place was offering

María Irene Fornés teaching playwriting at The Women's Project, 2000. Photo © by Martha Holmes.

—Change, a necessary part of life, is hard—at least for me. There are so
many consequences. The status quo is known and safe. But when I finally
decide, it is quick and I don't look back. . . . Sometimes, you must leave
home to grow, never mind your age!
—Julia Miles, Dialogues, Winter 1987

To celebrate its new identity, WPP went on a tear. In November 1987, it helped present Gail Kriegel's *Reverend Jenkins' Almost All Colored Orphanage Band* in New Orleans. In collaboration with the Los Angeles Theatre Center, it produced Marlane Meyer's *Etta Jenks* at the Apple Corps in April 1988, and come June, WPP opened new horizons through Mapping Theatrical Territories—its contribution to the First New York International Festival of the Arts headed by Martin Segal.

With a grant from the Rockefeller Foundation, and funding from the Festival that Pat Schoenfeld helped secure, WPP produced the work of non-American women for the first time in its history: the playwright Griselda Gambaro of Argentina; Mexican director Jesusa Rodriguez, who created and performed a piece called *Human Rights*. Suzanne Bennett thought that Joan of Arc might be a universal figure, and Miles asked theatre artists as various as Simone Benmussa of France, Yvonne Brewster of Jamaica and England, and Lou Nai Ming of China, to create their versions of the young woman who burned at the stake for her faith. Lavonne Mueller wrote *Letters to a Daughter from Prison: Indira and Nehru* about the tender, instructive relationship between the first Prime Minister of India, Jawaharlal Nehru, and his daughter. In the spring of 1989, director Vijaya Mehta took the play to India, and Miles and Mueller toured with it in Bombay and Delhi.

But if independence enabled WPP to explore new worlds, it also brought serious challenges. Miles needed a bigger staff, sophisticated marketing techniques, and a long-range plan if WPP was going to survive this transition. At a critical moment, the Ford Foundation came to the rescue. Urged on by Ruth Mayleas, the Foundation's program officer for the arts, in 1988 Ford gave WPP $200,000 over two years to improve marketing, promotion, and development so that WPP could achieve self-sufficiency and permanence.

The pressure on Miles was enormous. "The bigger the shop, the more who you are goes into running that shop," said director and playwright Joan Vail Thorne who had joined the Women's Project at its beginning. "Julia's regretted that. But she had to be sure that she was going to make this work, or there would be egg on the face of the feminist movement in a way. At the American Place, she just enjoyed the process. That was where she lived and loved being."

The American Place had provided a stable address for nearly ten years. Now WPP appeared to wander from one temporary home to another. After the Apple Corps there was a stop at the Judith Anderson on Theatre Row, then a respite at the YMCA on 63rd Street near Central Park West, where WPP became the resident company during the 1991–92 season.

For a time it looked as though the YMCA would provide a permanent home. "The YMCA wanted to do something with its little theatre," said Pat Schoenfeld, who was also on the Y's board at the time. "Women's Project pitched an idea, and the Y was receptive." WPP hired the theatre designer Roger Morgan and architect Leslie Armstrong to refashion the Y's existing theatre into a space that could become a thrust, proscenium, and arena stage. WPP raised money; it hoped to use the reconfigured theatre by the 1993–94 season.

But the plan fell through. "The board of an individual Y does not really have any power," explained Schoenfeld. "We were spinning our wheels." In 1995, the Y asked WPP to leave, and once again Miles hunted for a theatre and offices. "The staff was always scrambling for places to do rehearsals and productions," recalled Suzanne Bennett. "That became part of the work of the Women's Project." Finally, helped by the actor Tina Chen, who became WPP's second board president in 1995, WPP secured offices just off West End Avenue at 62nd Street.

There were personal changes, too, in the years immediately following the move. In 1989, Miles and Sam Cohn separated. Bennett, who had become a trusted colleague, left WPP to become artistic director of the Eureka Theatre in San Francisco. (She would return in 1994 as WPP's artistic associate.)

But despite the organization's nomadic existence, and the pressures of keeping a theatre vital and solvent, there were personal and professional triumphs. In December 1989, the League of Professional Theatre Women/New York, an advocacy organization that Miles had founded in 1982, honored her at Sardi's Restaurant. Colleen Dewhurst, who had acted in Lavonne Mueller's *The Only Woman General* in 1984 and was also on the board, sent an affectionate message:

> I wanted to say you have done more for women in the theatre than anyone I know because you care, you understand, and you recognize the talent when you see it.

> But more importantly, you don't address it as a competition, but as a vacuum in our theatre that needs to be filled, a place, a home. We women needed a place to test ourselves and find that we had much to offer, and that our civilization needed us.

Thanking the assembled group, Miles noted that the number of female playwrights produced in the not-for-profit American theatre had risen to 20 percent, and the number of female directors had risen to 25 percent.

Building on the Ford Foundation's assistance, in 1991 the Project reached out to public school students in New York City. "Ten Centuries of Women Playwrights," inaugurated by the playwright Marjorie Duffield, introduced teenagers to dramatists of the past and helped them write, direct, and perform their own plays about the present. "The program is an encompassing experience," said Fran Tarr who became education director in 1995. "Students read a play like Susannah Centlivre's *Adventures in Venice*, look at Centlivre as the voice of a particular world and contrast her society with theirs. Then they get to be the voice of their own society. The program empowers kids."

Throughout the 1990s, WPP discovered and presented new voices, although, because of space and money limitations, more frequently in conjunction with other theatres. Miles and the New Federal Theatre produced Cassandra Medley's *Ma Rose*, a fierce drama about the tormenting relationships among three generations of African American women. Kitty Chen, an actor who had turned to playwriting, wrote a comic but poignant family drama called *Eating Chicken Feet*, which WPP produced with Pan Asian Repertory. With New Georges, a young company devoted to work by women, WPP produced Kate Moira Ryan's *The Autobiography of Aiken Fiction* in which two teenage girls take to the road to escape their horrific families and have each other. "I don't think Julia had done that many gay plays before," said Ryan, "and this was pretty overt. I rewrote all the way through previews," she added, "and Julia was always smart about what should go, what should stay. Very hands-on and very loyal to the playwright. She's gruff, but I could always turn that around and make her laugh."

Strangely for a theatre committed to developing new plays, WPP had never offered an official Playwrights' Laboratory, where dramatists could concentrate on one scene or script in the company of other playwrights and in a safe environment. In the fall of 1992, Miles asked Sharon Houck Ross, playwright-in-residence at WPP while finishing her M.F.A. at the University of Iowa, to form just such a lab. Ross recalled that Miles and literary manager Susan Bougetz drew up a list of fifteen "emerging professional" writers, then Ross constructed a plan, and the Lab began meeting once a week at the YMCA, for three hours in the evening. Ross or Bougetz would take notes, which they passed along to Miles.

The spring 1993 issue of *Dialogues* published Ross's response to their initial efforts:

> It became apparent that most of us had exposed our work in places that were decidedly not safe. . . . All of us had war stories. An operational definition of "safe place" began to emerge. Although an individual always relinquishes some autonomy when joining a group, a safe place is one that accords more freedoms than it takes away. In a developmental lab, these freedoms should arise from respect for the author: her unique voice, her preferred style of learning, and her "ownership" of her own work.

That first year the focus was new, full-length plays. "A play could be read informally by all of us sitting around a table," said Ross, "or read by actors brought in by the writer; afterward, the group provided feedback. Usually, the writer would lead her own critique. A week or so later, I would follow up with a private meeting, to help the writer sort through the feedback and discuss a focus for the next revision." When Ross returned to Iowa in the spring of 1993, Bougetz led the Lab.

Kitty Chen, one of the Lab's original members, said that "Before the Women's Project, when someone gave me criticism, I took it personally. But in the WPP Lab, it was all peers. Julia was never there. Susan Bougetz said things in a helpful, gentle, supportive way. There was never the sense of 'This is wrong,' but instead, 'It might work better if. . . .'"

Chen remained in the Lab for five years. "I learned about my process," she said.

During the spring of 1993, the Lab paired some of the playwrights with directors to present a public performance called "Tandem Acts" at La Mama Galleria in the East Village. This spring festival of one-acts became an annual event for WPP. "We really wanted to nurture relationships between women artists," said Bougetz, "to get those numbers of women working up!"

As with the Directors Forum, the Lab subsequently underwent changes. Members eventually were limited to three years, and the Lab met twice a month instead of every week. When Lisa McNulty became literary manager in 1997, the Lab generally followed Dance Exchange founder Liz Lerman's steps for supportive critiquing in "Toward a Process for Critical Response." Karen Keagle, who took over as literary manager at the start of the 2000–2001 season, continued that approach—a lightly structured way of exchanging constructive comments about an artist's work in progress.

Questions inevitably lingered about whether the Playwrights Lab should be a learning ground or a launching pad onto WPP's stage, or both. But as Miles, Bougetz, and Sharon Houck Ross had intended from the beginning, the Lab had become, to the best of WPP's ability in an unsafe profession, a safe place.

✦ ✦ ✦

—Never was I so aware of being a woman, short, and young. . . . I decided the only solution was to outtalk everybody.

—Carey Perloff, Artistic Director, American
Conservatory Theater, San Francisco, at Women in
Theatre: Mapping the Sources of Power

The women, nearly five hundred of them, gathered in an auditorium at the New School on 12th Street and Fifth Avenue in Manhattan. The subject of WPP's symposium that November 1997 was Women in Theatre: Mapping the Sources of Power; the occasion was the twentieth anniversary of the Women's Project. Women from all theatrical fields were there, eager to hear colleagues talk about how far they had come, and the distance they still had to go.

A time traveler comparing 1997 to 1978 would have been impressed. Looking around at the audience and the panels, there were women representing every phase of theatrical creation: playwrights, actors, directors, designers, artistic directors and managing directors, fund-raisers and funding officers, university professors and critics. Nearly twenty years earlier Miles and her playwrights had been pioneers opening a new territory; now they could see that others had followed, to build where the Women's Project had cleared the way.

There had been setbacks. Since 1989, when Miles spoke to the League of Professional Theatre Women at Sardi's, the employment figures for female playwrights and directors in not-for-profit theatres had actually dropped to 15 and 18 percent, respectively. Merely two statistics, but they revealed what the women in that auditorium knew from their own experience: In the American theatre, they still lacked parity with men.

Yet one could not listen to the women that November without hearing their energy, realism, and determination. If they were saddened and frustrated by the struggle, even felt like giving up at times, they were also mapping strategies to gain new ends.

Ensuring WPP's own route to power, Miles doggedly pursued the acquisition of a theatre, finally discovering that an Off-Broadway proscenium house, Theatre Four on 55th Street between 9th and 10th Avenues, was for sale.

"Julia never got it out of her mind that she must have a theatre," said Pat Schoenfeld. "She is focused, and this focus is just undisturbable. It may take her forever, but it takes her where she wants to be."

In October 1998, with a $500,000 gift from Sally Bingham, WPP bought Theatre Four; the total cost was $1.5 million. Soon after, WPP embarked on a long-term campaign to raise money to modernize the building, an effort to which New York City and the State of New York pledged more than $2 million. Miles had attained one of her most tangible goals: Women's Project & Productions finally had its own home.

Eager to put her stamp on the new theatre, Miles began to produce there in the fall of 1998. Two productions moved to commercial Off-Broadway venues: Joan Vail Thorne's *The Exact Center of the Universe* and *Saint Lucy's Eyes* by a fresh voice named Bridgette A. Wimberly. Staged by Billie Allen, *Eyes* starred Ruby Dee as a former domestic who performs abortions to give young women back their lives.

Keeping pace with issues of concern to women, in 1999, WPP mounted Karen Hartman's *Gum*, which dramatizes the emotional and physical agony of a Middle Eastern girl forced to undergo a clitorectomy. Nor did WPP forget playwrights whom it had nourished in earlier years, like Darrah Cloud, Marlane Meyer, and Julie Jensen, whose *Two-Headed*, in 2000, was a lively celebration of female friendship.

Challenges remained as Women's Project & Productions entered the new millenium in its new house. But in the acquisition of its own building, and in the resolve which women had expressed that weekend at the New School, were tools for the future.

"Twenty-five years ago," Miles emphasized, "we saw a need to increase the number of women in the theatre in order to enrich the theatre and our culture. That need is still there. The Women's Project has graduated a generation of playwrights and directors, their voices have been heard and their work seen in theatres all over the country. They will continue to be heard, and so will we."

Alexis Greene is a theatre critic and author who lives in New York City. Her most recent book is a biography of the late Off-Broadway producer Lucille Lortel.

Lavonne Mueller

LITTLE VICTORIES

Linda Hunt and Caroline Kava in *Little Victories* by Lavonne Mueller, 1983.
Photo © by Martha Holmes. Jimmy Smits and Linda Hunt in *Little Victories* by
Lavonne Mueller, 1983. Photo © by Martha Holmes.

Author's Note

Once at a writers' conference, I encouraged women to write about war. I felt it was important for women to examine a subject matter dominated by men. After all, I said to the group, one of the greatest generals the world has known was a woman. I was astounded that nobody knew who that general was. This was the germ for Joan of Arc in *Little Victories.*

The germ for Susan B. Anthony came about in a more subtle way. I randomly picked up a biography of Anthony and was startled to find that she traveled out West at a time when few women were there. It was how she managed men that made her journey successful.

I chose to put Susan B. Anthony and Joan of Arc in a play because they both survived in a landscape of men. I also chose them because they were saints in the Kierkegaard sense. The *saint*, Kierkegaard stressed, is an antagonist to a particular or general kind of authority even while speaking in the name of another kind: the mystical. Saints live an obsessive message no matter what. And they are human as we are, and struggle with doubts as we do. One cannot forget the whimsical prayer of Saint Augustine beseeching the Lord to send him the gift of chastity . . . however, not just yet. And Cubans are fond of saying: *"Con los santos no se juega,"*—Don't even think about fooling around with the saints. Which all reverts back to the writer. Oh, if we didn't have saints, some of us would have to invent them.

Joan of Arc and Susan B. Anthony triumphed, yet they died believing themselves failures. It is possible to shake the world and not know it.

I was blessed with a marvelous cast. Linda Hunt stood proudly before her soldiers and made me believe she could lead the West Point men of her day into battle. Jimmy Smits flirted with Joan, guided her, yet respected his general and was ready to die for her. Caroline Kava smiled and sang her way into the rough tumbleweed world of the cowboys. Bryna Wortman, the director, mysteriously transformed the small stage into a combined panorama both medieval and Western. As I stood in the back of the theatre and watched the production, I thought of the preface that Ernest Hemingway wrote for *A Moveable Feast*: "If the reader prefers, this may be regarded as a work of fiction. But there is always the

chance that such a work of fiction may throw some light on what has been written as fact."

Susan B. Anthony died in 1906; women received the right to vote in 1920.
Joan of Arc died in 1431: She was canonized a saint in 1920.

—Lavonne Mueller

Little Victories was produced by the Women's Project of The American Place Theatre, in New York City, Julia Miles, Director. It was presented at American Place from January 26 through February 13, 1983.

Bryna Wortman directed. The set was designed by William M. Barclay, lighting by Phil Monat, costumes by Mimi Maxmen, and sound by Regina M. Mullen. Music was by Clay Fullum. The cast was as follows:

SUSAN B. ANTHONY	Caroline Kava
JOAN OF ARC	Linda Hunt
MARSHAL/CAPTAIN BATTAU	Terrence Markovich
HOTEL OWNER/TAILOR/BAR DOG	Bill Cwikowski
CAPTAIN LAVOUR/BEN	Jimmy Smits
SADDLE TRAMP/ARCHER/MINER	John Griesemer
VOICE OF JUDGE AND CARDINAL	Randy Spence

CHARACTERS

SUSAN B. ANTHONY
JOAN OF ARC
MARSHAL/CAPTAIN BATTAU
HOTEL OWNER/TAILOR/BAR DOG
CAPTAIN LAVOUR/BEN
SADDLE TRAMP/ARCHER/MINER
TAPED VOICES, including SUSAN'S MOTHER, JUDGE, CARDINAL

TIME

Last half of the 1880s and 1429.

PLACE

Various locations in the American West and in medieval France.

THE STAGING

The staging of the play should be simple and fluid so that whatever minimal elements are used in the setting—benches, crates, burlap curtains—can serve to create the worlds of both women. The "stove area" and "billiard room area" of the hotel in Act I, Joan's "battlefield," the Bar Dog's "bar," and Susan and Ben's "campfire" in Act II should be suggested rather than represented in a literal way.

The men's roles should be doubled or tripled as indicated in the list of characters.

Dedicated to the New Women:
Chris
Allie
Marya
Lisa
Stacey

Whatever you can do, or dream you can, begin it,
Boldness has genius, power and magic in it.

—Goethe

ACT I

At Rise: Susan enters and crosses to ladder—begins to swing a lasso as Mother's voice is heard.

MOTHER: *(Over speaker.)* Susan . . . Sus . . . an? *(Pause.)* Where is that girl? *(Susan continues to rope. After a few seconds.)* Stop that this minute. I just ironed that dress. *(Pause.)* Mind me, young lady. You're not in the Wild West . . . you're in Rochester. *(Susan continues to rope.)* I thought I told you to stop that.

SUSAN: A lot of people never mind their mothers.

Susan throws the lasso toward Joan who crosses and steps on the loop. Both girls remain in a freeze as the hotel area lights up.

Hotel Area

MARSHAL: *(Comes into hotel area. To Hotel Owner.)* You see a woman? Dark hair? Totin' these pamphlets? *(Pause. No answer from the Owner.)* History is traced wars to women like that. They incite folks to take up arms and rescue them. *(Pause. No answer from the Owner.)* I followed her through the heat on ten days now. Sun raised blood blisters on my face. *(Pause.)* You seen her?

Owner spits. Marshal and Hotel Owner remain in a freeze. Small sound of sheep bells is heard.

JOAN: *(To Susan.)* I'm hunting my sheep. They follow the wind.

SUSAN: *(Sing song.)* Leave them alone and they'll come home . . .

JOAN: Lost sheep never come home. You go after them!

SUSAN: I'll help you get them back . . . then we can go to the firehouse in town and watch the horses come out at six. *(Pause.)* We'll play firemen and save widow ladies and their babies from burning houses.

JOAN: *(Stops looking around for her sheep.)* Look at this . . . just like my place . . . only trees . . . a barn fallen in on itself . . . dumb cows bored with the pain of milk . . . dirty pigs. *(Pause.)* A big healthy calf was born today, and mother likes it better than me.

SUSAN: Mother calls me "savage" . . . her little "savage." *(Pause.)* I swing from so many trees, I've stretched my arms and I look awful in dresses.

JOAN: *(Abruptly.)* I have an eye that doesn't close. It doesn't even blink. *(Pause.)* I know about eyes. One always wants out.

Susan and Joan remain in a freeze.

Hotel Area

MARSHAL: You the owner of this place?

OWNER: Yep.

MARSHAL: Where's your deed?

OWNER: *(Takes out his gun.)* Here's my deed . . . 'n nobody's questioned it, either.

MARSHAL: *(Shows his badge.)* I'm the U.S. Marshal.

OWNER: I know you ain't no cowpuncher by the fancy way ya siddle up ta me. *(Pause.)* What'd she do?

MARSHAL: Broke the law. Voted.

OWNER: We wouldn't let that happen out here.

MARSHAL: Ya seen her? *(A long pause of silence.)* I kin haul ya in fer questions.

OWNER: Jist a minute. Hold on now. I gotta transfer my quid of tobacco ta the other jaw . . . 'n free my talkin' side.

MARSHAL: Well?

OWNER: Nope.

Spit. Then Marshal looks at him disgustedly. The Marshal strikes an official pose.

MARSHAL: *(Shouting.)* I'm here ta tell folks . . . no wagons start out beyond Dog Town 'less they got theirselves 100 men. Cause of the Indians.

OWNER: Yer talkin' loud 'nough fer Indians to hear.

MARSHAL: *(Still talking loudly.)* Sioux sure love ta capture them a woman.

OWNER: *(Loud.)* So I hear.

MARSHAL: A woman might find it better off ta be caught by a Marshal. *(He starts to exit.)* Injuns in the area—mind yer hair.

Marshal exits. Susan is standing watching Joan pluck a flower. After a pause, she walks to Joan.

JOAN: Loves me . . . loves me not . . .

SUSAN: *(Takes flower away from Joan.)* I pull purple skirts off morning glories. I love a flower's spine. A fortune teller came by our farm last week. He set me on the kitchen table and felt my head. Then he says: "You'll live a long time . . . and . . . and sleep in a lot of different beds!" My mother started right in crying . . . and Daddy, he told me I couldn't go any farther than the pasture posts without telling him.

JOAN: Mama says women who follow soldiers are whores. Girls like us are whores . . . in some places.

SUSAN: Who told you that?

JOAN: Uncle Tony's a sailor and he went to this island and child whores there got a special name. It means "small opening."

SUSAN: That's awful.

JOAN: Men don't think so. Do you think about getting married?

SUSAN: I watch the horses mate . . . and . . . it looks scary and thrilling . . .

JOAN: Maybe it's that way with people. Do you think about marriage?

SUSAN: I don't want to sit around and wait for anybody. I want to go away . . . and . . . find the big empty room that's the whole world. Sometimes I see a tired housewife bending over a washtub . . . and . . . well . . . it makes me want to be a man . . . just to help her. *(She looks at knife.)*

JOAN: Nuns never marry—and their veils cure headaches. I saw a beautiful parade today. With gold painted statues and six priests with red robes.

SUSAN: The only parades I ever see are old men . . . walking slowly in faded blues and faded greys.

JOAN: Those soldiers fought for their home.

SUSAN: Parades make me sad.

JOAN: *(Pause.)* How can you eat that thing? I hate oranges.

SUSAN: You do?

JOAN: They're putrid.

SUSAN: Summer's flesh is in an orange.

JOAN: Not to me. *(She makes a face. Susan looks at the orange carefully, turning it around. Then she puts the orange down on the ground in front of her and stares at it.)* Go on . . . you're the one eating it.

SUSAN: If I could taste this the way you do . . . I guess I wouldn't like it either. *(Pause. Rolling orange slowing in her hand.)* We're all so alone . . . aren't we?

JOAN: *(Pause.)* Can . . . you keep a secret?

SUSAN: Anything you tell me, I'll keep dark.

JOAN: I hear things. *(Joan takes Susan's hand and leads her to the side of the stage.)* Hear it? Soldiers' feet. Marching to war. Marching for France. Tramp . . . tramp . . . little pounding feet saying: "You come . . . you come . . . " *(She stops abruptly and looks at Susan. She holds out an arm.)*

See this arm? It's older than the other one. *(Pause.)* My mama tried to birth me for three days. This arm was all that poked out at first . . . till . . . till finally the rest of me came. Some day . . . some day I'll follow those soldiers . . . and march with this *(Holds out arm)* . . . to carry a big green hawk that attacks Englishmen when I tell it to. *(Pause. Jiggles arm to Susan.)* Touch it! *(Pause. Shakes the arm more strongly at Susan. After a pause, Susan touches Joan's arm.)* Promise . . . by my oldest arm, you'll go with me. And be bold with me.

SUSAN: *(Hesitantly.)* Go . . . where?

JOAN: Where we have to? *(Susan is silent. Joan shakes her arm at Susan again.)* Promise!

SUSAN: I'm afraid.

JOAN: The thing you're scared of is the thing you have to do. *(She is still silent. After a pause.)* Hurry. I don't have lots of time. *(Pause.)* Be a soldier with me. *(Susan silently stares.)* You got somebody better? *(Susan is still silent. Taunting Susan.)* You got anybody at all . . . fireman? *(Susan is still silent.)* Together. Partners. Stitched inside each other like a secret pocket in a spy's coat.

SUSAN: *(After a pause.)* I . . . promise.

JOAN: I was given this arm by heaven . . . *(Goes into her voices.)* Hear them . . . marching . . . left, right . . . left . . . right . . . right . . . left . . . right . . .

Joan and Susan march dreamily as the lights slowly fade on them.

Hotel Area

OWNER: You kin' come out now. *(Pause. Silence.)* I know yer there. *(He sniffs and holds up a finger to the wind.)* Women don't smell like a man. *(Susan goes from her childhood area to the hotel.)* They're after you like a fall buck.

SUSAN: I'm not an animal. I'm not some wild hog giving out rabies.

OWNER: What are you givin'?

SUSAN: These pamphlets . . . I want women to read them.

OWNER: Why?

SUSAN: So they'll vote. *(Pause.)* And this bale of paper. . . . I mean to fill it with names. Names of women from New York to California. Thousands of names to make the legislature change the laws.

OWNER: I never did like pressure. I got me pressured into marriage once.

SUSAN: Right now—I have to get to California. In a hurry. For a rally—a woman's rally that will bridge this country from East to West.

OWNER: You traveled in the West before?

SUSAN: First time.

OWNER: Travelin' in the West don't be easy on a woman . . . especially with a Marshal after her.

SUSAN: If I could have a room . . .

OWNER: It's cheaper ta get some fella take you to his room ta-night.

SUSAN: *(Firmly.)* My own room, please.

OWNER: *(Takes a deuce of diamonds card out of his pocket and hands it to her.)* Yer bed. *(He now takes her bags, all the time staring at her clothing.)* I tote bags fer women even if they ain't. *(Pause.)* Britches! You wear a stovepipe hat, too?

SUSAN: Just for weddings. *(She looks around.)* Dear Lord, I never knew there'd be no walls.

The Owner has taken her to another level. There is a billiard table and next to it a small table with a candle. A saloon piano, which is out of tune, is now heard.

OWNER: *(He takes a deuce of hearts which is hanging on the side of the billiard table and puts it in her hand along with the deuce of diamonds she is holding.)* Deuce of hearts and deuce of diamonds make a pair.

SUSAN: My bed? A billiard table? *(Pause.)*

OWNER: *(Pause.)* Miner bunks inna dry goods box in the hall. Paid me six bucks. *(Pause.)* Two dollars by the stove. *(Pause.)* Women don't come ta Horse Creek. *(He takes a string from an area near the billiard table.)* House facilities. *(He holds out the string which has a cup, toothbrush, comb, and soap on it.)* House facilities. Don't cost extra. Go on take it. Everybody uses it. *(She hands it back.)* Breakfast whenever ya get up. You'll find mountain bread on the stove after six. I do the cookin' here. *(Pause.)* Window ta the privy blew out, but we got us a Chinese boy ta stand there till it's fixed. *(Pause.)* Inny rats over two feet is caught by the management.

SUSAN: *(Looks around disgustedly. Then.)* I've slept on parlor chairs . . . on corn husk mattresses smelly from tobacco juice . . . on dirty train benches . . . but never . . . *(They both stare at the table. Pause. Susan faces the Owner.)* Mosquitoes—yes. And black deer flies. But . . . rats!

OWNER: Go back East, like you belong ta do. You jist hit the deep West!

SUSAN: Are you going to report me to the Marshal?

OWNER: Folks ta the West don't give out *no* information. Ta nobody. That's the only law around here. *(Pause.)* I don't like me no foreigners. *(Pause.)* If they're not women, Injuns, Mexicans—then they're strangers 'n that's jist as bad. *(Owner goes back to the stove area to sit. He then watches Susan from where he is sitting. Susan looks around once more, dejectedly, then lights a candle and pulls a curtain around the billiard table and begins to undress for bed. The Owner, snickering.)* Lady, spit out that thar candle or ivver man in this here hotel is gonna see you naked through them curtains.

Susan reaches unthinkingly for a billiard stick and holds it up in front of her breasts. The Owner laughs. Susan then blows out the candle. The area goes dark.

VOICE OVER SPEAKER: The State of New York calls Susan B. Anthony. *(Pause.)* Susan B. Anthony! Please take the stand.

The sound of the pounding of a court gavel is heard.

JUDGE'S VOICE OVER SPEAKER: What is your name?

SUSAN: *(Speaking from the now-darkened billiard table room.)* Susan B. Anthony, your honor.

JUDGE'S VOICE OVER SPEAKER: Where do you reside?

SUSAN: *(As she is scrambling in the dark for her jacket.)* Rochester, New York.

JUDGE'S VOICE OVER SPEAKER: Speak louder, please.

SUSAN: *(Lighting the candle. She can now be seen behind the curtain.)* Rochester, New York.

JUDGE'S VOICE OVER SPEAKER: Again.

SUSAN: *(Angrily.)* A man just got shot. Right next door to me.

JUDGE'S VOICE OVER SPEAKER: What can you say regarding your actions?

SUSAN: I have a stiff neck. *(Rubbing rear.)* Other parts of me are stiff, too.

JUDGE'S VOICE OVER SPEAKER: *(More firmly.)* What can you say regarding your actions?

SUSAN: I rode the Redbird Stagecoach all week. Next to the driver. On the outside. My skin's cracked and dry like old stone burned in the sun.

JUDGE'S VOICE OVER SPEAKER: What can you say regarding your actions?

SUSAN: I used to have good skin.

JUDGE'S VOICE OVER SPEAKER: What can you . . .

SUSAN: I voted the Republican ticket. Straight. Seven A.M.

JUDGE'S VOICE OVER SPEAKER: Whether you believe you have a right to vote or not is a question of law.

SUSAN: *(Defiantly.)* I did it, sir! I walked right in to that poll booth, and I did it.

Shocked voices and pounding of gavel is heard. The light goes dim on Susan's area. She sits on the billiard table.

Battlefield Area

Medieval music is heard. A Tailor comes on stage followed by Joan. The Tailor carries a basket of silk and plumes and a female dressmaker dummy. He puts the basket down and sets the form in position. Then he opens the basket and fluffs up the silks. Then he turns to Joan.

TAILOR: Joan . . . Joan of Lorraine. Ahh, your neck will have the best boiled leather . . . *(He strokes Joan's neck. Joan smiles.)* Then . . . I'll caress these lovely appendages in fine steel. *(He touches her breasts, counting.)* One . . . two . . . and thick rings of chain-mail under those deep, dark armpits. Beside these lovely moons . . .

JOAN: *(She is enjoying the stroking of the Tailor. She says dreamily as she strokes herself along with the Tailor.)* Yes . . . yes . . . more steel . . . more leather . . . more . . .

Lavour now comes on stage to see Joan and the Tailor.

LAVOUR: *(To Tailor.)* What in the hell are you doing?

The Tailor drops his hands.

JOAN: *(To Lavour.)* Did you swear, soldier?

LAVOUR: Get that lecher out of this camp.

The Tailor skulks off, bowing unctuously to Joan as he scurries off stage.

JOAN: Soldier, say "Martin" every time you want to swear.

LAVOUR: *(Pause.)* I'm your adjutant, not "soldier." *(He stands at attention.)* Captain Lavour.

JOAN: Enchanté. *(Pause. She looks at him startled.)* I didn't know my adjutant would be so . . . young. You smell funny.

LAVOUR: I don't smell of manure. I don't come from a farm.

JOAN: *(Happily. Sniffing his arm.)* Lemon soap. *(Pause. She goes on to touch his upper arm muscles.)* I bet you joust.

LAVOUR: I broke three lances fairly . . . in Reims.

JOAN: I've always wanted a knight to wear my scarf on his lance. *(She stares at him.)*

LAVOUR: *(Coldly.)* I'm not that kind of knight.

JOAN: *(She smiles, realizing she can command him. She begins to sort through the basket of silks and plumes. Holds up a green scarf.)* Maybe green. Sheep grass is not as green. *(She ties the green scarf around Lavour's arm.)* Where is he?

LAVOUR: Who?

JOAN: The captain that hates me. I saw him slouching near the wagon yard this morning. *(Captain Lavour remains silent. Joan turns to begin lifting up items from the basket.)* From the Dauphin. His personal plumes, scarfs . . . sashes. . . . *(She puts on more silks. She looks around royally.)* And he's promised me cannonballs—as many as I want.

LAVOUR: Cannonballs! Those things destroy trees and bushes. They make gashes in the ground. They don't kill men. *(He takes the cannonball from her.)*

JOAN: *(A pause as her face blushes in anger. She goes into a childish tantrum.)* I give the orders here. You soldiers are all alike. You don't think I know anything. Well I do. I know weapons when I see them. Don't bully me. I'll tell the Dauphin. Do you hear me? I'll tell the king. *(Stamping her feet.)*

LAVOUR: He's not the king yet.

He looks at this childish commander with contempt, then plants the cannonball in her arms. Then he briskly exits. Joan stares after him, half surprised and then slowly feeling childishly victorious. After a pause, she goes to the basket to sort happily through all her plumes and silks.

CARDINAL'S VOICE OVER SPEAKER: This inquisition will now begin. *(Pause.)* Please state your name before the cardinals present here in the name of the Holy Mother Church. Where were you born?

JOAN: *(She doesn't answer. She is too busy with her treasures.)*

CARDINAL'S VOICE OVER SPEAKER: Where were you born?

JOAN: *(Happily.)* Gifts. From the Dauphin.

CARDINAL'S VOICE OVER SPEAKER: Your birthplace?

JOAN: *(After a pause.)* Domremy.

CARDINAL'S VOICE OVER SPEAKER: What can you say regarding your actions?

JOAN: I lead armies to unite France. Because of you, Holy Fathers. *(Pause. Holding up a scarf.)*

CARDINAL'S VOICE OVER SPEAKER: Whether you have a right to lead armies or not is a question of this council.

JOAN: I love you all . . . I love the Holy Mother Church. And you love me. *(She exits carrying silks and plumes with her.)*

Hotel Area

The Owner is sitting by the hotel stove. He strums a guitar as the Saddle Tramp enters.

OWNER:

HORSE CREEK AIN'T CROSSABLE,
NOT EVEN HORSIBLE
HORSE CREEK AIN'T PASSABLE
NOT EVEN JACKASSABLE
HORSE CREEK AIN'T. . . . .

Susan comes into the stove area. The men stare at her.

SUSAN: I'm from the Billiard Suite.

SADDLE TRAMP: So yer the one that Marshal's lookin' for. You a bigamist?

SUSAN: I'm a voter. *(Saddle Tramp reacts dramatically.)* I didn't say I spread small pox. I said I voted. *(To Owner.)* I need a sheet. For my . . . bed.

OWNER: We had a rush of business fer dinner . . . *(Yanks sheet off a table and hands it to her.)* . . . 'n used it fer a tablecloth. *(Susan takes it gingerly.)* Youse 'at come from the East . . . we pamper you a spell. Sheet 'n tablecloth the first couple of days. *(Pause.)* We don't allow style as a regular thang.

SADDLE TRAMP: Welcome ta Hotel de Dirt.

SUSAN: Is there any water for washing in?

OWNER: A kettle full ta the back stove.

SUSAN: That won't be enough.

OWNER: You mean you're fixin' ta wash *all over*? *(Both men laugh at this.)* Damn that dog of mine. I've been scratchin' from Charlie's fleas all day. *(Pause.)* Wanna bet?

SADDLE TRAMP: Nice big fleas?

OWNER: *(Pause.)* Put up a dollar.

SUSAN: *(Looks at men firmly.)* I've seen that game. In False Bottom. *(Pause.)* You drop fleas in a pan and see which one of these grayback scrambles out first.

OWNER: That's right. *(Pause.)* Dollar a head.

SUSAN: I'm on.

OWNER: Bet's a bet. *(Knowing wink to Saddle Tramp.)* Don't put up money ya can't lose. *(Pause.)* I'll warn ya . . . this ain't no New York "Parchisi," "Hearts," or "Old Maid."

SADDLE TRAMP: *(Spits in a small hot fry pan.)* Pan's hot.

After a pause the Owner scratches his sleeve furiously. The two men both take fleas from the Owner's arm. Then the men hold out the fleas, hovering them over the hot frying pan. They wait for Susan. The two men look at Susan intently to see what she will do. There is a pause. After a determined silence, Susan courageously scratches the Owner's sleeve. She looks at his sleeve.

SUSAN: *(Takes a flea from the Owner's sleeve and dramatically hovers it over the pan.)* On three! One . . . two . . . three! *(They all drop the fleas in at once. Soon they are cheering. Susan too. After a pause.)*
OWNER: *(To Susan.)* Yers is out first. *(The men make a gesture to pay her.)*
SUSAN: I'll accept payment in bath water.

The Saddle Tramp turns the pan over and clears it.

OWNER: *(Cranky.)* Gotta be brought in from the creek. *(Pause.)* I need 'n feed Charlie, my dog . . . Charlie, my horse . . . 'n Charlie, the ox . . .
SUSAN: All your animals are named "Charlie"?
OWNER: It don't confuse me inny that way. *(Pause.)*
SUSAN: I've got to wake up early tomorrow. My stage leaves at dawn . . . and I just can't miss it. *(She starts to leave.)*
OWNER: If yer gettin' ready ta go ta California, then you'll be headed for Crystal Hills?
SUSAN: Yes that's right . . . in about a week . . . according to my map. There'll be a letter there from my friend.
OWNER: Crystal Hills, huh?
SUSAN: Yes.
OWNER: Nobody is told you about Crystal . . .

Saddle Tramp shakes his head gloomily.

SUSAN: Should they have? What's wrong with Crystal Hills? Is the Marshal there?
OWNER: Nope.
SUSAN: Indians?
SADDLE TRAMP: Nope.
OWNER: Is it real important that you go that way?
SUSAN: Yes. I told you I have a letter waiting for me at Crystal Hills.
SADDLE TRAMP: You kin' take the detour over Beaver Fork.
SUSAN: I'd lose seven or eight days that way.
OWNER: Sometimes a detour is worth it. Lotta people was determined ta get there . . . once.
SADDLE TRAMP: I knew me a wagon train of cavalry that . . . well . . . they ain't livin' ta tell the story.

SUSAN: Will you please tell me what this is all about!

OWNER: Hate ta see somebody alone took off for that place.

SADDLE TRAMP: God knows people in groups ain't fared no better.

SUSAN: What is this all about?

OWNER: Crystal Hills is . . . is so clear ya can't see 'em . . . 'n people is run smack into 'em head on 'n died.

SADDLE TRAMP: You'll see stacks of wagons which is broken their wheels by runnin' into 'em . . . bones of people 'n horses 'n birds with broken necks . . .

Susan stares at the men for a second and then the men can't hold out any longer and they begin to laugh.

OWNER: *(As he is laughing.)* Them hills is so . . . clear . . . they is invisible . . . *(Owner and Saddle Tramp exit. Joan enters.)*

SUSAN: *(Peeved. Pause.)* The West!

JOAN: It's not just the West.

SUSAN: You'd think I'd wise up to their jokes.

JOAN: I know.

SUSAN: *(Looking after men.)* . . . I'm always standing by watching somebody else do something.

JOAN: *(Pause.)* You won at fleas.

SUSAN: I walk up to a minister's house. To give him these pamphlets. And do you know what he says? *(After a pause.)* Are you the new hired girl? Did it ever occur to him that a woman standing at his doorstep just might be something else besides a . . . hired girl?

JOAN: Did he sign your petition?

SUSAN: *(After a pause. Smiling.)* . . . after I scrubbed down his porch . . . *(She chuckles.)* . . . OK . . . so he wasn't so bad. What about that jackass hotel owner . . . and that saddle tramp?

JOAN: *(Pause.)* My own first Sargeant asks me if I do only "sitting work." *(Pause.)* He sees me drinking in muddy tanks, right alongside the horses. He sees me stripping bark off the trees for my bed. *(Pause.)*

SUSAN: I wouldn't mind it so much . . . if . . . we could be on the trail together.

JOAN: But we are.

SUSAN: All the time. I'm lonely. I never thought I'd be lonely. *(Pause.)* It seems like here in the West, you come upon a stranger . . . share his or her food and home . . . and you're no closer to that person than a bird and a squirrel who happens upon the same tree branch.

JOAN: I saw a robin today and it made me think of home. *(Pause.)* My archers and lancers sit huddled together around the fire. They're homesick, too.

SUSAN: But they're homesick together. *(Pause.)* Maybe mother's right . . . maybe a woman can't take it—the traveling . . . the weather . . . I have bad dreams.

JOAN: Dreams! They're only cats and dogs of the sky.

SUSAN: . . . I dream . . . I never change anything. I see my face . . . old, weather-wrung. It's a homeless face. *(Pause.)* I'm afraid . . . afraid to stop . . . afraid to go on. *(After a pause.)* A Marshal's on my trail. *(Pause.)* If he gets me, I'll be hobbled like a horse. Taken back East on the same overland coach I came on. People gawking at every stage station. Finally thrown in a dark cell in Rochester. Tried with the speed of a miner's court. *(Pause.)* What if . . . I give up everything and lose? What if . . . I have no place to go . . . when I'm old?

After a pause, Joan picks up the communal brush still on the string and begins to brush Susan's hair. As she brushes.

JOAN: Maybe homeless is beautiful . . . maybe. Now . . . rest . . . rest . . . I'll brush your hair . . . then you brush mine. Women have always done that for each other. *(The light slowly goes dark. Joan quietly exits. Susan remains in semi-darkness. Sound of a court gavel is heard. Fade. Voices.)*

JUDGE'S VOICE OVER SPEAKER: Did Elizabeth Cady Stanton get you to wear men's clothing?

SUSAN: *(Angrily.)* I wear bloomers and logger socks because I ride a horse and I'm freezing cold.

JUDGE'S VOICE OVER SPEAKER: Did she?

SUSAN: It rains out here like . . . like a creek's fallen from the sky. A skirt drags in the mud. I refuse to get pulled down by the mud.

JUDGE'S VOICE OVER SPEAKER: Even women jeer at you.

SUSAN: Not all of them. At a boarding house in Big Bear, the lady owner told me to pick my room and order dinner, adding there'd be no bill. In French Lick, a miner's wife . . .

JUDGE'S VOICE OVER SPEAKER: You're Elizabeth Cady Stanton's lackey.

SUSAN: She writes my speeches.

JUDGE'S VOICE OVER SPEAKER: At home.

SUSAN: She makes the bullets. I fire them.

JUDGE'S VOICE OVER SPEAKER: But she stays home.

SUSAN: She has children. *(Pause.)* Seven of them. I don't believe there's a safe day in the month for her.

JUDGE'S VOICE OVER SPEAKER: Children . . . now that's the normal function of women, Miss Anthony, isn't it?

SUSAN: What's normal for a woman is something she must determine for herself.

JUDGE'S VOICE OVER SPEAKER: You, Miss Anthony, are unmarried, childless, dressed in men's attire, and traveling in a prairie of men. Am I correct?

SUSAN: Yes!

JUDGE'S VOICE OVER SPEAKER: Mrs. Stanton is married, a mother, attired as a lady of her social class, and living in her family home. *(Pause.)* How nice for her that you . . . you are in the West . . . delivering her speeches.

SUSAN: I met Mrs. Stanton when she first came to Rochester. For a lecture. It was the most thrilling speech I've ever heard. *(Pause.)* She's a lawyer's daughter, your honor. When she was five, she ripped out all the pages in her father's law books that discriminated against women. She's been "ripping" ever since. *(Pause.)* After that first speech, I followed her from city to city. I heard every speech she made. And . . . then . . . *(Pause.)* One day in Seneca . . . one August day . . . when heat lightning split the sky . . . we sat on her lawn talking . . . and she said: "Susan, you can help women. You!" *(Pause. Angrily.)* She picked me! Me! Out of hundreds of others. Don't you dare call me her lackey. I'm chosen! *(Susan remains standing for a moment. Susan's area goes dark.)*

ARCHER: *(He strums a guitar in one area near the battlefield and sings.)*
JOAN
JOAN
WITHOUT NO KNIVES
AT HOME
HOME;
   SHE CAN'T WINK
   SHE CAN'T SIGH
   A VIRGIN KEEPS HER CHERRY PIE
   KEEPS HER CHERRY PIE.

After a pause, Lavour comes in with Joan.

LAVOUR: Too many of your officers are refusing to follow you. More every day. *(Joan turns from Lavour and begins to strut.)* Desertion is increasing. Four corporals ran off with a full cart of supplies last night.

JOAN: *(Strutting.)* These spurs are five inches.

LAVOUR: The morning wind knocked down all the ammunition tents and blew off wagon covers.

JOAN: *(She struts again.)* Any traitor who comes near me will get it right between the legs.

LAVOUR: *(In contempt.)* My father always said: "The farther you get from Paris, the darker the bread."

JOAN: That means I'm a stupid farm girl, right? *(Pause.)* A few weeks ago, I was kicking cows home from pasture . . . but now. Silks! Plumes!

LAVOUR: Battle will stink a time in your nostrils.

JOAN: Is that a criticism of war . . .

LAVOUR: A criticism of fact. *(Pause.)* What is it you want . . . General?

JOAN: Want. I have no wants.

LAVOUR: Those who do not want something do not make war. They only endure it.

JOAN: Let me tell you something . . . Captain. I don't come from a fancy family in Paris . . . the way you do. I don't worry about low supplies of good wine . . . about losing my title . . . *(Pause.)* . . . You know what war means to me? *(Pause.)* A mule! *(Pause.)* We had a plow mule called Belle. She was born the same day I was. *(Pause.)* Stray English soldiers would come by our farm asking for pack animals to carry their cannons and arrows. We couldn't let them have Belle. She was all we had for the fields. We'd starve. *(Pause.)* So Daddy took Belle to the shed and . . . cut up her legs . . . till they were bleeding and she was limping . . . so the enemy wouldn't take her. *(Pause.)* Belle's legs would heal . . . we'd work her . . . till enemy stragglers came by . . . then we'd cut up Belle's legs again. *(Pause.)* We shared birthdays, Captain! *(Pause.)* And one day, after maybe the sixth time, I went to the shed where Belle was . . . all bleeding . . . and lame . . . and I started pounding the walls. I screamed and pounded till my fists were bloody as Belle's legs. *(Pause.)* I learned something about myself that day. I learned that . . . when I'm mad, I'm stronger than I ever knew I could be. When I'm mad, I don't feel pain. I endure. *(Pause.)* It's France that wants, Captain. *(Pause.)* Now . . . I have a battle to win. I'm tired . . . and I don't have much time.

LAVOUR: *(Demanding.)* Why are you so sure you're the right person to win France back?

JOAN: *(Points.)* See how the wind moves those twigs against the fallen leaves? *(Pause.)* I believe in mirages, Captain. Mirages have their real side. That same little whirling war is being waged . . . and I . . . *(She stamps her foot in the whirling leaves.)* . . . have won it.

Joan runs off stage before Battau arrives. Enter Battau.

BATTAU: *(After a pause, he enters.)* Some of our lancers stole tavern signs from town. They're drunk. Restless. *(Pause.)* I'm restless, too. *(Pause.)* You know what she's done now? *(Pause.)* Ordered half the line dismounted. She wants a flank movement on the other side of the river. *(Pause.)* No officer is going to walk into Orleans.

LAVOUR: If you're ordered to walk . . . you'll walk.

BATTAU: A farm girl tells us to walk. *(Pause. Laughs.)* I drew a map of this camp. I have it pretty well narrowed down.

LAVOUR: What do you have narrowed down?

BATTAU: Where her tent is. I'll put the scare of death in her.

Wood chopping is heard.

LAVOUR: I don't like treason. *(Pause.)* My grandfather . . . father . . . we've served France. Honorably. I don't intend to be the first in the family to commit treason.

BATTAU: We figure she's to the east of the wagon yard.

LAVOUR: Get rid of the map, Battau. *(Pause.)* The Dauphin's made her official head of this battalion. Until he comes to his senses, we'll follow her.

BATTAU: *(Holding out map.)* We got one big circle on the likely spot. *(Pause.)* She's a witch, you know that.

LAVOUR: You believe in goblins, too?

BATTAU: She's not normal. They say she sees things . . . hears things . . . She spooked the Dauphin! *(Pause.)* A witch, Lavour.

LAVOUR: A man . . . who graduated with me from the University of Paris . . . is now telling me he believes in witches.

BATTAU: You'll see. Check around. Babies in Rouen are being born deformed. People in Paris are losing teeth. *(He stares at Lavour for a second.)* All I want to do is kill a witch . . . that's all.

LAVOUR: She won't last ten minutes in battle. Let the English take her off our hands. They'd love to capture her. Think of the ransom they'll get.

Chopping sound is louder. Battau pauses to look, then:

BATTAU: *(He looks back out to the trees.)* What the hell's that?

LAVOUR: Somebody chopping wood. *(They both stare for several seconds.)* Do you think I want to ruin my career . . . maybe die because of a stupid farm girl? *(Pause.)* Trust me. *(Pause.)* If she isn't struck down when we breach the walls . . . she'll turn and run home to mother the minute the English cannons start popping.

BATTAU: *(Pause.)* Lavour, why are you doing this to me? Let me stop her.

LAVOUR: She has to be stopped officially. You know that. It's only a matter of time.

BATTAU: *(Looking at the tree in the distance.)* What the hell! What . . .

LAVOUR: That tree's about to fall.

BATTAU: Jesus . . . it's going to fall on my tent!

LAVOUR: Timber! *(Loud noise.)* It went on your tent, all right. *(Battau runs off to his destroyed tent. Joan comes on stage carrying a hatchet.)*

JOAN: I can cut a tree straight enough to drive a nail.

LAVOUR: I see. *(He can't help but be amused. He exits.)*

CARDINAL'S VOICE OVER SPEAKER: Please tell this court . . . if voices command you to wear men's clothing?

JOAN: I don't wear men's clothing by the counsel of any voices. I climb the underside of scaling ladders . . . using just my hands. The rest of me dangles in mid air.

CARDINAL'S VOICE OVER SPEAKER: What vision do you see?

JOAN: A long single line.

CARDINAL'S VOICE OVER SPEAKER: A line of . . . men?

JOAN: Yes. . . . Our men.

CARDINAL'S VOICE OVER SPEAKER: Men with natural heads?

Lavour enters.

JOAN: French heads. Please . . . come back . . . please . . . let me tell you more . . . about the glories I do in your name . . . . Captain *(Pauses, embarrassed.)* I need your advice . . . well, more like your help.

LAVOUR: *(Coldly.)* What is it, General?

JOAN: *(Slowly.)* How do you . . . ? *(He is watching her curiously.)* . . . How . . . *(Gathering courage.)* . . . how . . . do you . . . ride a horse?

LAVOUR: *(Stares at her in disbelief.)* You don't know how to ride a horse?

JOAN: I've only been in this army two weeks . . . do they really bite?

LAVOUR: Worry about the ones that kick at you when they run away. *(Pause.)* Horse bites are downright friendly. *(Looks at her disgustedly.)* Don't let the horse know that you are afraid.

JOAN: I won't be afraid.

LAVOUR: *(Calling.)* Archer! Archer! *(Archer comes running on stage.)* Over here. Bend over.

ARCHER: Which direction do you want my ass? *(He giggles.)*

LAVOUR: Get down on all fours. *(To Joan.)* Your horse. *(To Archer.)* She'll ride you.

ARCHER: *(Happily and lewdly.)* Ahhhh!

LAVOUR: I'm only doing this for France. *(To Joan.)* Every horse worth anything has a natural distrust of human beings. Especially soldiers. It wants nothing bigger than an oak leaf on its back. *(The Captain helps her straddle the Archer's back. Then the Captain takes a string from around the Archer's waist and puts it through the Archer's mouth as reins for Joan to hold. Then the Captain kicks the Archer so he will buck.)* Bucking is its way of making friends. So you both can get used to each other. Don't pull hard. That wrecks his mouth. *(To Joan.)* Head up! Up! You don't have to watch the horse.

Joan is riding, feeling all the passion between her legs. In a frenzy, she uses spurs. As she rides, she suddenly assumes command. She shouts authoritatively. Lavour watches amazed.

JOAN: Open the ranks! Let the English through! Group in single lines! No knight will be a shield for another! A single line! *(Pause.)* Close up those intervals! *(Pause.)* Knights in the front! Squires behind! Scale the wall!

ARCHER: Ahhhh! *(He bucks her off and rolls over on the ground in pain.)* She used them spurs on me! *(Pause.)* I'm bleeding. *(Pause.)* Find yourself another ass . . . fer soldiers pay . . . twelve lousy deniers a day. *(The Archer rolls away from her on the ground.)*

JOAN: *(Sits on the ground panting.)* I like that . . . oh, I like to ride a horse.

LAVOUR: Where did you learn to give commands like that?

JOAN: From peasant ignorance, Captain.

Lavour and Joan exit.

SADDLE TRAMP:

> I never change my underwear,
> I don't throw 'em away
> 'till they get so grimey
> I finally have to say:
> > Goodbye old sweat-stiff leggings
> > in all your pride of grime,
> > I've worn you for six years now
> > and that's a proper time.
>
> I never wash . . .

(Susan enters.) You traveling all alone?

SUSAN: Yes. What line goes through Indian territory?

SADDLE TRAMP: Miles-Deadwood Stage.

SUSAN: Not the kind of coach a lady would ride?

SADDLE TRAMP: Nope.

SUSAN: *(Smiles and points to the pan on her head.)* How's this? Will it fool the Indians?

SADDLE TRAMP: *(After a pause.)* They is savages—not morons.

Susan shrugs and takes off the pan hat.

SUSAN: Any food in Hotel de Dirt? Slice of bread? I missed supper.

SADDLE TRAMP: Built me some "trail stew." Ain't New York puff paste and cream fillins. *(He takes out a jar and empties it into a pot.)*

SUSAN: *(Pause. She holds out her hand.)* I'm Susan.

SADDLE TRAMP: Double Ugly. My "front name." *(Points to his face.)* I was cut in two places in a fight in Crow Canyon. I give a first-class funeral ta my real name long time ago. *(He continues stirring.)* So yer all by yourself?

SUSAN: Yes.

SADDLE TRAMP: I know what that is . . . being a cowpuncher . . . alone on the range . . . ridin' the fence line. Home's not where I throw my hat—but where I spread my blanket. *(He pours her a cup of coffee.)* Here, yodel this. *(Stares at her silently for a few seconds.)* Yer what we wranglers call a lone steer . . . prowlin' up and down the outside of a dusty cattle line. *(Pause as he tastes the stew. He motions to the pot.)* Go ahead Susan. *(Pause.)* It'll make ya steal yer own clothes, bite off yer own nose . . . watcha waiting for?

SUSAN: *(Stares at the pot. Reluctantly, she tastes it. She slowly smiles.)* Good. *(Eats another large spoonful.)*

SADDLE TRAMP: *(Gives her a big dish of the stew. Singing.)*

**THE COFFEE'S GOT CONSUMPTION
THE SPUDS IS HIT WITH FLU
THE FLAPJACKS SUFFER DROPSY
THE BEEF IS SCALPED BY SIOUX.**

(Susan laughs.) I like yer laugh. It don't sound like a man's . . . 'n you don't try 'n soften it like some women do. I guess we give you a lot of razzin' while back. *(He watches her eat.)* You eat that much all the time?

SUSAN: I read somewhere that plenty of good food wards off the cholera. *(She continues eating heartily.)*

SADDLE TRAMP: *(After a pause of watching her eat.)* So how ya like the West?

SUSAN: I love cowboys.

SADDLE TRAMP: *(Pleased.)* Yah?

SUSAN: When I was little, I roped sheets off my mother's clothesline.

SADDLE TRAMP: Big ones?

SUSAN: Big as boxcars. I still love sheet behavior of horses when the wind blows.

SADDLE TRAMP: Well, Susan, I'll tell ya . . . I have broke horses 'n they have broke me. *(Pause.)* But a horse, once he's yers, you ain't never gonna find a more loyal friend. *(He reaches in her soup and takes out a bone.)* I'll jist take this fer Plenty.

SUSAN: Your horse chews bones?

SADDLE TRAMP: Rolls 'em in her mouth like a dog. *(Pause.)* She's old now . . . 'n grayin' up around the ears. I kin loosen her cinch 'n drop the reins on the ground 'n she stays right next ta me. *(Pause.)* I catch her innywhere with a biscuit. *(Pause.)* She comes ta a river now—she won't even try ta swim—jist turns on her side 'n floats across. But she's the most horse I ever had.

SUSAN: Tell me . . . Double Ugly . . . what do you do when your horse gets . . . sick . . . useless?

SADDLE TRAMP: *(Reflects with a long pause. Then.)* I feed her. *(Pause.)* Some people don't feel fer critters, but I do. That's why I work with 'em. *(Pause.)*

SUSAN: Does it bother you . . . to think of cattle ending up on a plate?

SADDLE TRAMP: Nope. It's the way a critter's treated before he's eaten that bothers me.

SUSAN: *(Pause. Looking at him carefully.)* I stayed with some homesteaders in Calico Pass. The wife was sick . . . and do you know, Ugly, that they carried her right on her sick cot to the washtub to do their clothes—cause washing is women's work. *(Pause.)*

SADDLE TRAMP: Don't it occur to you to blame nature fer what is done to women?

SUSAN: Certainly not.

SADDLE TRAMP : A woman's body . . . how it's . . . formed . . . *(Gestures around his chest.)* . . . that's what is made your place in life. Nature don't make mistakes. These times scare me, Susan. Ya know they got them a machine fer hatching eggs by artificial warmth. A machine—ta take a mother's place. *(Pause.)* Now you talk about women votin'. Where's it all gonna end? *(Susan chews silently for a moment, then stops abruptly.)* That there's jist gravel in the beans.

SUSAN: *(She adjusts her mouth to accommodate the gravel. Then she stops again.)* What's this tasty meat?

SADDLE TRAMP: Wolf. *(There is a pause. She gives out a loud wolf howl . . . the Saddle Tramp laughs.)*

SUSAN: Wish the wolves around here were big enough to eat Marshals.

Pause, as Saddle Tramp watches her eat. Then.

SADDLE TRAMP: I think I'd like to hear you speak, Susan. Yep, I'd like that, all right. But I hit the trail early tomorrow . . . driving steer ta Fresno.

SUSAN: California?

SADDLE TRAMP: Yep.

SUSAN: Maybe . . . I could get you to sign my petition before you go. *(She hands him a paper. He just looks at the paper. After a second she hands him a pen.)*

SADDLE TRAMP: *(He refuses the pen with crooked hands.)* It takes me time ta git the crooks outta my hands from them bein' clamped 'round the saddle horn all day . . . 'n . . . well, I got ta think on somethang serious as this.

SUSAN: Think, then. All you want. And hear me speak in California. Cause I'll be all over that state . . .

SADDLE TRAMP: You know somethin' . . . you don't match. *(He tenderly touches the side of her face.)* One side of your face is darker 'n the other.

SUSAN: That's my window side . . . I get to the station early—for a window seat.

SADDLE TRAMP: *(He touches Susan's face again.)* I learn from horses to see how a person's eyes and ears work ta catch thangs . . . 'n Susan . . . all of yours is workin' fine—real fine like a good critters . . .

SUSAN: Double Ugly, you aren't going to try and kiss me?

SADDLE TRAMP: Why . . . no.

SUSAN: *(Sighs in relief and turns away from the Saddle Tramp. After a pause, she twirls around to face him.)* And why not! Aren't I pretty enough?

SADDLE TRAMP: A sweet hardy mountain flower.

SUSAN: Then why?

SADDLE TRAMP: Loner steer don't feel what the rest of the herd does.

SUSAN: I beg to differ with you, Ugly. These arms feel . . . these lips feel . . .

The Saddle Tramp slowly backs away from her and exits. Court gavel is heard.

JUDGE'S VOICE OVER SPEAKER: Susan B. Anthony . . . do you travel out West? *(Susan looks around nervously, straightening her hair.)* Answer, please.

SUSAN: The West is a curious place. Pigeon Creek . . . where there are no pigeons. . . . White Woman . . . with no women at all.

JUDGE'S VOICE OVER SPEAKER: Do you travel with men?

SUSAN: There's always a kind breakman who's willing to slow down the switch engine for a few minutes so I can jump aboard a flatcar or gondola and hook a free ride to the next town. Sometimes I run for the caboose . . . huffing alongside, my cape flapping. I throw my bags at the platform and lunge at the handrails. *(Pause.)* Too often the train glides away with my belongings. But my luggage is always left at the next depot up the line.

JUDGE'S VOICE OVER SPEAKER: *(More sternly.)* Do you only encounter men when you travel?

SUSAN: What does that have to do with this trial?

JUDGE'S VOICE OVER SPEAKER: Your character, Miss Anthony, is on trial.

SUSAN: Some days I only eat a crab apple and an ear of parched corn. *(Angrily.)* I'll have no danger of getting gout—the alderman's death. Is that character enough!

JUDGE'S VOICE OVER SPEAKER: Answer the question please. Do you see only men?

SUSAN: On a cold day, a trapper shoots a wolf, scalps the animal right then, and draws the warm skin on his head.

JUDGE'S VOICE OVER SPEAKER: This court would like to know where the trapper sleeps at night.

SUSAN: *(Angrily.)* You can ask that . . . when . . . when even little school-children out here carry guns to school.

JUDGE'S VOICE OVER SPEAKER: Is it true you're so close to men you hear their snores at night?

SUSAN: Not all men snore, your honor.

JUDGE'S VOICE OVER SPEAKER: When men cry in the night . . . from their nightmares . . . do you comfort them? *(Pause.)* Do you let down your long thick hair . . . lean over them with your comforting veil of hair . . .

SUSAN: I will not answer to this, sir. I refuse to answer these slanderous, irrelevant questions.

After a pause, Susan sits down angrily. She slowly turns to look at Joan. Joan is standing in the battlefield. Lavour goes to Joan.

LAVOUR: I saw you by the river.

JOAN: Testing the banks.

LAVOUR: Send a squire for that.

JOAN: A good soldier always makes his reconnaissance.

LAVOUR: How do you know that?

JOAN: I watch you, Captain. Has my riding improved?

LAVOUR: You've a talent for it.

JOAN: *(Smiles at Lavour.)* I have a good teacher. *(Pause.)* I ordered lancers to light hundreds of fires . . . so the English will think our camp is larger than it is.

LAVOUR: The food's improved.

JOAN: The men were complaining . . . I went to that ancient commissary sargeant and ordered beef—for the old soldiers in this unit. *(Pause. She mocks his ancient tone.)* "Ah . . . old soldiers," he says. How many old soldiers do you have?" *(Pause.)* I said—Plenty! And give them everything they deserve. *(Lavour chuckles. After a pause, Joan walks away to sit on the ground.)* I haven't slept in three days.

LAVOUR: Few generals do . . . before battle. *(Pause.)* Rumor is . . . the English are afraid of you. You're uncalculating . . . and naïve. You've nearly panicked them.

JOAN: *(Calling.)* Seven! *(Shakes dice.)* I smell sulphur.

LAVOUR: There's always sulphur in a camp. For trench-itch. *(Pause.)* A powerful mystery has formed around you. *(Pause.)* It's a weapon.

JOAN: *(Disappointed.)* Eight! *(Pause. She shakes dice again.)* Are there plenty of trumpets? Drums? I want all the music of a tournament. Ten! *(She calls her dice.)*

LAVOUR: You'll have music. I learned about war from tournaments. *(Pause.)* You . . . you just might pull it off.

JOAN: *(Pleased. Calling dice.)* Ah, seven!

LAVOUR: You've got a chance. More than a chance. You could take Orleans by simple boldness. *(Pause.)* Where did you get those dice?

JOAN: From the Dauphin. Pure ivory. *(Pause.)* It's the game of God. Chance belongs to Providence. *(Pause.)* Play with me.

LAVOUR: I have to watch the "watch." *(He starts to exit.)*

JOAN: Captain. *(Lavour stops.)* I was alone for years in the hills . . . with only sheep and cows. I finally have my own army now . . . 10,000 men . . . and still nobody talks to me. *(Pause.)* Don't leave. That's an order. *(After a pause.)* Captain, are you afraid? *(Pause.)* Is . . . is a knight ever afraid before battle?

LAVOUR: Knights are afraid.

JOAN: I thought so. *(Pause. Takes a breath.)* Because I am. *(Pause.)* What do you think about . . . Captain? *(Lavour turns and stares at the ground.)* What does a soldier from Paris think about . . . before battle?

LAVOUR: My father took me hunting when I was young. *(Pause.)* Once . . . we were ambushed by English Knights . . . my father, me, a young peasant boy who acted as my father's page. *(Pause.)* We were ready to eat our catch of rabbit . . . when suddenly . . . . English arrows flew at us. Father and I escaped into some heavy willows; our heads pushed close to the roots so we couldn't be seen. But the peasant boy didn't make it. He was killed. *(Pause.)* I was frightened . . . afraid to move . . . but I could hear a soldier say: "I'll have a French Chair while I eat" . . . I could see through the brush . . . he pulled the dead boy by the heels, dragged the little carcass toward the fire . . . and sat on him. *(Pause.)* The English soldier ate our food and sat on a runt of a child . . . a scrawny poor boy . . . no older than you. *(After a pause.)* Now . . . I see a child . . . and I'm fierce for France.

JOAN: Captain . . . you see mirages, too. *(Pause.)* Follow me . . . follow me with all your heart. I can win. Will you help me?

LAVOUR: *(Softly.)* Yes. *(Pause. Strongly.)* Yes!

Lavour walks to the standard at the side of the stage and brings it back to Joan. Susan slowly walks to the tree stump at C. She picks up the hatchet. After looking at the hatchet for a moment, she says to the Saddle Tramp.

SUSAN: Please . . . cut my hair before I go.

The Saddle Tramp walks to her and takes the hatchet. Susan kneels and throws her long hair over the tree stump. He stares at her hair. (Pause.)

JOAN: Captain, I am peasant France. *(She hold up her standard triumphantly.)*
LAVOUR: Yes!

The Saddle Tramp now brings the hatchet down on Susan's hair. Just as the hatchet touches her hair, the stage goes dark.

END OF ACT I

ACT II

SUSAN: *(Enters from the back.)*
COME ON . . .
NOW,
COME ON . . . .
NOW, SEE WHAT'S NEW
I'VE SPLIT THE SKIRT
SPLIT IT RIGHT IN TWO
AND . . .
THERE AIN'T NO HORSE THAT
CAN'T BE RODE . . . AND
THERE AIN'T NO MAN THAT CAN'T
BE THROWED

(To Bar Dog.) You open to speakers? *(Bar Dog just looks at her.)* I've been on the road for six months and I've seen nothing but tent-saloons since Medicine Bow. *(Pause.)* I'd sure like to speak in here. *(Pause. Bar Dog looks at her blankly.)* I came over the Soda Springs Road. The Miles Deadwood Stage sunk up to its springs in slime.

BAR DOG: Where's your baggage?

SUSAN: We had to lighten up. I lost all my clothes, books, old letters. *(Pause.)*

BAR DOG: *(Looks at "Wanted" poster.)* Well . . . if it ain't Susan B. Anthony, the chantoozie.

SUSAN: The speaker.

BAR DOG: Yer, . . . wanted. *(Whistles to the back room.)* Hey . . . the woman outlaw's here . . .

SUSAN: . . . speaker! *(She looks around nervously, then sees a poster and rips it off the wall.)* That should make me a real good draw.

BAR DOG: A Marshal came through here yesterday putting the "Wanted" sign up.

SUSAN: I know the Marshal's close. I can smell his Kill-Dad Tobacco. I've been smelling his tobacco since Echo Canyon. *(Pause.)* He draw the beard on me too?

BAR DOG: I did that.

SUSAN: You draw a good "beard" Mr . . . Mr . . .

BAR DOG: Kibby. Kibby Newt.

SUSAN: Susan B. Anthony. How about it . . . Kibby? Can I speak here tonight?

BAR DOG: I don't like no howling woman ta my establishment. Man's gotta have a quiet place ta drink after drivin' cattle or minin' ore all day.

SUSAN: I promise not ta "howl."

BAR DOG: Two months ago, I let a preacher talk from Pierre Hole . . . 'n he blew a ram's horn fer two hours straight before he damned us all ta hell. Then he drunk up some cowpoke's bottle of French brandy. Nearly had a mass-a-cree in here.

SUSAN: I promise . . . no mass-a-crees.

BAR DOG: I tell ya . . . it jist ain't the wilderness no more like it used ta be. I got me a claim shack this year 'n 'fore I knew it somebody was buildin' a sod hut ten feet from my privy. Yep, land's all took. Even the beavers is thinnin' out.

SUSAN: One hour. That's all. Let me speak for one hour.

BAR DOG: Thangs is quiet. Ain't been nobody shot in three days. *(Pause. He fingers the newspaper.)*

SUSAN: *(Takes the newspaper and looks at it. After a pause.)* The Caribou Sentinel. Yipeeeee! It says here the state of Kansas cast 9,000 votes for Woman's Suffrage. That's the first time it's been put to a popular vote. *(Pause.)* Kibby, let me tell the folks in this town about women's right to vote.

BAR DOG: My wife says she ain't gonna vote . . . even if this here state says she can. I do the votin' in the family . . . jist like I earn the wages.

SUSAN: Does your wife pray?

BAR DOG: Sure.

SUSAN: You tell your wife . . . what's your wife's name?

BAR DOG: Jane.

SUSAN: You tell her Susan B. Anthony said: "Jane, you do your own praying—you do your own voting." Tell Jane something else. A woman's brain is 100 grams lighter than a man's. Dante's brain was 100 grams lighter than Byron's. Does that mean Dante shouldn't vote?

BAR DOG: Can't say I know 'im.

SUSAN: Dante wrote the *Divine Comedy.* Maybe the greatest poem ever written.

BAR DOG: What's he ever done fer the West? *(Pause.)* I'm a bar dog. Can't say as I read me Dante. I kin look inna neck of a bottle of whiskey 'n tell the age jist like a cowpoke can tell the age of horse by lookin' in its mouth. I ain't never been ta the East. Afraid ta go. I'd get there 'n start wearin' celluloid collars 'n cuffs 'n never be worth a cuss no more.

SUSAN: Be the first man in your town, Kibby, to stand up for Freedom of Speech. Let me . . .

BAR DOG: I had me a man come in from New York jist last week. He says: "I think I'll have a cocktail." I said—ya don't think in here—ya drink . . . 'n it comes straight—in a tin cup.

SUSAN: I'm asking for an hour . . . give me half an hour!

BAR DOG: So ya eat ice cream ta the East? I ain't never et none, but a North Platte fella had some once 'n told me it give bout as much feed as loping a rough horse 'ginst a west wind with a funnel in yer mouth.

SUSAN: Thirty minutes . . .

BAR DOG: Is it true they keep water coolers filled with champagne ta fancy New York hotels?

SUSAN: I don't know about fancy hotels. I stoked a train from Navaho Twins for a free ride. Sometimes I stack wood for lunch.

BAR DOG: I use buffalo chips. *(Pause.)* Help yourself ta a free biscuit. I shot at 'em every morning ta see if they're soft 'nough ta eat.

SUSAN: Kibby Newt . . . do you believe in these United States?

BAR DOG: My daddy fought for fourteen dollars a month and the Union.

SUSAN: Then you believe in the Constitution of this country.

BAR DOG: My daddy was in the seventy-ninth regimental band. He serenaded Ulysses S. Grant hisself.

SUSAN: Then you do believe in Freedom of Speech. *(The Bar Dog just stares at her.)* Give me thirty minutes, Kibby.

BAR DOG: *(Pause.)* Fifteen.

Lights go dark. Lights come up on Battau who is seen struggling in a mud hole.

BATTAU: Ahhh . . . get me out of here . . . *(Joan enters.)* Help! Get me out of this mud hole. *(Pause.)* My page is dead. I can't move in all this armour.

Joan walks to Battau.

JOAN: Captain—at last we meet. *(Battau looks at her, embarrassed.)* I'll pull you out. *(She takes some rope and moves toward Battau.)*

BATTAU: Don't come near me with rope.

JOAN: It's the only way I can pull you out.

BATTAU: You make a rope . . . snake around a man till . . . it chokes him.

JOAN: That's not true. *(Pause.)* I make a rope snake across the Loire.

BATTAU: I heard about that.

JOAN: A very narrow part of the Loire. You could cast that far yourself.

She gets closer to him displaying the rope.

BATTAU: Don't tie me up. Spit toads, but don't tie me up . . . like a . . .

JOAN: Traitor? *(Pause.)* Here, grab my foot, then. For a start.

BATTAU: I heard about your "foot," too. *(Joan stares.)* It pulls off, and you grow another . . .

JOAN: I hate to tell you this, but I'm not a witch. It will take a great deal of brute strength to pull you out.

BATTAU: How do you know? *(Pause as Joan stares at him.)* Uh, huh! You know . . . because you got "second sight." Admit it.

JOAN: I know . . . because I pull my cow out of mud holes all the time. Back home. *(Pause.)* A cow can't be pulled from behind.

BATTAU: Don't get in back of me!

JOAN: If you pull a cow's tail . . . tug her out that way . . . you . . .

BATTAU: You want?

JOAN: Pull off her tail.

BATTAU: Don't come near me!

JOAN: So. I come in at the front.

BATTAU: *(Calls.)* La . . . Vour!

JOAN: Why are you calling my Captain? I'm here.

BATTAU: *(Calls.)* Lavour!

JOAN: I'll have you out in no time.

BATTAU: Don't take another step . . . stay away. *(Pause.)* They all got cows.

JOAN: Who?

BATTAU: Witches.

JOAN: I think it's bats they have.

BATTAU: What's the difference?

JOAN: I'd say a lot of difference.

BATTAU: *(Even more suspicious.)* Oh?

JOAN: I hate milk . . . but . . .

BATTAU: But what?

JOAN: Back home . . . when the morning frost is on the pasture grass . . . and I'm barefooted . . . and my feet are cold, you know what I do?

BATTAU: Fly?

JOAN: *(Comes close to Battau.)* I told you, I'm not a witch. Keep it a secret, though. *(Pause.)* Don't you want to know what I do?

BATTAU: OK . . . OK . . . tell me. Just stand back. *(She stands back.)*

JOAN: When the cow drops a steaming green cowpie, I run and stand in it to warm up.

BATTAU: *(In disgust.)* Ogggg! *(Pause. Calls.)* Lavour!

JOAN: Major, I'm going to put this rope around your waist.

BATTAU: *(Meekly.)* I'm a Major?

JOAN: One thing I've learned in the Army . . . no man refuses a promotion. *(She pulls him from the mud. Battau now steps out of the rope, trying hard to regain his stature.)* I'd be more careful if I were you, Captain.

BATTAU: Captain? You promoted me!!

JOAN: Strategy. *(Pause.)* And *Captain* . . . don't kill me . . . in case I have to save you again.

The Captain stares at her sternly. After a few seconds he smiles.

BATTAU: Well . . . we both hate the English, anyway.

Joan exits. Battau exits. Enter Ben and Susan. Ben is sketching.

BEN: A beautiful moonlight night.

SUSAN: I'm afraid I don't like moonlight nights. It's when the Indians raid.

BEN: Is that why you can't sleep at night?

SUSAN: I'm not used to hearing tom-toms all night . . .

BEN: And the splashing of oars . . .

SUSAN: And the war songs of braves, Mr. Caleb.

BEN: After ten days on the Miles Deadwood Overland . . . intimately thrown together by every bump in the road . . . I think we're entitled to call each other by our first names. *(Pause.)* Ben. Please.

SUSAN: Susan. *(Pause.)* Ah, yes, the Miles Deadwood Stage. Five miles an hour except when the horses are frightened by Indians.

BEN: Then it's thirty miles an hour while the harness holds.

SUSAN: Thanks again for getting that soldier to change seats with me. I hate to ride with my back to the horse.

BEN: I could see you were having a bad time of it.

SUSAN: I get sick riding backwards.

BEN: Especially with silly frills poking at you. That Southern Belle sat next to you all the way from Eagle Rock to Meeteetse.

SUSAN: When she finally got out . . . I used a ruler to measure the empty space she left. Five feet ten inches! *(They laugh.)*

BEN: Why don't you take the Butterfield? It's roomier.

SUSAN: And the nickel-plated harness shines in the sun.

BEN: And it stops at hotels.

SUSAN: That's the long way.

BEN: Ah, a lady in a hurry.

SUSAN: I hurry when I can, but the West is deceptive. Nothing here is located where it really is.

BEN: The West is a . . . mystery. Trains are spreading civilization into the wilderness . . . everywhere, little depots, eating houses . . . and the old Conestoga Wagon rolls along the Boseman Trail and ends mid-journey at a station for modern pullman cars. The nineteenth century and the middle ages meet each other daily on the prairie.

SUSAN: *(Takes the sketch from Ben.)* Is that . . .

BEN: You.

Ben exits. Susan begins to sand a piece of wood. Joan enters.

SUSAN: You haven't been around in weeks.

JOAN: I come when I can: My time is short. We're outside Orleans now.

SUSAN: This last stretch of prairie's been pretty tough.

JOAN: We're building a tower. It goes forward on rollers . . . right up to the city walls. The latest thing in military arsenal.

SUSAN: I've got to put a fence rail on the forward axle. The wheel's broke . . . just when I'm so close to California.

JOAN: But all it is is putting old things together. Everything that is, was. Like the machine that flings stones through the air. The wind's been shooting things through the air for thousands of years now.

SUSAN: I've over 10,000 names now. A woman on crutches clomped her way up a muddy street to be the first person in this state to sign up. In one town, a husband beat his wife for signing this. Not just women's names. Men too. They say the legislature isn't laughing at me anymore. They say Washington, D.C., might be afraid of Susan B. Anthony.

JOAN: We've got them scared, all right. My captain says the English think I got "powers." They're shaking in their shoes. He brought me a bouquet of wild onions today.

SUSAN: Your Captain?

JOAN: With a blue ribbon around them. You know, so I don't get scurvy. *(Pause.)* He throws breadcrumbs to the song sparrows.

SUSAN: Can he fight?

JOAN: Oh, yes!

SUSAN: That's the important thing, isn't it?

JOAN: Yes. *(Pause.)* But . . . now and then I'm breathless, when he gets too close.

SUSAN: I'm breathless . . . more than now and then. *(Pause.)* I rode a stage for ten days with a land surveyor. He reads Dickens and Shakespeare. He sketches. *(Pause.)* We laughed. Ate together. He played a little brass harmonica. *(Pause.)* He's the kind of man . . . who . . . who can sit up all night and whistle for dancing. He can make me forget everything . . . the rally . . . the vote.

JOAN: *(She sings songs teasingly.)*
> OH, HO,
> GOT A BEAU!
> OH, HO
> GOT A . . .

SUSAN: What about Lavour?

JOAN: Soldiers walk so funny . . . arched back. . . . When Lavour rides, he looks at his shadow. Soldiers always do that. A nice sunny day is their mirror.

SUSAN: You should see a cowboy ride his horse . . . one foot out of the stirrup . . . way over cocky to one side.

JOAN: That's what my first sergeant calls "too much mane and tail."

SUSAN: I saw a cowboy mount his horse at the rack in front of my hotel, ride across the street to the post office, dismount and tie his horse, mail a letter, then mount again and ride the horse back across the street to the hotel, get off, tie the horse and go to his room. *(They chuckle. After a pause.)* I had a long wait with a prairie farmer at the depot outside Comb Wash, and I gave him my whole speech. About the virtues of women. What our vote means to mankind, etc. A good sixty minutes worth. *(Pause.)* When I finished . . . he said: "When I'm feeding the steer and drive the wagon load of hay there and find jist one, I don't unload the whole thing for him." *(Pause.)* A Westerner always speaks by way of his animals.

JOAN: What about that artist land surveyor who sketches?

SUSAN: Oh, he's different. He reads poetry to me . . . sits close. Oh, I love a man's smell: train smoke, sweat, horses, sunshine. *(Pause.)* Sometimes I think . . . stay with him. Don't go to California. Take his warmth. *(Pause.)* Then I think of all the people who signed my petition. They depend on me. *(Pause.)* And there are the women waiting to sign my petition. And I know there's a truth stronger than the single pulse of my life! *(Pause.)* What are those lights in the hills?

JOAN: Signal fires. . . . Deserters trying to get more of my lancers to run off . . . I've got to go.

Joan exits. Ben enters.

BEN: Susan, sit by the fire with me.

SUSAN: Shall we throw on some more logs?

BEN: The white man builds a big fire and stands way back. The Indian builds a small fire and sits up close. *(They sit before the fire and Ben begins to sketch.)* I'll miss our lively talks, Susan. Tomorrow morning, you take a boat . . . I catch a train. There's no guarantee I'll have any good conversation.

SUSAN: Trains are packed with interesting people.

BEN: Pretty ones? *(He shows her his sketch.)*

SUSAN: *(Shyly.)* You've drawn the hair much too full.

BEN: Did you know Choctaw widows mourn by never combing their hair. For the full term of their grief.

SUSAN: What made you come to love the Indians?

BEN: Their fragileness. *(He continues drawing.)*

SUSAN: I don't think Indians are fragile.

BEN: Their race is.

SUSAN: Sioux steal cattle and molest homesteaders.

BEN: There are outlaw Indians just as there are outlaws among us. *(Pause.)* The early French explorers named them "Sioux." It means "Little Snakes." *(Pause.)* They call themselves "Dakotas" now. *(Pause.)* I've met over a hundred different tribes and maybe twenty thousand Indians, and I've never been threatened with any violence.

SUSAN: I should think the Indian is doing well enough. We have federal agencies set up for them. That's more than women have.

BEN: Ahhh . . . but think . . . who's the first lady of this land.

SUSAN: *(After a long pause.)* The squaw?

BEN: Of course. *(Susan smiles.)* The Dakotas have a saying. "No one should go far in the desert who can't sleep in the shade of his arrows." You have to know the desert to understand that. *(Pause.)* A good quiver full of arrows is as valuable as a horse. *(Pause.)* Stick the arrows in the sand by their points and lie with your head in the shade of their feathers. *(Pause.)* Remember that.

SUSAN: *(Smiling.)* I will. *(Looks at the sketch.)* I still say you made the hair too . . . full.

BEN: Ordinarily, I'd give you the sketch. But I want to keep it myself. Do you mind?

SUSAN: No.

BEN: *(He touches the hair on the sketch.)* There's a forest in a woman's hair. A calm which isn't silence hides inside. *(He looks at her slowly, then reaches out to touch her hair.)* Why did you cut it? *(A boat whistle is heard.)* The boat . . . *(Pause.)* Let it go by.

SUSAN: I've got to get to California.

BEN: *(Caustic.)* The rally . . . the "big" rally. *(Now more softly.)* Some day, what you're doing will seem inevitable. *(Looks at Susan affectionately.)* Marry me. We'll study Indians together. We'll build a house.

SUSAN: *(Weakly.)* A house?

BEN: With a porch.

SUSAN: *(Dreamily.)* And stone chimney . . .

BEN: A home—not a squatter's cabin.

SUSAN: . . . with baskets full of flowers hanging from the ceiling . . .

BEN: A two story house . . . .

SUSAN: . . . .with shelves for books. And muslin curtains. . . . *(Susan looks briefly at Joan.)*

BEN: Your house . . . to grow old in . . . yours! *(Pause.)* You'll win, Susan. You'll win . . . and when you have the rights as men do, who will care about you then?

SUSAN: Oh, Ben, I'm tired . . . I'm so tired . . .

Ben moves closer to her and puts his face in her hair.

BEN: Let me put my face in this hair . . . dark as the eclipse and scented with rain. *(He puts his face to her hair . . . then moves slowly to kiss her. After a pause, they break apart.)*

SUSAN: *(Annoyed by her feelings.)* I'm happy. *(Pause.)* Dear God, I'm happy.

The boat whistle is heard.

BEN: Tear up the boat ticket, Susan. Women will win . . . it's the ordinary course of history.

SUSAN: But I'm part of that history. *(Pause.)* I was chosen. And I promised. *(Pause.)* Every day I see the strings and snags of women's hair in the brush . . . all along the trail. *(Backing away from Ben and moving to the boat area.)* They say . . . women's hair gets caught in the brush. Pioneer women. *(Pause.)* And I keep hearing their silent voices. *(Pause. Susan moves closer to the boat area.)*

BEN: *(The light goes dark on Ben as he says.)* Susan . . . go with me . . . I have arrows enough . . .

Susan slowly goes to the boat railing as Ben exits. Boat whistle is heard. Susan is now standing by the boat railing. As Joan is hurriedly going by.

SUSAN: Joan . . . Joan . . .

JOAN: I'm in a hurry.

SUSAN: Mrs. Stanton wrote that the Married Property Bill was passed. Think of it. Women now have a purse of their own. *(Pause.)* What do you mean you're in a hurry? You just got here.

JOAN: I don't have time . . . they're waiting.

SUSAN: The Committee on Woman's Suffrage that I tried to get into Congress was defeated. *(Pause.)* I need to talk . . . I *need* somebody . . .

JOAN: They're waiting.

SUSAN: Please . . . just a minute. *(Pause.)* A minute! You owe me that! *(Joan remains, but she is decidedly looking out toward the battlefield. After a pause.)* The Committee I tried so hard to get into Congress—Wham! Done in.

JOAN: You told me.

SUSAN: Aren't you even sorry?

JOAN: Of course I'm sorry.

SUSAN: What about the Married Property Bill!

JOAN: Good.

SUSAN: Just . . . *good*?

JOAN: *(Looking off nervously to the battlefield.)* Don't you think I'd like more time?

SUSAN: I . . . I need to talk about the small things . . . the little stupid everyday things . . . the things we used to laugh about . . . *(Joan is impatiently looking toward the battlefield.)* . . . I haven't earned a dollar in six days . . . .I smell like a smoked side of bacon . . . I can grease a fry pan on my cape . . . I let a dog sleep on my feet to keep them warm. *(After a pause.)* I saw a bride today. She sat in a chair outside the Church. And her husband knelt in front of her, and put his arms around her—chair and all.

JOAN: Susan . . . I have to go. *(She exits.)*

SUSAN: *(Says as she watches Joan go off.)* . . . He put his arms around her . . . chair and all. *(Boat whistle sounds again. Pause. Susan picks up her pamphlets to continue her journey. Singing as she exits.)*

> COME ON NOW
> COME ON NOW
>   SEE WHAT'S NEW
> I'VE SPLIT THE SKIRT
> SPLIT IT RIGHT IN TWO
>   AND THERE AIN'T NO HORSE THAT
>   CAN'T BE RODE,
>   AND THERE AIN'T NO MAN
>   THAT CAN'T BE THROWED.

The Miner and Bar Dog enter singing.

MINER and BAR DOG: *(Singing.)*
   LAST NIGHT I GOT LAID BY THE FIRE
   AS I HUNKERED DEEP DOWN BY THE BURRS,
   I WONDERED WHY MY SWEET YOUNG COWGIRL
   DIDN'T TAKE OFF HER LONG SILVER SPURS.
   SILVER SPURS . . .
   SILVER SPURS . . .
   I GOT LAID WITH LONG SILVER SPURS.

MINER: I want rusted in the boiler. I want the jimjams. I want me so drunk, I'm gonna open my shirt collar ta piss. *(Pause . . . pounds the bar.)* Kinda hooch Indians trade their wives fer.

Susan enters the bar saying to the audience and Bar Dog and Miner.

SUSAN: This speaker you see here now is one jump ahead of the Marshal. Stick around. I can get arrested any minute. *(Pause.)* No throwing of turnips, cigar stumps, beets, old quids of tobacco, or lampblack. *(Pause.)* A rally is going on here in California. Open up your ears and hear me.

MINER: My brother's wife is in this here California rally . . . 'n she is left my brother 'n nine hired hands by theirselves with nobody ta holler 'em in at night.

BAR DOG: Women oughta stay at home . . . where they got it easy.

MINER: Mules 'n women are jist alike . . . they don't know whether ya treat 'em good or not.

BAR DOG: Hey . . . you got something 'ginst mules? *(Bar Dog and Miner chuckle.)*

SUSAN: Now . . . ah . . . this country's in the middle of a contest for equality . . . a contest that . . .

BAR DOG: Set me up fer a bitin' contest. With a snake. I'll give the critter a handicap. He kin bite me first.

SUSAN: . . . a contest that will ensure the constitutional rights of all citizens.

MINER: Hit's Sunday. Don't you ivver shut down?

SUSAN: I don't have any Sundays . . . now I know you're decent gents and want to do the right thing . . . and the right thing to do is give a fair chance to all. But the cards are marked. The dice have ten sides. The dealer's dealt us out.

MINER: *(He sing songs.)*
   HER HEART IS IN NEW YORK
   BUT HER BUTTE IS IN MONTANA
   GOD HOW SHE LOVES THE HARD-SHELLED
   BAPTIST LEMONADE

SUSAN: I know you're decent gents and want to do the right thing . . . and . . .

BAR DOG: Save part of yer breath fer breathin'.

SUSAN: . . . And the right thing is a fair chance . . .

MINER: Ya can't sell a thousand-foot claim on a vest pocket specimen . . . 'n ya can't sell us on no women votin' with jist you up there.

SUSAN: In the state of Kansas, that good state, they voted for women's suffrage.

MINER: Jest grasshopper yerself back ta Kansas, then. *(Both snicker.)*

SUSAN: In the state of Kansas . . . if you would consult the newspaper . . . I can give you the newspaper . . .

MINER: Give us limb! We don't wanna buy it—jist rent it. *(The men laugh.)*

SUSAN: In the state of Kansas, the legislature is coming to terms with Civil Rights for females. In the language of the law that means . . .

MINER: *Limbs* is our language.

SUSAN: *(Trying to continue.)* Civil Rights! In the language of the law, that means . . .

MINER: While yer "long windin' it" up there, gold is sinkin' in the ground by the inch.

MINER and BAR DOG: *(Chanting.)* Limbs! Limbs!

Susan swings her leg up on a beer keg.

SUSAN: *(Sings.)*
  COME ON, NOW
  COME ON, NOW
    SEE WHAT'S NEW,
  I'VE SPLIT THE SKIRT
    SPLIT IT RIGHT IN TWO
  AND THERE'S AIN'T NO HORSE THAT
    CAN'T BE RODE
  AND THERE AIN'T NO MAN
    THAT CAN'T BE THROWED.

(Pause. Susan moves closer to the men. The men have been startled by her song and she now has their attention.) Do you know what baseball is? *(Men grunt in agreement. Pause.)* My brothers were allowed to play baseball. But not me! Because I was a girl and baseball is not "polite." *(Pause.)* So you know what I did? I hid behind the trees and bushes on the farm, and I spied on my brothers. I watched them pitch a ball, then I'd go to some deserted place behind the pasture and I'd throw a hundred speeding baseballs into the fence posts. But I knew I couldn't really be a good player until I got on the team, because baseball is a team sport. When you hide and try to steal knowledge, you have to take second best. *(Pause.)* So I went out in the open, and I got in the game. When my brothers yelled at me, I just stood tight to the base. And I learned to

play that game as it should be. And I ran the bases hard. And sometimes we won and sometimes we lost. But we all played; that's the American Way.

The Bar Dog and Miner are impressed.

MINER: *(Extends his hand to her.)* Limpy Bob.

BAR DOG: *(Extends his hand to her.)* Three Deuces.

SUSAN: *(Shakes hands with men.)* Susan B. Anthony!

BAR DOG: Anthony . . . Anthony . . . *(To Susan.)* You know somebody called Double Ugly? He come through here with some cattle.

SUSAN: Is he here? *(Looking around.)* Ugly? Ugly?

BAR DOG: He done took off. He left this here lariat and gun fer you. He said . . . "tie 'em up and shoot 'm 'iffen they don't behave." *(Pause.)* He also said somethin' bout signin' some paper fer ya.

SUSAN: My petition! He signed it! Oh, Ugly! Ugly!

Marshal enters.

MARSHAL: OK—everybody freeze! *(Miner and Bar Dog run off and exit leaving Susan who tries to hide.)* I seen you . . . Susan B. Anthony! *(Pause.)* Come on out! *(After a pause, Susan slowly comes forward.)* So yer the Susan that voted. *(Pause.)* I've chased you so hard I feel like I was run through the syrup cane mill. I come through mountain snow on a dog sled. Winds was strong and dead trees was fallin' everywhere. Only way I could keep them dogs goin' was give 'em whiskey every mile.

SUSAN: How did you know I was here?

MARSHAL: You went back on yer course. Nine cases outta ten, a criminal does that. Just like a stalked bear or lion. It's the age-old thang in nature to deceive by doublin' back. *(He takes some bark out of his pocket and begins to write.)* When I make a catch, I record it ta my book . . . 'n if I don't have no paper, I use birch bark. *(After a pause.)* So you're *her*. I lost you fer awhile in the Alkali Flats near Frenchtown.

SUSAN: You've been hot on my trail since Horse Creek.

MARSHAL: That's right.

SUSAN: . . . Elkhorn . . . Mount Idaho . . . Squaw Gulch, Woods Flat, Otter Lake, Mother Lode . . .

MARSHAL: . . . Big Hole, Bumble Bee, Yankee Fork, Wilson Bar, Carson Hill, Walla Walla. I seen their smoke signals. Sioux is followin' ya too.

SUSAN: When I see a column of smoke in the sky, I just send an answering smoke signal back. Indians aren't all that unfriendly, Marshal.

MARSHAL: *(Shocked.)* You send 'em back an answer?

SUSAN: Of course, I don't know what I say. *(Pause.)* If a woman's so stupid and insignificant she can't vote, why take all the bother to haul her back East?

MARSHAL: Seein' a little rattlesnake in yer path . . . ya wouldn't let it move off cause it's too small ta bite.

SUSAN: Do you have daughters, sir?

MARSHAL: Five. None of 'em bigamists!

SUSAN: Neither am I.

MARSHAL: None of 'em for "free love."

SUSAN: Neither am I.

MARSHAL: Woman that comes out ta these parts by herself is half bigamists or half free love, or both, one ta the other.

SUSAN: Can tell you haven't been to my lectures.

MARSHAL: What good is all this done ya? People is jist come out against you more 'n ever. *(Pause. He hands her a flyer.)* California just killed women's right to vote.

SUSAN: *(Looks at flyer and reads.)* One Hundred and ten thousand For— One Hundred and thirty-seven thousand Against—It was close. *(After a pause.)* What good does this arrest do you?

MARSHAL: *(Looks at her defiantly.)* I cross many a river with cattle. Sometimes their leader turns back and the whole bunch begins ta swim in a circle. That circle's gotta be broke—or they all drown.

SUSAN: I've got women swimming in a circle. Is that it? *(Pause. Angry.)* Why don't you people out here ever talk *direct.*

MARSHAL: You don't buy a horse is got brands on it all over. That's a sure sign it's been owned by a lotta cow dogs 'n ain't been loyal ta inny of 'em.

SUSAN: God only knows what that means. *(Pause.)* Marshal, we've been through a lot together. You're not going to . . . to . . . shackle me, are you? *(She holds out her hands to him.)*

MARSHAL: *(After a pause.)* Hell, no! *(Pause.)* But being a girl ain't gonna save you. Yer under arrest.

SUSAN: I've got good outdoor wrinkles from the sun. Some indoor wrinkles, too. I'm no *girl.*

MARSHAL: *(After a pause.)* You ready, then? *(Pause.)* Jesus, she jist answered the Sioux back.

SUSAN: Ready.

MARSHAL: I hear ya sing, too.

SUSAN: Marshal, you're going to hear my song from here to Rochester.

Susan and Marshal exit. Soft battle drums. Joan and Lavour enter.

LAVOUR: *(Pause. Looks at her tenderly.)* Nervous?

JOAN: A little.

LAVOUR: Excited?

JOAN: A little.

LAVOUR: *(Pause. Looks at her lovingly.)* I think . . . I'll watch you take Orleans today.

JOAN: *Watch* me?

LAVOUR: *(Teasingly.)* Well . . . I'm tired . . . you know it rained all night. I had to get up early and dig a trench around my tent.

JOAN: *(Smiling.)* Didn't we all. *(Pause. Fondly.)* When I look back . . . I expect to see you, Captain . . . I want to see you . . . swinging that shining sword . . .

LAVOUR: I'll be there.

She now kneels down before him and begins to put leg armour on his legs. As she does, she says.

JOAN: You're right. There's always the stink of death in my nostrils. *(Pause. Still dressing his leg armour.)* All that can must carry torches . . . and tell the men to be careful of canon holes—they're filled with water. They're little rivers. *(Pause.)* What is the last count of sergeants?

LAVOUR: Four thousand.

JOAN: Save them for the wall. Use our knights for the sieges.

Lavour now begins to put armour on Joan.

LAVOUR: Follow the drums . . . do you hear me? And stay to the back.

JOAN: I can't do that.

LAVOUR: You must stay to the back.

JOAN: The closer you get to battle, the safer it is. You know that. The dead are always far out.

LAVOUR: Please . . . don't take chances. *(Pause. As he finishes dressing her armour.)* It's such a curse of a war, a bloody curse of a war. I long for the war of my ancestors. *(Pause. Lavour has finished dressing her armour.)* Please . . . stay to the back.

JOAN: The army needs its infantry. You know that.

LAVOUR: Do you have the map? *(Pause.)* The map I gave you . . . with the terrain . . . the position of the wall . . . with the . . . .

JOAN: *(She holds out her two hands and cups them together, palms upward.)* This is my map. *(Pause.)* These life lines are the gulches and creeks angling to the center of the drawbridge . . . where we assemble the archers. The end of the Loire drops down to a trickle out where my palms meet. Toward those little wrinkles there, the lancers settle in with the stone machines. I cock my thumbs, and they're towers looking down on the land below—our moving towers.

LAVOUR: *(He takes her hands and puts them to his lips and kisses them.)* Please . . . please . . . don't take chances.

Lights begin to dim as battle drums are heard.

JOAN: My Captain . . . will you be the first with me . . . to enter Orleans?

LAVOUR: No . . . this is your history.

A Lancer comes on stage carrying a standard, and hands it to Joan. The Archer comes in. Joan stops in a victory position.

JOAN: If this is my glory, then I grieve for God's. *(She exits.)*
ARCHER: She's over the wall.
LAVOUR: Follow her!

The Archer, Lancer and Lavour exit . . . chanting "Joan, Joan, Joan." Joan returns to the stage to plant her standard. Susan comes on stage echoing the "Joan" chant.

SUSAN: Joan . . . Joan . . . *(Happily.)* You took Orleans! *(They embrace. Pause. Susan pulls away.)* I'm going back to stand trial.
JOAN: With your victories.
SUSAN: LITTLE VICTORIES.
JOAN: Petitions . . . the Marriage Property Bill . . .
SUSAN: Little Victories. . . . Women can't vote. Maybe they never will.
JOAN: Maybe . . . they will.
SUSAN: I need you. *(Pause.)* Who will brush my hair . . . when it's gray.
JOAN: I don't know what it's like to fight when you're fifty . . . sixty . . . seventy . . . eighty years old.
SUSAN: I'll miss you.
JOAN: And I'll miss you. *(Pause.)* Reach. *(Pause.)* I reached out for you with this, my oldest arm. I found you.
SUSAN: I turned back. I found you.
JOAN: Reach. *(Pause.)* I had to.
(Pause. Points to audience.)
It's just another prairie. *(Pause.)* You won't be alone. *(Pause.)* The future will help you. *(Pause.)* Take the dark.
(Susan reaches out to audience as the lights go dark.)

END OF ACT II

CURTAIN

Mary Gordon Murray, Alaina Reed, Charlaine Woodard, Randy Graff, and Roo Brown in *A . . . My Name Is Alice*, 1984. Photo © by Carol Rosegg, Martha Swope Associates.

Author's Note

In the fall of 1982, Joan Micklin Silver asked me to help her find positive, up-beat songs and sketches for actresses who were participating in a NARAL (National Abortion Rights Action League) benefit that was being held at Circle in the Square. To our surprise, we came up empty-handed. We found marginal scenes but no songs (all were of the he-left-me-and-now-I'm-miserable variety). Most of the material we found was void of humor. A show in which women could find humor in their lives, not only about men but also about their families and their careers, seemed extremely timely.

We started by contacting all of the women writers we knew and asked them to contribute material. Because many of them had writing partners who were men, we realized that male writers with the right sensibility could also write for the project. Once the word got out that men were welcome (including male/male writing teams), they began to approach us with ideas. The mission became finding humorous and meaningful selections for and about women, regardless of who wrote them. For more than a year, we met with writers three mornings a week with the goal of assembling a revue. These brainstorming sessions helped us identify the issues that we wanted to examine.

In the summer of 1983, we took the first round of material (about thirty-five selections) to Julia Miles at the Women's Project. She agreed that the timing was perfect for such a project. By November we began our first workshop of *A . . . My Name Is Alice*. We culled the selections down to twenty-eight. The workshop was tremendously successful and led to further revisions and refinement of the piece. February 1984 saw our second workshop (with twenty-five selections) and by April the show moved to the Village Gate, where it played for more than a year.

The joy of *A . . . My Name Is Alice* is that it allows women to laugh at themselves. The beginnings of most social movements are fueled by anger at injustice, and the women's movement of the late twentieth century was no exception. But there comes a moment when those fighting the battle can take a breath and laugh. It is through humor that we often make our biggest strides. Joan and I hope that *Alice* has accomplished this in some small way.

—Julianne Boyd

Act I

ALL-GIRL BAND lyrics by David Zippel; music by Doug Katsaros: Copyright © 1983 David Zippel and Doug Katsaros. All rights reserved.

A . . . MY NAME IS ALICE POEMS by Marta Kauffman and David Crane: Copyright © 1984 Crane and Kauffman. All rights reserved.

AT MY AGE lyrics by June Siegel; music by Glen Roven: Copyright © 1983 Roven and Siegel. All rights reserved.

TRASH lyrics by Marta Kauffman and David Crane; music by Michael Skloff: Copyright © 1984 Skloff, Crane and Kauffman. All rights reserved.

FOR WOMEN ONLY POEMS by Marta Kauffman and David Crane: Copyright © 1984 Crane and Kauffman. All rights reserved.

GOOD THING I LEARNED TO DANCE lyrics by Mark Salzman; music by Stephen Lawrence: Copyright © 1983 SJL Music Co. All rights reserved.

WELCOME TO KINDERGARTEN, MRS. JOHNSON lyrics by Marta Kauffman and David Crane; music by Michael Skloff: Copyright © 1984 Skloff, Crane and Kauffman. All rights reserved.

I SURE LIKE THE BOYS lyrics by Steve Tesich; music by Lucy Simon: Copyright © 1984 Sigh and Moan. All rights reserved.

MS. MAE by Cassandra Medley: Copyright © 1984 Cassandra Medley. All rights reserved.

GOOD SPORTS
"DETROIT PERSONS" by Susan Rice

"EDUCATED FEET" by Carol Hall: Copyright © 1984 Daniel Music LTD. All rights reserved.

THE PORTRAIT lyrics and music by Amanda McBroom: Copyright © 1981 McBroom Music. Used by permission. All rights reserved.

BLUER THAN YOU lyrics by Winnie Holzman; music by David Evans: Copyright © 1983 Holzman and Evans. All rights reserved.

Act II

PRETTY YOUNG MEN lyrics by Susan Birkenhead; music by Lucy Simon: Copyright © 1984 Calougie Music and Algebra. All rights reserved.

DEMIGOD by Richard LaGravanese: Copyright © 1984 Richard LaGravanese. All rights reserved.

THE FRENCH SONG lyrics and music by Don Tucker; monologue by Art Murray: Copyright © 1977 Murray and Tucker. All rights reserved.

PAY THEM NO MIND lyrics and music by Calvin Alexander and James Shorter: Copyright © 1965 Calvin Alexander/Gujim Records. All rights reserved.

HOT LUNCH by Anne Meara: Copyright © 1983 Anne Meara. All rights reserved.

EMILY, THE M.B.A. lyrics by Mark Saltzman; music by Stephen Lawrence: Copyright © 1983 SJL Music Co. All rights reserved.

SISTERS lyrics by Maggie Bloomfield; music by Cheryl Hardwick: Copyright © 1983 Bloomwick Publishing. All rights reserved.

HONEYPOT lyrics by Mark Saltzman; music by Stephen Lawrence: Copyright © 1983 SJL Music Co. All rights reserved.

A . . . My Name Is Alice was originally produced by the Women's Project at the American Place Theater in New York City in 1983. It was conceived and directed by Joan Micklin Silver and Julianne Boyd with set design by Adrianne Lobel, lighting design by Ann Wrightson, costume design by Mimi Maxmen, choreography by Yvonne Adrian, and musical direction by Jan Rosenberg. The production stage manager was Renee F. Lutz. The cast was as follows:

Lynnie Godfrey
Randy Graff
Polly Pen
Alaina Reed
Grace Roberts

Contributing authors include Calvin Alexander, Susan Birkenhead, Maggie Bloomfield, David Crane, David Evane, Carol Hall, Cheryl Hardwick, Georgia Bogardus Holof, Winnie Holtzman, Doug Katsaros, Marta Kauffman, Richard LaGravenese, Stephen Lawrence, Amanda McBroom, Anne Meara, Cassandra Medley, David Mettee, Art Murray, Susan Rice, Glen Roven, Mark Saltzman, James Shorter, June Siegel, Lucy Simon, Michael Skloff, Steve Tesich, Don Tucker, and David Zippel.

CHARACTERS

FIRST ACTRESS:	Mature, thirtyish black woman. Earthy, but with a strong ironic edge.
SECOND ACTRESS:	Twentyish urban type. Sexy and sometimes neurotic.
THIRD ACTRESS:	Twentyish black woman. Dancer with high energy and sparkling personality.
FOURTH ACTRESS:	Fiftyish. Warm, motherly type with a mischievous sense of humor.
FIFTH ACTRESS:	Late twenties/early thirties. Cosmopolitan, sophisticated woman with a secretly zany side.

ACT 1

The house lights go down and the stage is dark. Lights come up as the First Actress enters center stage. As the song progresses, the dancing becomes spirited, reminiscent of a syncopated marching band.

All-Girl Band

FIRST ACTRESS:
  IT WAS ONE OF THOSE DAYS
  WHEN YOUR MIND IS A MAZE.
  I WAS TRAPPED IN THE DOUBT OF MY LIFE.
SECOND ACTRESS: *(Enters from upstage center.)*
  I WAS DOING A QUIZ
  FOUND IN *COSMO* OR *MS.*
  WHEN THE MUSIC WENT OUT OF MY LIFE.
BOTH:
  BUT I'M NOT THE TYPE TO FACE THE BLUES ALONE.
FIRST ACTRESS:
  SO I DUSTED OFF MY FLUTE.
SECOND ACTRESS:
  AND SLIDE TROMBONE—
BOTH:
  AND JOINED AN ALL-GIRL BAND.
  NOW I JAM FROM THE NIGHT TILL MORN.
  I JOINED AN ALL-GIRL BAND.
  NOW I CAN BLOW MY OWN HORN!
THIRD ACTRESS: *(Enters center stage.)*
  I WAS FED UP WITH RULES
  AND THE ROOMFUL OF FOOLS
  AT MY OFFICE WAS DRIVING ME NUTS.
  WELL I NEEDED SOME PEACE
  OR AT LEAST A RELEASE
  OR I'D KICK IN THEIR IFS, ANDS, AND BUTTS.
  BUT AT FIVE I PUNCH THE CLOCK AND NOT MY BOSS
  AND I RUN HOME TO BECOME DIANA ROSS.
ALL:
  I JOINED AN ALL-GIRL BAND
  AND THE FEELING IS JUST WHAT I NEED.
  I JOINED AN ALL-GIRL BAND.
THIRD ACTRESS:
  FROM NOW ON I'M SINGING THE LEAD!

Fourth and fifth actresses enter from downstage left and right, respectively.

ALL:
  WE'RE SHAKIN' OUR MARACAS.
  WE'RE MAKING NEWS,
  MAKING MUSIC THAT'S RHYTHM AND BLUES.
  TOGETHER WE'RE MUCH BETTER THAN SO-SO—
  EACH OF US IS A VIRTUOSO!

FOURTH ACTRESS:
  I WAS HITTIN' THE SKIDS.
FIFTH ACTRESS:
  I WAS SICK OF MY KIDS.
FOURTH and FIFTH ACTRESSES:
  DISCONTENTED TO JUST BE A WIFE.
FIFTH ACTRESS:
  IF I SPENT ONE MORE DAY
  WITH THE DAMN P.T.A.,
  I WOULD DROWN IN THE CAR-POOL OF LIFE.
FOURTH ACTRESS:
  THEN WE GAVE UP PLAYING
  MAH JONG,
  BRIDGE
FIFTH ACTRESS:
  AND GIN.
FOURTH ACTRESS:
  NOW I PLAY THE BASS GUITAR.
FIFTH ACTRESS:
  AND VIOLIN.
ALL:
  WE JOINED AN ALL-GIRL BAND
  AND THE MUSIC INSIDE OF US SINGS.
  WE JOINED AN ALL-GIRL BAND,
  NOW LOOK WHO'S PULLING THE STRINGS!

  WE JOINED AN ALL-GIRL BAND,
  AND THE HARMONY SPARS THROUGH THE NIGHT.
  WE JOINED AN ALL-GIRL BAND
  ALICE IS GOING ALL RIGHT!

A . . . My Name Is Alice Poems

Spoken with piano under.

FIFTH ACTRESS:
  A . . . My Name Is Alice
  And my husband's name is Allan
  And we live in Alabama
  And we sell apples.
FOURTH ACTRESS:
  A . . . My Name Is Alice
  And my husband's name is Albert
  And I live in Albuquerque
  And I get alimony.

THIRD ACTRESS:
A . . . My Name Is Alice
And I work as an attorney
For Applebaum, Bemshick and Cohen
And do I have anxiety!
SECOND ACTRESS:
A . . . My Name Is Alice
And I live in an apartment
And I live in it alone
And it's kind of antiseptic
And my boyfriend's an accountant
And he's kind of antisocial
And I want to be an actress
But I couldn't get an agent
So I sell Avon.

Chime does "ding-dong."

FIRST ACTRESS:
A . . . My Name Is Alice
And my husband's name in Adam
And his girlfriend's name is Amy
And my lover's name is Abbie
And her husband's name is Arnie
And his boyfriend's name is Allen
And my analyst's name is Arthur
And we're working on my anger.

All-Girl Band Tag

ALL: *(Singing.)*
WE JOINED AN ALL-GIRL BAND
AND THE HARMONY SOARS THROUGH THE NIGHT.
WE JOINED AN ALL-GIRL BAND.
FIRST and SECOND ACTRESSES:
NOW I CAN BLOW MY OWN HORN.
THIRD ACTRESS:
FROM NOW ON I'M SINGING THE LEAD.
FOURTH and FIFTH ACTRESSES:
NOW LOOK WHO'S PULLING THE STRINGS.
ALL:
ALICE IS DOING ALL RIGHT!

BLACKOUT.

At My Age

Lights come up to discover Vicky standing by a chair stage left, primping. Throughout the song, she and Karen play to an imaginary mirror, miming different motions such as combing hair, putting on mascara and lipstick, etc.

VICKY:
 THIRTY-TWO YEARS YOU LIVE WITH A MAN
 AND YOU LOSE HIM.
 THERE YOU ARE
 WITH HIS PICTURE AND A HOUSEFUL OF MEMORIES.
KAREN: *(Enters and stands right of center stage, primping.)*
 FIFTEEN YEARS OLD
 AND I'VE NEVER EVEN GONE STEADY.
 ALL MY GIRLFRIENDS
 THINK IT'S KIND OF WEIRD.
VICKY:
 DIDN'T WANT TO START AGAIN.
KAREN:
 COULDN'T WAIT TO START.
 HE'S SO GORGEOUS
 AND HE'S GOING OUT FOR TRACK.
VICKY:
 OUT OF THE BLUE AUNT SARAH CALLED.
 "I'VE GOT SOMEONE FOR YOU.
 WALTER'S DEAD—
 SITTING HOME WON'T BRING HIM BACK."
 AND IT'S MY FIRST BLIND DATE . . .
KAREN:
 MY FIRST REAL DATE . . .
VICKY:
 AT MY AGE.
KAREN:
 AT MY AGE.
VICKY:
 I'M NOT READY.
KAREN:
 I'VE BEEN READY FOR SO LONG.
VICKY:
 WHAT'LL WE DO FOR A WHOLE LONG EVENING?
 WHAT DO YOU SAY TO A PERFECT STRANGER?
KAREN:
 WHY DOES THIS KINKY HAIRCUT LOOK ALL WRONG?
 WONDER IF MOM'S CHANEL SMELLS TOO STRONG?

HOW COULD I KNOW THAT MY BROTHER
WOULD GET HIM TO CALL ME?
THEN HE PHONED
AND I COULDN'T GET MY VOICE TO COOPERATE . . .
VICKY:
 FIFTEEN YEARS OLD
 IS WHAT I SUDDENLY FEEL LIKE—
 CLAMMY HANDS
 AND THAT LONG-FORGOTTEN ACHE.
KAREN:
 PARALYZED AND TERRIFIED.
VICKY:
 NOT A THING TO WEAR . . .
 HE'S FROM SCARSDALE.
KAREN:
 SHOULD I TRY TO SMOKE?
 MAYBE HE'LL GET HIS FATHER'S CAR.
VICKY:
 HE'S FIFTY-EIGHT YEARS OLD
 AND A BROKER—
 SO HE'LL PROBABLY GO FOR BROKE.
 AND IT'S MY FIRST BLIND DATE . . .
KAREN:
 MY FIRST REAL DATE—
 IT'S CRAZY!
VICKY:
 IT'S CRAZY!
KAREN:
 WILL HE LIKE ME?
BOTH:
 WILL HELLO BE JUST GOOD-BYE?
VICKY:
 WHAT'LL I DO IF HE WANTS TO KISS ME?
KAREN:
 WHAT'LL I DO IF HE TRIES TO FRENCH ME?
VICKY:
 KISSING IS NOT THE PROBLEM.
KAREN:
 I MAY DIE!
BOTH:
 WHAT'LL I DO IF HE DOESN'T EVEN TRY?
 IT'S ALL SO NEW—
 IT'S A FIRST ALL RIGHT!

KAREN:
LIKE ALGEBRA OR CHAUCER.
VICKY:
LIKE THAT FIRST NIGHT.
BOTH:
AND HERE I AM – ANOTHER FIRST.
WELL, IT WON'T BE THE LAST,
BUT IT MAY BE THE WORST!
KAREN:
MY FIRST REAL DATE.
VICKY:
MY FIRST BLIND DATE.
KAREN:
WHO'S NERVOUS?
VICKY:
WHO'S NERVOUS?
BOTH:
I HOPE I DON'T START ACTING LIKE A FOOL.
KAREN:
MY FIRST REAL DATE . . .
VICKY:
MY FIRST BLIND DATE . . .
KAREN:
AT MY AGE.
VICKY:
AT MY AGE.
KAREN:
HE'LL THINK I'M A WIMP.
VICKY:
OLD FASHIONED OR ODD.
KAREN:
MY I.D.!
VICKY:
MY NEW BAG!
BOTH:
HE'S HERE! OH MY GOD!
BE COOL . . .

Both stand and take a few steps downstage.

HELLO.

BLACKOUT.

Trash

Lights come up to discover Mindy sitting stage left, reading a paperback novel. A desk is set downstage right.

VOICE OVER: "Jacqueline—She had the kind of beauty that made men burn with desire. She was every woman's envy and every man's dream. Yet she was possessed by a lover whose cruelty was ravishing torment."

Mindy puts down the first novel and picks up a second from the table beside her.

VOICE OVER: "Babette—The world was her bedroom. From the beaches of St. Tropez to the boardrooms of Manhattan's super-rich; from the back streets of Florence to the pyramids of Cairo; from the Casinos of Las Vegas to the jungles of Peru. Babette, she was a woman who couldn't stay put."

Mindy puts down the paperback.

MINDY: Mindy—She had everything. An exciting job as a receptionist for a woman's shoe manufacturer, a studio apartment in Queens, a boyfriend of limited qualities, and yet somehow she knew, there had to be more.

As the song intro begins she stands and crosses to center stage.

MINDY: *(Singing.)*
SHE DRESSED AND TOOK THE DOUBLE R,
AND PRESSED INSIDE THE CROWDED CAR,
REGRETTED HAVING LEFT THE LIMOUSINE AT HOME.
SHE HID BEHIND HER *DAILY NEWS*
AND WONDERED WHAT HAD MADE HER CHOOSE
THIS CRAZY LIFE OF DANGER, SEX AND BOOZE
AT KAPLAN'S SHOES.

SHE FOUND HER OFFICE DOOR UNLOCKED—
SHE HELD HER BREATH AND GENTLY KNOCKED.
SHE HEARD A SOUND AND HID BEHIND HER DESK.

Mrs. Kaplan enters.

HER RIVAL ENTERED DRESSED IN RED,
AND MINDY SWORE SHE'D SEE HER DEAD.
SHE GRABBED THE ROLODEX AND RAISED IT,
BUT INSTEAD THE WOMAN SAID:

MRS. KAPLAN: *(Speaking.)* Mindy, type this up for me, and I'll need three copies. *(Sees Rolodex over Mindy's head.)* Oh, and can you get me Milton Glaser's phone number?

Mrs. Kaplan exits.

MINDY: *(Singing.)*
WHY CAN'T MY LIFE BE TRASH?
WHY CAN'T I WAKE UP TO SCORCHING ROMANCE?
TORN FROM THE PAGES OF COLLINS OR KRANTZ?
OH, WHY CAN'T MY LIFE BE TRASH?

Howard enters upstage center and crosses to Mindy.

THEN HOWARD RUSHED INTO THE ROOM,
AND MINDY SENSED IMPENDING DOOM
HE SLIPPED AN INVOICE IN HER IN-BOX AND HE SMILED.
HOWARD: *(Speaking.)* Hi, Mindy. *(Howard flexes his muscles as he sings.)*
SHE MARVELED AT HIS FINE PHYSIQUE,
HIS BULGING PECS THAT LEFT HER WEAK,
SHE WATCHED HIM FLEX
WITH THOUGHTS OF SEX
AND MINDY TRIED TO SPEAK.
SHE TOUCHED HIS CHEEK.
MINDY: *(Touches his cheek.)* You have something here, Howard.
HOWARD: Oh. Tuna salad. Listen, Mindy. I've been thinking . . . I think
maybe we should start seeing other people. I mean we work in the same office
and all, and we've been seeing each other for three years now, and I dunno . . .
MINDY: *(Singing, as she pushes Howard offstage.)*
WHY CAN'T HE TREAT ME LIKE TRASH?
(Speaking.) We'll talk about it later, Howard. *(Singing)*
WHY CAN'T HE PULL ME TO STRONG SPANISH HIPS?
TAKE ME AND TEAR OUT MY HEART WITH HIS LIPS?
UNLEASH ALL I'VE HELD IN ME?
COMPLETELY SIDNEY SHELDON ME??

Stanley enters, carrying a briefcase. He has a trucking walk and a snappy style.

MINDY: May I help you?
STANLEY: Stanley Henderson. I have an appointment with Mrs. Kaplan.
Leather samples. *(Indicates briefcase.)*
MINDY: Have a seat. *(Sees thick paperback book that STANLEY has pulled out
and is reading.)* Oh, I've been meaning to read that—how is it?
STANLEY: Pretty good. I liked *Forbidden Tears* a lot better.
MINDY: *(Into intercom.)* Mrs. K, your ten o'clock appointment is here.
STANLEY: *(To himself.)* From the moment he laid eyes on her he knew he
had to possess her.
MINDY: Pardon?
STANLEY: Nothing. He knew that behind that icy exterior lived a hot-
blooded siren, sensuous and exotic.

Mindy has meanwhile taken a stick of gum from her desk and has slunk to the other side of Stanley.

MINDY: Gum? *(Stanley shakes his head.)* Her heart was pounding. She looked at him again and raw passion welled within her.

STANLEY: He met her gaze, and his eyes danced with cruel amusement. *(His eyes do so.)*

MINDY: She had to turn away . . . How does he do that? *(She mimics Stanley's eyes.)*

STANLEY: He approached her slowly, and touched her arm. *(He crosses to Mindy.)*

MINDY: Sending shivers up her spine.

STANLEY: He held her close. *(Mindy is wrapped in Stanley's arms. They sing romantic nothings to each other.)*

STANLEY: Aaahhh . . .

MINDY: Aaahhh . . .

STANLEY: Aaahhh . . .

MINDY: Aaahhh . . .

STANLEY: Aaahhh . . .

MINDY: Aaahhh . . .

MINDY: Mindy closed her eyes, secure at last in the strength of his firm embrace.

STANLEY: But of course theirs was a love that was never meant to be.

MINDY: *(Puzzled.)* Oh, yeah? Why's that?

STANLEY: Because of the secret pact they had made years before aboard the Baron's yacht.

MINDY: *(Thinking fast.)* Ah, the Baron's yacht, yes, but . . . but she was suffering from amnesia then and has only recently begun to piece together the puzzle of her former life.

STANLEY: Perhaps. Then of course she remembers that she was a lady of the evening then, and he a simple priest. *(He assumes priestly pose.)*

MINDY: *(Desperate now.)* But things have changed! Now she's a world-famous fashion model! *(She poses.)*

STANLEY: And he's the Pope!

MINDY: Oh. *(The intercom buzzes and the fantasy is over.)* Mrs. Kaplan will see you now. *(Stanley prepares to leave.)* We always have tomorrow. *(She drapes herself on the desk.)*

STANLEY: I already read it. It's not very good. *(He exits. Mindy returns to her desk and sits dejectedly.)*

MINDY: Broken and defeated, Mindy sat down at her desk. She filed some invoices, wrote out a disbursement, sharpened a pencil . . . *(Singing.)*

WHY CAN'T MY LIFE BE . . .

(Inspiration hits. She presses the intercom button. Speaking—) Howard, it's Mindy. Can you come in here? I got a book I want you to read.

BLACKOUT.

For Women Only #1

A single spot comes up C. stage as a Poetess enters, carrying a huge elaborately covered book.

POETESS: A poem. From my collection, "For Women Only." *(She recites.)*
I am woman.
A crippled bird.
The ledge is cold,
My wings are clipped.
He did it.
He did it.
I was his pretty Polly.
Pity Polly.
Pity pretty Polly
Doesn't want a cracker.
I am woman.
A crippled bird.
F-flap

The light starts to fade.

F-flap
F-flap
F-

The light is out.

Good Thing I Learned To Dance

The lights come up as an Actress enters and tap dances at C. stage. She sings.

ACTRESS:
LITTLE GIRLS CANNOT RESIST A TAP CLASS.
LITTLE GIRLS BY SIX CAN KEEP A BEAT.
I DON'T THINK I EVER MISSED A TAP CLASS.

WHO'D'VE GUESSED WHAT SOUNDS COULD COME
FROM FEET?

GOOD THING I LEARNED TO DANCE.
GOOD THING I LEARNED TO DANCE.
LITTLE GIRLS ARE NOT SUPPOSED TO SHOUT,
SO I STAYED WELL-BEHAVED.
I KEPT MY BAD SELF SAVED
FOR TWICE A WEEK WHEN I COULD LET IT OUT.

Her mother's voice is heard from offstage. After each admonishment, the girl reacts with a tap pattern.

MOTHER: *(Speaking.)* Now, don't be showing off in front of your friends, acting fast. *(She taps.)* You just tap dance yourself into that kitchen and do those dishes! *(She taps.)* I'm gonna do a tap dance upside your head if you don't get into bed! *(She taps violently. The girl ages to early adolescence.)*
ACTRESS: *(Singing.)*
TEEN-AGE GIRLS LOVE JUNIOR HIGH SCHOOL SOCIALS.
LOTS OF TIMES WE WENT WITHOUT A DATE.
TEEN-AGE BOYS WERE SHY AT MY SCHOOL SOCIALS.
I WAS GONNA SIT AROUND AND WAIT? UH-UH!

GOOD THING I LEARNED TO DANCE.
GOOD THING I LEARNED TO DANCE.
TWO BY TWO THE GIRLS WOULD START TO SHAKE.
THE BOYS WOULD STAND AND STARE.
WE'D BE TOO COOL TO CARE,
WHILE THEY FIGURED OUT WHAT MOVE TO MAKE.

Speaking while dancing with invisible partner.

You like this move, Clara? It's called the Four Corners. They're trying to get this on "Shindig." When Mary Alice does it, she goes all up in the air. *(Demonstrates.)* If that doesn't get those boys across the gym, they are dead . . . Oh, Clara, they are dead! *(She checks out crowd.)* Ohhh, look at Joyce Webb, dancing by herself. Y'know, it's true about Joyce. I'm in her gym class and I saw for myself. She sent away for these pills to enlarge her breasts, and you know what happened? Her nipples disappeared! *(She ages again, and is now a contemporary woman. Singing—)*
GROWN-UP WOMEN HURRY TO THE CITY.
I HAD NOTHING LEFT BUT DREAMS TO LOSE.
AIMLESSLY I WANDERED THROUGH THE CITY,
DANCED AT NIGHT TO KICK AWAY MY BLUES.

GOOD THING I LEARNED TO DANCE.
GOOD THING I LEARNED TO DANCE.

LATE ONE NIGHT A STRANGER CAME MY WAY.
HE FLASHED HIS CARD AND SMILE.
HE SAID "YOU MOVE WITH STYLE,"
AND THAT'S HOW I GOT WHERE I AM TODAY!

She doffs, her skirt to reveal an exercise leotard. She exercises throughout. Speaking—

And stretch and breathe,
and stretch and breathe.
Welcome ladies, to the Beverly Hills branch
of Boogie for Beauty.

And one, and two . . .

Come on ladies, if you want to slim up, you got to get down.
If you want to remove it, you got to groove it!
You've got to rock to lose those rolls!

She sings.

GOOD THING I LEARNED TO DANCE.
GOOD THING I LEARNED TO DANCE.
GOOD THING I LEARNED . . .
IT'S A GOOD THING I LEARNED TO DANCE!

BLACKOUT.

Welcome to Kindergarten, Mrs. Johnson

Lights up on simple schoolroom set. Ms. Thomas is at her desk, stage L. She is wearing a bright smock. As Mrs. Johnson enters, Ms. Thomas crosses to her.

MS. THOMAS: Welcome to kindergarten, Mrs. Johnson.
MRS. JOHNSON: How do you do? It's a pleasure meeting you. Janie has told me so much about you.
MS. THOMAS: It's a shame you couldn't make it last week with the other mothers.
MRS. JOHNSON: I'm sorry. I was speaking at a conference in Zürich.
MS. THOMAS: Well, come along. *(Crosses back to her desk.)* I've been observing Janie very closely. Have a seat. *(Mrs. Johnson starts to sit in a miniature kiddy chair and nearly falls off onto the floor. Ms. Thomas, oblivious to her difficulty.)* Sit up straight. *(She sings.)*
SHE'S A VERY BRIGHT GIRL, MRS. JOHNSON.
SHE WORKS BEYOND POTENTIAL—
A MODEL FOR HER PEERS,
EXPLORING AT A LEVEL

THAT IS WAY BEYOND HER YEARS
AND I'M SORRY
BUT IT'S GETTING ON MY NERVES.

MRS. JOHNSON: *(Speaking.)* I'm sorry. . . .

MS. THOMAS: *(Speaking.)* Don't fidget, Mrs. Johnson. *(Crosses to Mrs. Johnson, singing.)*

SHE'S A DIFFICULT GIRL, MRS. JOHNSON.
SHE HELPS THE OTHER CHILDREN—LORD KNOWS WHERE IT
    WILL LEAD,
AND I'VE LEARNED THAT WHEN MY BACK IS TURNED
SHE'S TEACHING THEM TO READ.
I'M TO SAY THE LEAST DISMAYED—
WHAT DOES SHE THINK THIS IS, THIRD GRADE?

SHE'S INDEPENDENT.
SHE'S ASSERTIVE.
SHE'S ALWAYS SELF-ASSURED.
NOW I DON'T KNOW WHERE SHE'S GETTING THAT
BUT IT'S NOT TO BE IGNORED—
AND IT GENERALLY STARTS AT THE HOME.

(Ms. Thomas sits back at her desk. Speaking—) Did you know that Janie's the only child in class with an even reasonable self-image? Now who's responsible for *that*?

MRS. JOHNSON: *(A bit thrown.)* I am.

MS. THOMAS: I'm sorry?

MRS. JOHNSON: *(Louder.)* I am.

MS. THOMAS: I am *what*?

MRS. JOHNSON: I am, Ms. Thomas.

MS. THOMAS: Good. Well, how do you expect her to be intimidated by simple authority?

MRS. JOHNSON: Well, I . . . *(Starts to sit on her hands.)*

MS. THOMAS: Keep your hands where I can see them. *(Mrs. Johnson jerks her hands up. Ms. Thomas sings.)*

NOW, I'M NOT SAYING YOU'RE A BAD MOTHER
EVEN THOUGH YOU MISSED OUR PAGEANT
AND THE HALLOWEEN PARADE.
NO, NO ONE'S SAYING YOU'RE A

Produces Bad Mother flash card.

BAD MOTHER,
BUT YOUR COOKIES AT THE BAKE SALE,
WELL, THEY CLEARLY WEREN'T HOMEMADE.

MRS. JOHNSON: *(Abashed; speaking—)* They were Pepperidge Farm Mint Milanos.

MS. THOMAS: The other mothers baked.

MRS. JOHNSON: I know, but . . . but I hate baking.

MS. THOMAS: Janie was humiliated!

MRS. JOHNSON: She never said a thing to me!

MS. THOMAS: Well . . . *(Singing.)*
YOU'RE A BUSY LITTLE BEE, MRS. JOHNSON,
ZIPPING OFF TO ZÜRICH.
I HEAR NEXT WEEK IT'S ROME.
IS THERE REALLY ANY WONDER
THINGS ARE SUFFERING AT HOME?

Mrs. Johnson starts to protest.

OH, THERE'S NO NEED TO OBJECT.
IT'S ALL HERE IN JANIE'S ARTWORK—
YOU CAN SEE THAT I'M CORRECT.

She produces a large pig made out of a Clorox bottle and decorated with hearts. She shows it to Mrs. Johnson.

MRS. JOHNSON: *(Speaking.)* It's a pig! Made out of a Clorox bottle!

MS. THOMAS: Oh, come on, Mrs. Johnson. There are domestic problems written all over this pig. I know what I'm talking about. I've taken psychology courses.

MRS. JOHNSON: *(Starting to stand.)* But . . .

MS. THOMAS: *(Raising pig over Mrs. Johnson's head.)* If you have something to say you raise your hand! *(Mrs. Johnson sits abruptly, Ms. Thomas sings.)*
NOW, NO ONE WANTS TO BE A—

Ms. Thomas flashes card at Mrs. Johnson.

MRS. JOHNSON:
BAD MOTHER.

MS. THOMAS:
AND I THINK WE CAN DO BETTER
IF WE JUST MAKE UP OUR MINDS,
'CAUSE WE ALL KNOW WHAT HAPPENS TO A—

She flashes card again at Mrs. Johnson.

MRS. JOHNSON:
BAD MOTHER!

MS. THOMAS:
AND THERE'S EVERY INDICATION
THAT THIS SUITS YOUR SITUATION.
HERE IS MY EVALUATION—
TAKE IT HOME AND HAVE IT SIGNED!

She picks up an evaluation with "Bad Mother" marked on it and pins it on Mrs. Johnson, who is crushed.

(Speaking.) Now, wasn't it nice meeting and getting a chance to chat like this?
MRS. JOHNSON: *(Fighting back tears.)* Uh-huh.
MS. THOMAS: Did you know we have these parent–teacher conferences every Monday at four o'clock?
MRS. JOHNSON: *(Shaking head.)* Un-uh.
MS. THOMAS: Well, I hope I'll be seeing you again very soon. *(She replaces the pig.)*
MRS. JOHNSON: Ye-yes, Ms. Thomas.
MS. THOMAS: That'll be all. *(Mrs. Johnson tears out of the classroom.)* No running in the halls. *(She sees the next mother waiting.)*
Welcome to kindergarten, Mrs. Feldman. Have a seat.

BLACKOUT.

I Sure Like The Boys

Lights discover an Actress stage R. The song is lyrical, full of the innocent sensuality of a young woman discovering sex.

> I SURE LIKE THE BOYS WHO LIKE TO DANCE REAL
> SLOW.
> WHERE THEY LEAD IS WHERE I GO.
> DIP ME DOWN, SPIN ME ROUND,
> WE'LL MAKE HISTORY IN THIS LITTLE TOWN.
> I SURE LIKE THE BOYS WHO LIKE TO DANCE REAL
> SLOW.

Crosses slowly to stage L.

> I SURE LIKE THE BOYS WHO LIKE TO DRIVE REAL SLOW.
> NO RUSH, YOU KNOW WE'LL GET THERE. PARKING BY THE
>   LAKESIDE,
> HEADLIGHTS IN THE MOONLIGHT—
> ONE LOOK AT ME AND OFF THEY GO.
> KISS ME REAL SLOW.

> NO RUSH, YOU KNOW.
> FEEL EVERY CORNER,
> TRY EVERY SPOT—
> HERE ARE MY LIPS, MY HAIR, MY EYES, MY HEART.
> I SURE LIKE THE BOYS
> WHO LIKE TO DANCE REAL SLOW.

the grill a little bit more. Make sure the metal tips of the comb glow red, red hot. That's the onliest way to do me a good press. Wigs! No, I don't like them wigs and fake braids strung down the back or those corn-rows with the ring-lets and the what not, like you see so many of the people walking around to-day—trying to make believe they're Polynesian royalty. *(Laughs.)* Like this gal I seen coming home out the train the other night. Let's see, was it Wednesday? Yes, it was Wednesday, cause Wednesday's my choir practice night and . . . Oh, Mt. Zion, yes that's right, right there on Convent Avenue, that's the one. Oh, Ebenezer Baptist? Why yes, I know your church. That was Reverend Gaines' old church before he passed, bless his heart. Yes, I heard about it. Fell right out of the pulpit, didn't he? Well, you never know, when your time is up, when the call comes, you just got to go. That's right, amen! . . . Now let me tell you about this gal. Honey, she was fine. One of our peoples, fine as wine. Had on real sharp clothes for days, hair all coiffed real fluffy, all these long pretty curls down her back. She was one of them long-leggedy gals. Had her hemline jacked up to there so she could show off them shapely hams. *(Ms. Mae demon-strates.)* She would criss-cross them this way, then criss-cross them that way. Then she commenced to a-tossing and a-flinging, and a-flinging and a-toss-ing. Child just sending up smoke signals something awful. Had all the men folk skittish. Yes she did! Well, anyway, we're ridin' along on the train, and we stopped at 59th Street and the door flew open. Peoples comin' and goin', and in walked this nobody character. You know—one of them faceless folk you don't pay too much attention to. Well, anyway, this Mr. Faceless had his stuff timed out precise and on the button, because before you could blink twice this shadow-of-a-lowlife had done jumped up, snatched off the woman's hair, leaped out the door and the train took off! Yessir! If I'm lying I'm flying! There she sat with her whole head nekked! I just can't describe it—but let me tell you! She was the most pitiful sight! Little teeny piggy twigs all over her nappy head. Her real live hair wasn't as long as a baby maggot. You know those teeny stubbles with the twisted knots so short they don't have tips? Yes, "buckwheat bubbles"! That's what we used to call 'em. And you know she was humiliated, 'cause it's a long haul from 59th Street to 125th before she could jump off and hide herself. And to top it all off, wouldn't you know that this would be the one car in the whole entire train just brimmin' over with all God's white folk in creation, all goin' uptown—I don't know where—past Harlem. And why they had to choose this car on this particular night with this child shamed low, I'll never know. I felt so put out with her sittin' up there in the open lookin' like that. And here them white folk ain't hardly got used to seein' us in the rough, much less knowin' what to make of this chile sittin' up there lookin' like a burr-headed pickaninny from off the plantation! And the few colored peoples there was, they're dippin' their heads down into their necks tryin' to look off and away, and then the white folk tryin' to look into their faces to see how they're supposed to react. Child, it was all too embarrassing. I just wanted to reach into my handbag to seek out a scarf or hankie to help the poor thing out of her misery, like any good Christian woman should . . . but then, I didn't know the girl . . . I thought she might feel worse, get the wrong idea. That's why I tell my grands, and my great-grands and my nieces and all of me and mine that that's what you get for totin' somethin' fake. Wear your real hair and go about your business. Don't cop no stick-up attitude, no false pride, 'cause the Lord will lay you low, yes he will! Hallelujah! *(She once more becomes aware of herself in the mirror.)* Oh, my, this is turning out real fine. I like that, I like that. I can see where I'm gonna be comin' from now on. Come on around here where I can see you. *(She motions beautician around.)* Now, you must stop by Mt. Zion Church one of these Sundays. *(Lights start to fade as gospel music begins under.)* In fact, let me have your address, cause we're having a church raffle for our building fund and I'll send you a stub for you and your husband. . . .

LIGHTS ARE OUT.

Detroit Persons

> *Lights come up as the Detroit Persons burst in from the various entrances, bouncing basketballs and performing tricks with them. Sport show music plays underneath. Rosie Cassidy, an older woman, tries to quiet them down as showtime approaches.*

ROSIE: All right, ladies . . . five seconds to air time . . . three . . . two . . . one . . . Hi Sports! Rosie Cassidy here! Welcome to the ZBS Cavalcade of Sports. Tonight I have here with me America's foremost female exhibition basketball team, the Detroit Persons. The Persons have been kind enough to take a few moments off from their whirlwind cross-country tour to share some of their intimate thoughts with us. Now, I notice there are only four of you here today. Where is your star forward, Nadine Johnson?

SHERIDAN GRACE: *(Crosses to Rosie.)* Oh, Nadine . . . she's doin' a thing for coke.

ROSIE: *(Misunderstanding.)* How wonderful . . . a commercial.

SHERIDAN: Uh-uh honey. This ain't no endorsement. She doin' time for coke. *(Crosses away.)*

ROSIE: Aha. *(Crosses to Vonelle.)* So ladies, tell me . . . *(She places her hand companionably on Vonelle's shoulder. VONELLE turns her head and glares at Rosie's hand.)* As an exhibition team . . . *(Sees the glare and snatches her hand away.)* Right . . . as an exhibition team, you're on the road an average of two weeks every month. How does this affect you personally?

VONELLE: Bricks get laid more than me, Rosie.

SHERIDAN: Yo, Spike here has it good. Her husband travels with her.

ROSIE: *(Crosses to Spike.)* Spike Martin. What a well-rounded person you are. I understand that along with a husband and two children, you have also managed to obtain a master's degree in English literature from Yale.

SPIKE: That's right, Rosie. See, for me it was a toss-up between seventeenth-century metaphysical poetry and sports.

ROSIE: Well, how did you come to choose the sports over the poetry?

SPIKE: I started to go for my PhD., but my mind kept returning to athletics. I missed the feeling I used to get when I stole bases as a kid. You know, the thrill of sliding in there with my spikes flying . . . *(She begins to build in intensity as ROSIE gestures to the off-camera director to cut.)* The elation of sinking my metal cleats into the vulnerable flesh of my opponent. The high I got when the ruby red blood began to gush out of the veins, when the face contorted into a horrible mask of excruciating pain, when the helpless body writhed on the ground in spasms of anguished nausea, when . . . *(Spike rips open her jacket to reveal spiked leather bands.)*

ROSIE: *(Desperate.)* Hence, the name "Spike."

SPIKE: Hence. *(Vonelle dribbles her ball down to Rosie.)*

ROSIE: Vonelle Grace, I understand you made a tremendous comeback from injuries to play basketball this year.

VONELLE: That's right, Rosie. My whole body like to give out on me.

ROSIE: But now you are in tip-top shape. What gave you the will to go on? *(Sheridan has been quietly moving to directly US. of Rosie.)*

VONELLE: Well, I'd have to give credit to my sister Sheridan here. *(They slap hands loudly just behind ROSIE's head, startling her.)* Whenever I got real down, she'd say to me, "Honey, just pick yourself up, go out there on the court, and hurt somebody." *(She pitches her basketball into ROSIE's stomach.)*

ROSIE: *(Doubled over in pain.)* Thank you, Vonelle. You're an inspiration to us all. *(She sees the next player approaching.)* Wanda Handwerger, you've been playing professional basketball in this country for over seven years. . . .

SHERIDAN: And she still don't speak so good English neither . . .

Wanda glares.

ROSIE: Do you feel there are any significant differences between men's and women's basketball?

WANDA: *(In a heavy accent.)* Say again, please?

ROSIE: *(Very slowly.)* Do you see any differences in men and women basketball players?

WANDA: Ah! Our cycle. They do not have.

ROSIE: I beg your pardon?

WANDA: My voman's body. One or two days a month I find myself to cry out at the referee for every close call. I veep when I miss the yump shot. I am very cross with my boyfriend. Male players do not have this, I think. *(She clicks her tongue.)*

ROSIE: Thank you, Wanda. Now I understand you have planned a special demonstration for us today. Is that right?

WANDA: Oh, yes, by golly. We want to expose ourselves on national tee wee.

SPIKE: Exposure, Wanda, we want exposure.

The players pile their basketballs on Rosie, who exits as they break into a spirited dance that incorporates basketball tricks. They sing.

Educated Feet

SHERIDAN:
  WE GOT HUSTLE.
  WE GOT HEAT.
OTHERS:
  WE GOT HUSTLE,
  WE GOT HEAT.
SHERIDAN:
  LEARNED OUR FIGHTIN'
  ON THE STREET.
OTHERS:
  DIRTY FIGHTIN'
  ON THE STREET.
SHERIDAN:
  AND TO MAKE IT REAL COMPLETE—
ALL:
  WE LOOK GOOD ENOUGH TO EAT.
  WE GOT ED-U-CA-TED FEET,
  WE GOT EDUCATED FEET.
SPIKE:
  WE GOT SPICE AND
  WE GOT SPUNK.
OTHERS:
  WE GOT SPICE AND
  WE GOT SPUNK.
WANDA:
  BOOGIE ON DOWN THE
  COURT AND DUNK.
OTHERS:
  BOOGIE ON DOWN THE
  COURT AND DUNK.

VONELLE:
  BOUNCE THE BALL AND SEE IT FLY.
ALL:
  WATCH THE COMPETITION CRY.
  WE GOT ED-U-CA-TED FEET.
  WE GOT EDUCATED FEET.

  WE'RE SAYIN' PH.D.
  WE'RE SAYIN' M.B.A.
  WE'RE SAYIN' VIC-TO-RY,
  WE'RE SAYIN' HIP, HIP, HIP
  HOORAY!

  WE'RE GONNA GIVE YOU
  SOMETHIN' SWEET.
  GONNA GIVE' YOU
  ATH-A-LETE.
  WE GOT ED-U-CA-TED FEET,
  WE GOT EDUCATED FEET.
WANDA:
  WE GOT WIM AND
  WE GOT WERVE.
ALL:
  WE GOT VIM AND
  WE GOT VERVE.
WANDA:
  WE GOT BRAINS AND
  WE GOT NERVE.
OTHERS:
  WE GOT BRAINS AND
  WE GOT NERVE.
WANDA:
  WE GOT MUSCLES WE CAN FLEX.
ALL:
  WE ARE NOT THE WEAKER SEX.
  WE GOT ED-U-CA-TED FEET,
  WE GOT EDUCATED FEET.

  WE'RE SAYIN' PH.D.
  WE'RE SAYIN' M.B.A.
  WE'RE SAYIN' VIC-TO-RY,
  WE'RE SAYIN' HIP, HIP, HIP
  HOORAY!

WE'RE GONNA GIVE YOU
ATH-A-LETE.
WE GOT ED-U-CA-TED FEET.
WE GOT ED-U-CA-TED

(Speaking.) Feet, don't fail me now!

BLACKOUT.

For Women Only #2

The Poetess enters US.C., and crosses DS. slowly, once again lugging the book.

POETESS: Another poem from my collection, *For Women Only*.
I am woman.
A neglected plant.
Hanging by the window
Waiting to be watered.
He did it.
He did it.
I was his philodendren
Calling out:
"Won't somebody talk
to me?"
I am woman.
A neglected plant.
D-droop

Lights begin to fade.

D-droop
D-droop
D-

LIGHTS ARE OUT.

The Portrait

Lights come up to discover an Actress sitting stage L. She sings.

THERE'S A PICTURE IN A SILVER FRAME
HANGING DUSTY ON MY WALL.
AND TWO PEOPLE WITH THEIR EYES THE SAME
HOLDING DAISIES, I RECALL.

AND THE BABY IN THE SAILOR DRESS
AND THE PIGTAILS—THAT WAS ME.
AND THE OTHER WAS MY MOTHER
ON OUR EASTER BY THE SEA.

PEOPLE TELL ME THAT I'M JUST LIKE HER,
AND I WONDER WHAT THEY SEE.
SHE WAS A LADY, LACE AND CAMEO,
NOT THE GYPSY THAT IS ME.
SHE SPENT HER EVENINGS MAKING POETRY.
I SPEND MY NIGHTS MAKING TIME.
AND WONDER, AM I LIVING?
PARTLY HER DREAMS, PARTLY MINE?

WHAT WOULD SHE THINK OF THE TOO MANY MEN,
THE LIES I GET LOST IN, AGAIN AND AGAIN,
THE TEARS IN THE MORNING, THE BOOZE
AND THE BLUES IN THE NIGHT.

IT'S BEEN YEARS NOW SINCE I'VE SEEN HER FACE,
HEARD HER FOOTSTEPS ON THE STAIR.
BUT JUST LATELY IN MY DREAMS AT NIGHT
I WILL CALL HER, AND SHE'S THERE,
LOOKING PRETTY, LIKE SHE USED TO,
BEFORE TIME AND TEARS TORE HER APART.
AND SHE TELLS ME THAT SHE LOVES ME,
THEN SHE LEAVES ME IN THE DARK.

MAMA DON'T LEAVE ME, MAMA DON'T GO
YOU KNOW THE ANSWERS TO ALL I DON'T KNOW.

Stands, crosses to C. stage.

MY DREAMS COME UP EMPTY AND MY HEART'S LYING DEAD ON
   THE FLOOR.
MAMA DON'T LEAVE ME, MAMA PLEASE STAY.
MAMA I NEED YOU TO SHOW ME THE WAY.
I'M LOST AND I'M LONELY
AND I CAN'T FIND MY WAY ANYMORE—
MAMA,
MAMA.

THE LIGHTS FADE.

Bluer Than You

Three actresses enter US.C. Throughout the song, each tries to top the others in blueness.

FIRST ACTRESS:
  WHAT CAN I SAY? I GUESS THIS HASN'T BEEN MY DAY . . .
SECOND ACTRESS:
  WEEK . . .
THIRD ACTRESS:
  DECADE.
SECOND ACTRESS:
  I'M DISTURBED . . .
FIRST ACTRESS:
  I'M DISTRAUGHT . . .
THIRD ACTRESS:
  I'M DISTRESSED. . . . I'M OVERWROUGHT.
SECOND and THIRD ACTRESSES:
  YOU'RE OVERDOING IT.
ALL:
  I'M UNHAPPY AND I DON'T KNOW WHY.
FIRST ACTRESS:
  I WOULD HAVE TO GET DOWN
  TO GET HIGH.
THIRD ACTRESS:
  SO WOULD I.
SECOND ACTRESS:
  ME TOO!
ALL:
  I'M BLUE!
FIRST ACTRESS:
  MY MAN HE UP AND QUIT ME,
  MY CLOTHES NO LONGER FIT ME
  'CAUSE I'M STILL COOKIN' FOR TWO.
  NO ONE WILL DATE ME.
  EVEN GAY MEN SEEM TO HATE ME.
  I'M BLUER THAN YOU.
THIRD ACTRESS:
  YOU THINK YOU'RE HURTIN', HONEY,
  THE LAST TIME I MADE MONEY

WAS OCTOBER OF SEVENTY-THREE.
MY SHRINK'S ON THE EQUATOR,
DIAL-A-PRAYER SAID "CALL BACK LATER."
I'M BLUER THAN SHE!
SECOND ACTRESS:
OH, THE THINGS I'M SMOKIN'
SINCE I LOST MY FAVORITE BOY.
ALL MY NAILS ARE BROKEN,
SO WHAT'S LEFT TO ENJOY?
ALL:
OY!
FIRST ACTRESS:
I'M IN SUCH A QUANDRY.
SECOND ACTRESS:
I HAVEN'T DONE MY LAUNDRY.
THIRD ACTRESS:
I DON'T HAVE A LAUNDRY TO DO!
FIRST ACTRESS:
MY CO-OP'S GOING RENTAL.
SECOND ACTRESS:
AND MY HAIR'S TURNIN' GREY.
FIRST and THIRD ACTRESSES:
DAY BY DAY—
THIRD ACTRESS:
MY SATIN SHEETS ARE SHREDDING.
FIRST and SECOND ACTRESSES:
WE'RE INVITED TO A WEDDING.
ALL:
I'M BLUER THAN THEY . . . ARE

The following is spoken.

THIRD ACTRESS: Am I blue? Are these tears in my eyes telling you? . . .

SECOND ACTRESS: I mean . . . I mean my man calls me such terrible names.

FIRST ACTRESS: Your man speaks to you?

THIRD ACTRESS: *(Trying to break in.)* If I could just . . .

SECOND ACTRESS: I mean, I get up in the morning and I say, "Come right in heartache and have a seat."

FIRST ACTRESS: You can get up in the morning?

THIRD ACTRESS: Listen . . . .

SECOND ACTRESS: I got a right to sing the blues.

FIRST ACTRESS: Well, I know I got a right to sing the blues.

THIRD ACTRESS: Well, I don't know if I've got a right, but I do have a letter of recommendation. . . . *(The others ad lib an argument as she reads her letter.)*
"Being possessed of multiple emotional trauma, it is here by recommended
that . . . *[actress's name]* . . . sings the blues to the fullest extent allowable by
the laws of this state."

They sing.

ALL:
OH—I'VE MADE A WRECK OF
MY LIFE IN EVERY WAY,
SO—I'M PAGING CHEKOV.
I'M A BLUES-ED UP MAMA—
USE ME IN A DRAMA.
SECOND ACTRESS:
DON'T EVER TRY TO HEAL ME.
FIRST and SECOND ACTRESSES:
DON'T NORMAN VINCENT PEALE ME.
ALL:
JUST LEAVE ME IN MY JUICES TO STEW.
THIRD ACTRESS:
I'M GONNA BE AS MAUDLIN
AS THE LAW WILL ALLOW.
FIRST and SECOND ACTRESSES:
AND HOW!
ALL:
'CAUSE I GOT A CONFESSION,
THIS IS A GREAT DEPRESSION.
I'M BLUER THAN THOU!
YA SHOULDN'T EVEN KNOW FROM
WHAT I'VE BEEN THROUGH. . . .

I'M BLUE—AIN'T THESE TEARS TELLIN' YOU?
I'M BLUE—I'M BLUER THAN YOU.
I'M BLUE—I'M BLUE.

I'M BLUER THAN
BLUER THAN
BLUER THAN
BLUER THAN YOU . . . . DON'T ASK!

They exit, griping and complaining.

END OF ACT I

ACT TWO

Watching the Pretty Young Men

Lights come up to reveal three chairs set in a semicircle. Cocktail lounge music plays under as ARLENE, ROZ, and HELEN enter, clutching purses.

ARLENE: Are you sure the parking lot is open all night? The last train is at 10:40 and if we miss it we'll be stuck here all night . . .

ROZ: *(Cutting her off.)* Arlene, will you stop already? The parking lot is open all night. Now *this* is a great table!

They begin to settle into the chairs.

HELEN: I didn't know we'd be so close to the stage.

ROZ: They say there is one guy here who is really . . . *(She makes a suggestive gesture.)*

ARLENE: *(Trying to exit.)* I have to call the sitter. *(The others stop her.)*

ROZ: I don't believe it.

HELEN: Arlene, you're making me nervous. Sit down.

ROZ: Anybody has to go to the ladies' room do it now while I order the drinks. *(The lights dim as an anticipatory chord is heard. The women slump in various attitudes of anticipation and embarrassment.)* Too late.

ARLENE: Oh, my God.

HELEN: Oh, my God.

ROZ: Oh, my God.

ALL: *(Singing.)*
OKAY, ALL RIGHT,
THIS IS GONNA BE THE NIGHT.
I GUESS WE'RE IN FOR QUITE AN EXPERIENCE—
CURTAIN UP, THERE GOES THE LIGHT.
AND OH, MY GOD! JUST LOOK AT THAT!
A G-STRING AND A COWBOY HAT!

The following is done first as individual solos, then repeated as a round.

ROZ:
HEY, HEY, HEY, YOU'RE DRIVIN' ME CRAZY
WHEN YOU MOVE SO LAZY, YOU MOVE SO HOT!
ARLENE:
MOTHERS DON'T GO TO THIS KIND OF SHOW.
THEY STAY HOME WITH CHILDREN AND BAKE
CUPCAKES A LOT.

HELEN:
COME AND SHOW YOUR MAMA HOW SWEET YOU ARE
AND SHE'LL TAKE YOU RIDING IN HER CADILLAC CAR.

Helen takes a pair of binoculars out of her bag. Arlene nudges her and she puts them away.

ALL:
THIS CAN'T BE ME,
I CAN GUARANTEE.
IT SEEMS SO WELL, YOU KNOW, UNINHIBITED.
WHO'D HAVE THOUGHT I'D EVER BE.
AND OH, MY GOD JUST LOOK AT THOSE!
I WONDER HOW THEY'D LOOK IN CLOTHES!

Roz stands and starts to walk toward the performers. Arlene pulls her back. The following is done as a round, with each person moving on to the next verse on each progression until they arrive back at the original verse.

ROZ: *(Verse 1)*
HEY, HEY, HEY, YOU'RE DRIVIN' ME CRAZY
WHEN YOU MOVE SO LAZY, YOU MOVE SO HOT.

When Helen sings this verse, she pulls out a telescope to look at the men.

ARLENE: *(Verse 2)*
BABY IS BAD, AND MAMA IS GLAD
'CAUSE IT'S OH, SO WICKED WHEN YOU SHAKE IT A LOT.
HELEN: *(Verse 3)*
COME AND SHOW YOUR MAMA HOW SWEET YOU ARE,
AND SHE'LL TAKE YOU RIDING IN HER CADILLAC CAR.

Helen takes out her car keys and waves them at the dancers.

ALL: *(They pull themselves together after their display.)*
OKAY I'M SHY.
I THINK I'D DIE
IF SOMEONE SAW THE WAY I'M BEHAVING NOW,
SAW THE LOOK THAT'S IN MY EYE.
AND OH MY GOD! THERE'S MARY STEIF,
WITH MRS. SCHWAB, THE RABBI'S WIFE.
ROZ: *(Pointing to the rabbi's wife.)*
HEY, HEY, HEY IT'S DRIVING THEM CRAZY
WHEN THEY MOVE SO LAZY, THEY GET SO HOT.

ROZ and ARLENE:

IF THEY KNEW WE SAW THEM HERE, OOH.
THEY'D BE SHOCKED AND HORRIFIED
AND HEAVEN KNOWS WHAT.

HELEN:

STILL AND ALL. MY DEARS, THE ODDS ARE EIGHT TO TEN
COME NEXT WEDNESDAY NIGHT, WE'RE GONNA SEE THEM
AGAIN!

The three ladies become very demonstrative, throwing money at the dancers, swing-ing their purses in mid-air, and jumping onto the chairs.

ALL:

HEY, HEY, HEY, YOU'RE DRIVING ME CRAZY
WHEN YOU MOVE SO LAZY, YOU MOVE SO HOT.
HEY, HEY, HEY, YOU'RE DRIVING ME CRAZY
WHEN YOU MOVE SO LAZY, YOU MOVE SO HOT.

The stage lights dim and the house lights come back up. The women pull themselves together.

WATCHING ALL THE PRETTY YOUNG MEN—
WE ARE WATCHING ALL THE PRETTY YOUNG MEN.
WATCHING ALL THE PRETTY YOUNG MEN,
WATCHING . . .

ARLENE: Next Wednesday, girls?

They nod in eager agreement, singing—

ALL THE PRETTY YOUNG MEN!

BLACKOUT.

Demigod

A Woman enters and crosses to C. stage.

WOMAN: I know you're gonna go. . . . I know it. I've been thinking a lot about what you said and I believe that you love me too. . . . And I understand that she gives you something else, something you need I guess is what you said. I wanted to apologize for yesterday. I was so confused, you know. I didn't know what to do with myself. . . . I mean, two years . . . what does a person do? Do I have a nervous breakdown? Do I start a new career? Do I go and have an affair with O.J. Simpson? I mean what do I do? I felt so ugly, Frank, and I don't mean just looks, I mean ugly . . . you know? Then you held me and touched the back of my neck and kissed me and said the things you said, and I felt a lot better. So, I did our laundry, like I always do on Sundays. And in the middle of folding our bedspread, I noticed your jock strap in the washing machine. Drowning in the wash cycle. It was twisting and turning, being mangled and manipulated into all sorts of painful positions. It looked as if it were crying out for help, poor little thing. Then the strangest thing . . . I imagined you were still in it . . . the jock strap I mean. I got hysterical. I mean I couldn't stop laughing. I thought it was the funniest thing I ever thought of. . . . People started staring at me. . . . A woman came up to me and said I should be careful not to inhale too much of that fabric softener. . . . Then all of a sudden I heard your voice. So I ran over to the machine, lifted the lid, and I could hear you in there, choking on the Clorox 2 and the Lemon Fab. But I couldn't make out what you were saying, so I yelled, "Frank, what is it, what are you saying?" And the manager of the laundromat yelled back, "I'm gonna call the police if you don't stop screamin' at your wash, lady!" It made me think, Frank. It made me think that maybe I'm not handling this too well. I can't drop two years of being lovers and go back to being friends. We never were friends, Frank. We slept together on the first date, remember? And I know you wanted to leave on good terms, like telling me you still love me and all, but I really think it'll be easier for me if we break up as enemies. It'll be better for me just to hate you openly instead of being so adult about it, don't you think? I mean, why be adult about it? So we can meet for lunch and laugh about all this? So you can tell me about your lovers and I can tell you about my lovers? So we can sleep together for old times' sake? I don't want to be your friend, Frank. I loved you, but I never said I liked you. And if being adult means throwing me away for that slut-rag you picked up on the goddamned train platform, then the most mature thing I could do for you would be to rip your face off. (*She mimes doing so.*) Oh, yes! That feels much better!

BLACKOUT.

The French Monologue

An Actress enters DS. R., wearing a beret and carrying a lighted cigarette in a long elegant holder. She is very, very French. She speaks directly to the audience in a thick French accent.

ACTRESS: Hello you . . . remember me? Chanteuse Rose? The little girl with the big voice who died for love—twice a night? Oh, how I love to sing of love—*en Français* of course. French is the language of love. Of course, I was not always French. Until I was thirteen, I was German. Being German was nice—I liked the sausage—but in my heart I knew something was missing. So, at thirteen I decided to change. For a while I was Danish. *Comme ci, comme ça*—I liked the pastry. Then I was very many things. I was Irish. Italian, Rumanian, Polish but always, no matter how good the food, or how high the mountains, I knew something was missing—*l'amour n'est-ce pas?* I needed to sing of my broken heart, to die for love—twice a night. And for this I needed a slit in my skirt, a beret on my head, long cigarette, champagne, stiletto heels—I needed, I *needed* to be French. French—my Papa was right. When I was a little girl, he used to come into my room, kneel by my bed, and whisper into my ear, he would say "Heidi—I was still German then—Heidi, you're different, you should be French." And then he would sing me a little lullaby that never failed to help me to sleep, and so my friends, tonight I would like to sing for you my Papa's lullaby to me that he sang, *en Français* Monsieur?

Piano player begins as she turns US. and a single spot picks her up.

The French Song

ACTRESS:
PARLEZ-VOUS FRANÇAIS, CHANSON PARIS—
FILET MIGNON, N'EST-CE PAS?
MON AMI, CHAISE LOUNGE. CAFÉ À CRÈME,

ESCARGOT, YUM-YUM, POURQUOI?
BEAUJOLAIS, DÉCOR. CHEVROLET COUPÉ—
MERCI, MADAME POMPIDOU.
JEAN COCTEAU TOUT DE SUITE.

The lights gradually fill the stage.

MON DIEU POTPOURRI—
AH DAT'S A NICE-A RAGOUT.
À LA MODE, À LA CARTE.
VIVE LA FRANCE.
BON APPETIT, LA GUERRE
CREPES SUZETTE, LAFAYETTE
PARDONNEZ-MOI.
C'EST LA VIE, VIN ORDINAIRE.
QU'EST-CE QUE C'EST, COUP DE GRACE—
GO MOW ZE LAWN.
MAURICE CHEVALIER, QUEL BOEUF,
VERSAILLES EN CHANTÉ LA PLUME DE MA TANTE.
CHATEAUBRIAND, C'EST TOUGH.

LIBERTÉ, EGALITÉ, FRATERNITÉ—
FAUT PAS AU COCO CHANEL.

VOULEZ-VOUS COUCHER
AVEC MOI CE SOIR?
NO BIDET EN LE HOTEL.

The lights narrow to just the C. stage spot.

COQ AU VIN, IMMEDIATEMENT—
ARC DE TRIOMPHE
MON PLAISIR, CHAMPS D'ÉLYSÉES
COURTERIER C'EST NOM
MERDE IN LE CHAPEAU.
J'ACCUSE, JACQUELINE BOUVIER!

Spoken.

Good-night Papa!

She exits US. C. as lights blackout.

Pay Them No Mind

An Actress enters US. C. The song starts low-key and gradually builds until it is triumphant at the end.

ACTRESS:
PEOPLE LAUGH EACH TIME THEY SEE US PASSING BY
AND THEIR WHISPERING MAKES YOU FEEL LIKE YOU
WANT TO CRY.
KEEP ON WALKING BY MY SIDE, DON'T LOOK BEHIND—
YOU SEE, I LOVE YOU, SO PAY THEM NO MIND.

PEOPLE SAY OUR LOVE AIN'T GONNA LAST TOO LONG,
AND THEY POINT AT US AS THOUGH WE'VE BEEN
ONLY CARRYING ON.
KEEP ON LOOKING IN MY EYES, AND WE'LL BE FINE.
'CAUSE I LOVE YOU, SO PAY THEM NO MIND.

STAY WITH ME AND LET THEM SEE,
LET THEM KNOW THAT YOU LOVE ME.
IF IT'S TRUE, WHO CARES WHAT THEY DO,
'CAUSE I DON'T NEED ANYONE BUT YOU.

IT'S YOU AND ME, WE'RE GONNA MAKE IT ALL ALONE.
SO LET THEM LAUGH AT US, WE'RE GONNA BUILD
A WORLD ALL OUR OWN.

HOLD ON, HOLD ON TO ME, THEY'LL LEARN IN TIME.
HOW I LOVE YOU, SO PAY THEM NO MIND.

STAY WITH ME AND LET THEM SEE,
LET THEM KNOW THAT YOU LOVE ME.
IF IT'S TRUE, WHO CARES WHAT THEY DO,
'CAUSE I DON'T NEED ANYONE BUT YOU.

IT'S YOU AND ME. WE'RE GONNA MAKE IT ALL ALONE.
SO LET THEM LAUGH AT US, WE'RE GONNA BUILD
A WORLD ALL OUR OWN.
HOLD ON, HOLD ON TO ME, THEY'LL LEARN IN TIME.
HOW I LOVE YOU, SO PAY THEM NO MIND.

STAY WITH ME AND LET THEM SEE,
LET THEM KNOW THAT YOU LOVE ME.
IF IT'S TRUE, WHO CARES WHAT THEY DO,
'CAUSE I DON'T NEED ANYONE BUT YOU.

IT'S YOU AND ME, WE'RE GONNA BUILD A WORLD
ALL OUR OWN.
HOLD ON, HOLD ON TO ME, THEY'LL LEARN IN TIME.
KEEP ON WALKING BY MY SIDE, DON'T STOP, DON'T
LOOK BEHIND YOU.
HOLD ON, HOLD ON TO ME, THEY'LL LEARN IN TIME.
HOW I LOVE YOU, SO PAY THEM NO MIND.

BLACKOUT.

Hot Lunch

The Workman enters DS. L. and sits on a bit of construction debris. He wears a hardhat and carries a metal lunchbox that he eats from. He ogles the imaginary girls that walk by.

WORKMAN: Wowee, would I like a taste of that . . . beautiful, baby, beautiful . . . Hey don't ignore me, honey; you're not that pretty. . . . *(A woman enters and crosses past him.)* Wowie, look at them gazoombas! I'd like to show you a taste of heaven, honey bunny.

WOMAN: *(Very polite.)* Excuse me, would you repeat what you just said to me?

WORKMAN: *(Startled.)* Huh? Oh sure. I said I'd like to show you a taste of heaven, honey bunny.

WOMAN: What else? You said something before that I couldn't quite make out.

WORKMAN: *(Getting annoyed.)* I don't know. I said you got a great pair of legs or something. I forget.

WOMAN: *(Matter of fact.)* No, no, I don't think you said legs. . . . It was something more like daroombas.

WORKMAN: Hey lady, walk on by will ya? I'm eating my lunch.

WOMAN: Yes, and I'm very sorry to disturb you, but try to remember what you said. It's very important to me. . . . Now, it sounded like . . .

WORKMAN: *(Very softly.)* Gazoombas.

WOMAN: Sorry, I didn't get that.

WORKMAN: Gazoombas! Now will you please leave me alone? I'm on my lunch break.

WOMAN: I know, I know I'm infringing on your time and I apologize for it, but what are gazoombas?

WORKMAN: Aw, just a word. A made-up word. No big deal. Look if you're pissed off I'm sorry, okay? I said gazoombas, so what? You got a nice shape. Since when is it a crime to give a compliment?

WOMAN: Yes, yes, I understand your motivation. It's just the word, *gazoombas.* I'd never heard it before. What exactly does gazoombas refer to?

WORKMAN: *(Embarrassed.)* You know. *(Indicates up.)* Up there. *(She looks up.)* Your chest, lady.

WOMAN: *(Relieved.)* Oh, thank goodness. I kind of thought that's what you meant, but I wasn't quite sure.

WORKMAN: Well, that's what I meant, okay? No offense. *(He begins to pack up.)*

WOMAN: Of course not. *(She sits very close to him abruptly.)* So, you like my tits.

WORKMAN: *(Startled, he jumps up.)* Hey, cool it, will you? I work here!

WOMAN: Sorry, I just wanted to know if you really appreciated my mammaries.

WORKMAN: Lady, would you excuse me? I gotta get back on the job. *(He tries to go past her and she stops him with her hands on his shoulders.)*

WOMAN: Of course, how stupid of me. But before you go, I'd like you to see my gazoombas! *(With back to audience, she opens her blouse to him.)*

WORKMAN: Lady, lady, cover yourself! What are you doing!

WOMAN: I thought if I showed you my gazoombas, you'd show me your wogabongo. *(He covers his crotch with the lunchbox.)*

WORKMAN: Wogabongo?

WOMAN: You know . . . your pecker, dick, schlong, Johnson . . . wogabooongo!!!

WORKMAN: *(Trying to leave.)* You're a wacko lady!

WOMAN: Why am I a wacko? You like my gazoombas, I like your wagabongo. I just want that taste of heaven you promised me. Why, with my gazoombas and your wogabongo, we could make great shtahpoonko!

WORKMAN: *(Calling to his unseen coworker.)* Hey, Joe! Joe! Help! Help!

WOMAN: *(Really going for him.)* C'mon, Wogabongo, squeeze my gazoombas!

WORKMAN: *(Running for the exit.)* Help, Joe, call the cops! I got a nut-case down here! Help!

WOMAN: *(Chasing after him.)* Oh, baby boy, I can't wait to show you my chubookie!

WORKMAN: Oh, my God!!!!

He exits. The Woman, thoroughly pleased with herself, straightens herself up, dusts off her hands, and exits in the other direction, happy with a job well done.

BLACKOUT.

For Women Only

The Poetess enters US. C. and crosses DS., once again lugging the book.

POETESS: The final poem from my collection. Autographed copies will be available in the lobby following the performance.

I am woman.
A dying swan.
Dancing, dancing, dancing.
My toe shoes torn.
My tutu, too.
He did it.
He did it.
(And he knows who he is.)
That weekend he took her skiing
in Aspen—
That's when he did it.
A love bullet through my feathered breast.

Thumps book.

I am woman.
A dying swan.

Ach-ch

Lights start to fade.

    Ach-ch
    Ach-ch
    Ach-

LIGHTS ARE OUT.

Emily the M.B.A.

This is performed in the style of a tough sixties girl-group. The four women in this group are just as tough—they wear suit jackets and carry briefcases.

CHORUS: *(Singing.)*
    DOO-DOO-DOO-DOO-DOO.
CHORUS LEADER: *(Speaking.)* Emily majored in finance. She trained for the fastest track. First in her class, summa cum laude, she was:
EMILY: *(Singing.)*
    THE ACHIEVER OF THE PACK.
CHORUS LEADER: *(Speaking.)* Emily's class was distinguished. For the first time the school was co-ed. The valedictorian was Emmy. . . .
ALL: *(Singing.)*
    AND AT GRADUATION SHE SAID:
EMILY: *(Addressing her class.)*
    NOW WE GO FORTH INTO BUSINESS,
    NOW WE ARE MS. M.B.A.
    WE MUSTN'T LOSE SIGHT OF OUR MS-NESS.
    LET'S ALL TAKE A VOW TODAY:

Each Chorus Member, as she starts to sing along with Emily, takes a vow.

    REMEMBER WE'VE GOT TO BE DIFFERENT,
    REMEMBER WE'VE GOT TO BE NEW,
    REMEMBER WE'VE GOT TO CHANGE ALL OF IT,
    BUT BE SURE WHAT GETS CHANGED
    ISN'T YOU.
CHORUS LEADER:
    EMILY SOON WAS RECRUITED
    BY TRON-MEGA-TECH-DATA-BASE.
    BOW-TIED AND CORPORATELY SUITED,
    SHE INSCRIBED ON HER ATTACHE CASE.

EMILY:
> REMEMBER WE'VE GOT TO BE DIFFERENT.

CHORUS:
> DOO-DOO-DOO-DOO.

EMILY and CHORUS LEADER:
> REMEMBER WE'VE GOT TO BE NEW.

ALL:
> REMEMBER WE'VE GOT TO CHANGE ALL OF IT,
> BUT BE SURE WHAT GETS CHANGED
> ISN'T YOU.

The Chorus dances with their briefcases as they sing "Go, go, Emily!"

FIRST CHORUS MEMBER: *(Speaking in sixties street-fighting bad-girl style.)* Did Emily progress vertically through the corporate structure?

CHORUS LEADER: Best believe it, girl. Within a year she was handling acquisitions.

SECOND CHORUS MEMBER: *(Challenging.)* Oh, yeah? How did Emily deal with takeovers?

EMILY: I was good-bad, but I wasn't evil.

FIRST CHORUS MEMBER: Yeah, well how did Emily play corporate politics?

CHORUS LEADER: Close . . . very, very close.

They hurl their briefcases offstage. Then they continue the song.

CHORUS LEADER:
> BUT EMMY'S PROGRESS STARTED SLOWING
> HER CAREER BEGAN PLATEAU-ING.

Emily begins to get worried.

EMILY:
> OH, NO!

CHORUS:
> OH, NO! OH, NO!

CHORUS LEADER:
> SHE THOUGHT A LITTLE SELF-ENHANCEMENT
> MIGHT REVITALIZE ADVANCEMENT.

EMILY:
> OH,YEAH!

CHORUS:
> OH, YEAH. OH, YEAH.

CHORUS LEADER:
> SOMETHING REALLY SPLASHY,
> THAT'S WHAT SHE WOULD DO.

EMILY:
> ENGINEER A FLASHY

ACQUISITION COUP.

ALL: *(Getting excited by the idea.)*
 OOOH-OOOH-OOOH-OOOH . . .

CHORUS LEADER:
 WHERE WAS THE PROSPECT EMILY WONDERED
 THAT WAS RIPE FOR GETTING PLUNDERED?

EMILY:
 UNDER.

CHORUS:
 UNDER, UNDER.

CHORUS LEADER:
 WHERE WAS THE OUTFIT SO FORSAKEN
 IT WAS ACHIN' TO BE TAKEN?

EMILY:
 OVER.

CHORUS:
 OVER, OVER.

CHORUS LEADER:
 SHE FOUND THE FIRM TO STOMP ON,

Emily smiles.

 THE COMPANY TO SINK.
 THE ONE THAT SHE WOULD TROMP ON WAS . . .

EMILY:
 WOMAN TRONICS INC!

The Chorus is horrified at Emily doing in a company run by women.

CHORUS:
 OH, NO, NO, NO, NO, NO, EMILY!

They back away from Emily.

 REMEMBER, DOO-DOO-DOO . . .

EMILY: *(Speaking to Chorus.)* What do you mean, "No, no, Emily." I'm not going to pass this up just because it's a company run by women. You're asking me to put my career on the line. A male executive wouldn't have to think twice about this. *(Delivering the big one.)* Business is business!

CHORUS LEADER: *(Singing.)*
 THE TAKE-OVER STRUGGLE WAS STRESSFUL!

CHORUS:
 STRESSFUL!

CHORUS LEADER:
 BUT TO EMILY WINNING WAS ALL!

CHORUS:
 WINNING, WINNING WAS ALL!

CHORUS LEADER:
  SHE SAID WHEN HER PLAN WAS SUCCESSFUL—
CHORUS:
  WHAT'D SHE SAY?
EMILY:
  LET'S GO THERE AND WATCH THEM CRAWL!

During the following dialogue, the Chorus acts out the action as the Chorus Leader narrates it. The chorus sings "No, no, Emily" under.

CHORUS LEADER: Emily and two guys from upper management took off in a company car to close the takeover deal. On the way, they broke out a bottle of Chivas, and a toast was proposed: To Emily!
  CHORUS: *(Toasting.)* Emily!
  CHORUS LEADER: One toast followed another as dark clouds filled the sky! Was it the rain or was it the Regal? No one saw the sign that said: Danger! Bridge Collapse!
  ALL: Watch out watch out watch out watch out!

Pandemonium breaks out. The Chorus whirls and shrieks. Lights flash on and off. Car crash sound effect. Emily spins offstage. When all is quiet, a lone hub cap clatters across the stage. The group reforms and begins a slow funeral march. The Chorus sobs gently as the Chorus Leader sings.)

CHORUS LEADER:
  THAT EVENING THEY PULLED FROM THE WRECKAGE
  THREE TWISTED BODIES, ALL DEAD.
  AND THEY FOUND IN THAT CORPORATE EXECAGE—
CHORUS: *(Speaking.)* What they find?
CHORUS LEADER:
  AN INSCRIBED PIECE OF LEATHER THAT READ:
ALL: *(Once again taking the vow.)*
  REMEMBER WE'VE GOT TO BE DIFFERENT.
  REMEMBER WE'VE GOT TO BE NEW
  REMEMBER WE'VE GOT TO CHANGE ALL OF IT.
  BUT BE SURE WHAT GETS CHANGED

  OH, NO, NO,
  ISN'T
  OH NO NO NO NO NO NO NO,
  ISN'T YOU!

BLACKOUT.

Sisters

An Actress enters and sits C. stage. She sings.

MY SISTER AND I, WE SHARE AN APARTMENT IN QUEENS.
WE MOVED FROM THE VILLAGE WHEN IT WENT WAY BEYOND
    OUR MEANS.
HER HUSBAND DIVORCED HER AND LEFT TOWN IN SEVENTY-
    ONE.
HE SAID THAT HE NEEDED A YOUNGER GIRL WHO WAS MORE
    FUN.

I LOST MY JOEY, LET'S SEE, YES, IT'S EIGHT YEARS TODAY.
THE HURT WAS SO BAD THAT I'VE LOCKED ALL MY MEM'RIES
    AWAY.
WE TRY NOT TO FOCUS OUR EYES OR OUR HEARTS ON THE
    PAST,
OR MENTION NOSTALGICALLY HOW TIME GOES FLYING
    SO FAST.
SHE WAS THE PRETTY ONE, I WAS THE ONE WHO COULD
    SING.
I SOUGHT THE FAME AND THE LOVE I THOUGHT BEAUTY
    COULD BRING.
SHE SEEMED SO SURE OF HERSELF, WHILE I FELT SO
    AFRAID,
SHE THOUGHT IF SHE HAD MY TALENT SHE'D SURE HAVE IT
    MADE.
NEVER CONNECTING, WE LIVED OUR ADULTHOODS ALONE,
SHE WAS SELF-SATISFIED, I PROUD TO BE ON MY OWN.

FUNNY HOW LIFE BRINGS THE BEST OF US DOWN TO OUR
    KNEES.
FUNNY HOW HEARTS CAN PERCEIVE WHAT THE EYE
    NEVER SEES.

SOMEHOW WE TOUCHED IN THE DARKNESS OF
    LONELY AND OLD.
JEALOUSY FADES WHEN TWO STORIES ARE ALREADY TOLD.
JOY TIPTOES IN SOMETIMES AS LIFE'S SURPRISES ARRIVE.
MY SISTER AND I—WE ARE SHARING THE END OF OUR LIVES.

The lights slowly dim.

Honeypot

A single spot comes up to reveal a blues singer decked out á la Billie Holiday, with a flower in her hair. She sings in various blues' styles.

HONEYPOT:
OH, WON'T YOU HELP ME,
WON'T YOU HELP ME PLEASE?
I GOT AN ACHIN'
THAT'S SHAKIN'
ME DOWN TO MY KNEES.

OH, WON'T YOU TELL ME
WHAT THIS MIGHT BE?
IS IT THE SAME OLD THING THAT'S
ALWAYS WRONG WITH ME?

Lights come up to reveal the interior of a psychotherapist's office. The doctor is very "modern" and serious, and takes notes occasionally.

DOCTOR: *(Speaking.)* Well, I'm here to help. So please, feel free to say exactly what's on your mind.

Honeypot sits by the doctor's desk.

HONEYPOT: *(Singing.)*
I WANT SOME SWEETMEAT, DADDY.

COME AND DIP IT IN MY BOWL.
I NEED THAT JELLY ROLL, DADDY.
COME ON AND FILL MY DONUT HOLE.

MY COFFEE'S BEEN SITTIN'
FOR WEEKS ON THE SHELF.
IF YOU DON'T COME BY AND GRIND IT
I MUST DO IT MYSELF.

I NEED THAT SWEETMEAT, DADDY . . .
DOCTOR: *(Speaking.)* I'm not sure I understand exactly, Miss . . .
HONEYPOT: Honeypot.
DOCTOR: Yes, well. Miss Pott, I was wondering if . . .
HONEYPOT: No, Honeypot's my first name. Honeypot Watkins, the blues singer.

Riff on the piano.

DOCTOR: Well, Honeypot, you seem to have some sense of your personal desires, but I wonder if you could tell me *exactly* what it is you want.

HONEYPOT: *(Singing.)*
  I WANT SOME SWEETMEAT, DADDY,
  COME ON AND DIP IT . . .

DOCTOR: *(Speaking.)* Honeypot, I'm going to be frank. You're trying to articulate your sexual needs, aren't you?

HONEYPOT: *(A bit embarrassed.)* Well, yes, Doctor, I guess I am. . . .

DOCTOR: Fine. But what I'm hearing is a lot of talk about food. Do you think you could discuss sex without referring to the contents of your refrigerator?

HONEYPOT: I think so.

DOCTOR: Well, then, why don't I ask you again? What is it exactly you want?

HONEYPOT: *(Singing.)*
  WHEN MY OVEN'S OVERHEATED
  I NEED MY FIXIT MAN.
  WHEN MY LOCK NEEDS OPENIN',
  I'M SURE HE'S THE ONE WHO CAN.

  HE'S GOT A MONKEY WRENCH
  THAT I LOVE TO USE.
  DON'T KNOW HOW I'D LIVE
  WITHOUT HIS SCREWS.

  OH, HE'S MY HANDY, DANDY
  FIXIT MAN,
  YEAH, YEAH, YEAH . . .

DOCTOR: *(Interrupts, speaking.)* Let me ask you . . . do you often find yourself associating sex with food and hardware?

HONEYPOT: No, I really haven't noticed that.

DOCTOR: Then do you think we could try once again? You know, Honeypot, we're all a little embarrassed to really discuss sexuality. That's a perfectly normal response.

Honeypot is relieved.

But if you'd like to try to work through that . . .

HONEYPOT: Oh, yes, I'd love to try to work through that.

DOCTOR: Please, feel free. What sorts of sexual activities do you most enjoy?

HONEYPOT: *(Singing.)*
  HE COMES TO MY STABLE,
  GRAZES IN MY HAY.
  HE REARS UP, NICE AND HIGH
  AND OHHH . . . .
  I LIKE IT THAT WAY, YEAH, YEAH!
  I LIKE IT THAT WAY, YEAH, YEAH. . . .

DOCTOR: *(Speaking.)* Try not to mention horses.

HONEYPOT: *(Groping for another approach, speaking.)* Okay . . . *(Singing.)*
DIVE DOWN, DADDY
YOU NEVER MISS A STROKE.
WHY DON'T YOU
DIVE DOWN, DADDY . . .
DOCTOR: Try not to mention swimming.
HONEYPOT: *(Speaking.)* Okay. Uhhh . . . *(Singing.)*
I GOT A REAL THING FOR THAT THING
IT REALLY MAKES MY SPIRIT SING.
I GOT A REAL THING FOR THAT THING. . . .
DOCTOR: *(Getting excited.)* All right, what thing is that exactly Honeypot?
HONEYPOT: Well, you know what I mean, his . . . oh you know.
DOCTOR: His penis. Right?

Honeypot is horrified.

HONEYPOT: Ahh! Yes, his monkey wrench!
DOCTOR: Yes, his monkey wrench. But you mean something else when you say that.
HONEYPOT: *(Forcing out the word.)* His . . . p . . . penis?
DOCTOR: Yes. Now, what would you like him to do with the penis?
HONEYPOT: *(Singing.)*
DADDY, MY DOOR'S WIDE OPEN.
WHY DONT YOU COME ON INSIDE?
DADDY, MY DOOR SWINGS EASY . . .
DOCTOR: *(Flatly.)* You can think before you answer, you know.
HONEYPOT: *(Trying to please.)* Doctor, I think I know what you mean.
DOCTOR: *(Excited.)* Yes?
HONEYPOT: I think I want the penis . . .
DOCTOR: Yes?
HONEYPOT: *(Speaking.)* In my . . . *(Singing.)*
SUGARBOWL . . . .
DOCTOR: *(An accusatory silence.)*
HONEYPOT: *(Softly.)* Vagina.
DOCTOR: This is very important, Honeypot! Are you feeling yourself becoming more aware of what it is you really want? That it isn't wrenches and donuts?
HONEYPOT: Yes, I think so.
DOCTOR: Can you tell me about it?
HONEYPOT: *(Speaking.)* Yes, I believe I can. *(Singing operatically, and standing in a classical singing pose.)*
I'D LIKE EXTENDED FOREPLAY. DADDY,
NOT MERELY GENITAL CONTACT AS SUCH.

THEN PROCEED WITH ACTUAL PENETRATION, DADDY.
I'D ENJOY THAT VERY MUCH.

I'D LIKE TO EXPERIENCE SEXUAL RELEASE CONCURRENTLY WITH
YOU.
I'D PREFER A MULTIPLE CLIMAX
BUT THE OTHER KIND WILL DO.
CONSIDER SEX JUST ONE ASPECT OF ME AS A PERSON,
DADDY . . .

DOCTOR: *(Speaking.)* Wonderful progress, Honeypot.

HONEYPOT: Thank you. Doctor.

DOCTOR: With regular therapy, within five years you should have a sex
life as good as the typical American woman.

*A look of horror passes over Honeypot's face. She slips back into her blues style of
singing.*

HONEYPOT:
COME BACK HERE, DADDY.
AND PUT THAT MONKEY WRENCH IN MY BOWL!

She exits.

LIGHTS FADE.

Friends

*Two Actresses are discovered sitting a little apart. Throughout the piece, as they
gradually age, they occasionally change position in their chairs. They do not look at
each other until the very end.*

OFFSTAGE VOICE: Are you still on that phone?

FIRST ACTRESS: *(Speaking.)*	SECOND ACTRESS: *(Speaking.)*
	You hang up first.
Okay . . . you still there?	
	No fair. I did last time.
Well . . .	
(Singing.)	*(Singing.)*
DON'T FORGET,	
CALL ME IN THE MORNING.	
	BE MY FRIEND.
TELL ME WHAT YOU'RE	
GONNA WEAR TO SCHOOL	
	THOSE STUCK UP GIRLS.

HELP ME WITH MY MATH.
I'LL DO YOUR ENGLISH.

THE BOYS

PLEASE DON'T TELL
  YOUR BROTHER
I THINK HE'S COOL.
DON'T FORGET,   DON'T FORGET
CALL ME IN THE MORNING   CALL ME IN THE MORNING

(Speaking.)   *(Speaking.)*

                             Maid of Honor?

Of course!
Matron of Honor?

                             Oh, wow.
                             Lamaze?

I'll try.
Aerobics?

                             I'll try.

(Singing.)   *(Singing.)*

                             DON'T FORGET.
                             I NEED YOUR PLUMBER'S
                               NUMBER.

THE CHILDREN.   MEET YOU AT THE
                             PLAYGROUND
                             AROUND ONE.

OH, GOD, THE HOUSE.   HOW DO YOU FIND TIME
                             TO READ A NOVEL?

                             THOUGHT I'D WORK
                               FREELANCE
MY HUSBAND.   BUT WOMAN'S WORK IS
                               NEVER DONE.
                             WELL,
DON'T FORGET,   DON'T FORGET,
CALL ME IN THE MORNING   CALL ME IN THE MORNING

YOU REMEMBER MY
FIRST LOVE
MY DRESS SIZE
MY BIRTHDAY
MY DIVORCE

OF COURSE I DO
AND YOU KNOW I CAN'T
   EAT GARLIC
AND MY SON-IN-LAW
   BORES ME.

AND SOMETIMES MAYBE
I DO TOO.

OF COURSE YOU DO.

WELL SOMETIMES
I GET SORE AT YOU.
BUT WHAT THE HELL,

WHAT THE HELL,
WHAT ARE FRIENDS FOR?

WHAT ARE FRIENDS FOR?

WHAT ARE FRIENDS FOR?

WHAT ARE FRIENDS FOR?

BE MY FRIEND.

BE MY FRIEND.

(Speaking.)

(Speaking.)

The kids are moving to Denver.

Let's go back to school

(Singing.)

(Singing.)

I NEED A FRIEND.

I NEED A FRIEND.

(Speaking.)

(Speaking.)

I can't believe he's gone.

You did everything you could.

(Singing.)

(Singing.)

I'LL BE YOUR FRIEND
I'LL BE YOUR FRIEND
MY FRIEND, MY FRIEND.

I'LL BE YOUR FRIEND
I'LL BE YOUR FRIEND
MY FRIEND, MY FRIEND.

DON'T FORGET, I'LL
COME AND SEE YOU
  SUNDAY

                HELLO, FRIEND.

THINK OF SOMEPLACE
  NICE
YOU'D LIKE TO GO.

                A CUP OF TEA.

YOUR GINSENG TEA
IS QUITE A PICK-UP.

                CUP OF TEA.

I MAKE A CUP
WHENEVER I FEEL SLOW.

                MEMORY
                IS FUNNY THOUGH.

TASTES FUNNY THOUGH.
YOU LISTEN TO THOSE
  NURSES, NOW   MY FRIEND,
YOU KNOW.   I KNOW.

AND DON'T FORGET,
CALL ME IN THE MORNING.   FIRST THING IN THE MORNING.

The two women look at each other for the first time.

DON'T FORGET,   DON'T FORGET.
CALL ME IN THE MORNING.   CALL ME IN THE MORNING.

LIGHTS FADE OUT.

A special light comes up. The Third Actress walks into it.

THIRD ACTRESS: *(Speaking.)*
  A . . . My name is Alice . . .
  And I'm all right!
  Amen!

Lights come up on the full stage as the music starts.

ALL GIRL BAND: *(Reprise.)*

FOURTH ACTRESS: *(Enters US. C. singing.)*
  IF YOUR LIFE IS A MESS,
THIRD ACTRESS:
  IF YOU'RE BORED WITH SUCCESS,
FIRST ACTRESS: *(Enters US. C.)*
  IF YOUR SHRINK TRIES TO PUT YOU AWAY . . .
SECOND ACTRESS: *(Enters DS. R.)*
  IF THEY THROW YOU IN JAIL,
ALL:
  OR YOU'VE BROKEN A NAIL,
FIFTH ACTRESS: *(Enters DS. L.)*
  OR YOU'VE DENTED YOUR NEW CHEVROLET! . . .
ALL:
  WE HAVE GOT SOME SOUND ADVICE TO PULL YOU THROUGH.
  THERE'S A VIRTUSO LOCKED INSIDE OF YOU!

  COME JOIN OUR ALL-GIRL BAND.
  IT'S THE FEMINIST WAY TO RELAX.

  COME JOIN OUR ALL-GIRL BAND
  WE NEED A TUBA AND SAX!

  COME JOIN OUR ALL-GIRL BAND
  AND THE HARMONY SOARS THROUGH THE NIGHT.
  COME JOIN OUR ALL-GIRL BAND.
FIRST and SECOND ACTRESSES:
  NOW I CAN BLOW MY OWN HORN!
THIRD ACTRESS:
  NOW I AM SINGING THE LEAD!
FOURTH and FIFTH ACTRESSES:
  NOW LOOK WHO'S PULLING THE STRINGS!
ALL:
  ALICE IS DOING ALL RIGHT!

Jam session.

ALL:
  ALICE IS DOING ALL RIGHT!

BLACKOUT.

María Irene Fornés

ABINGDON SQUARE

Madeleine Potter and John Seitz in *Abingdon Square* by María Irene Fornés, 1987. Photo © by Martha Holmes.

Author's Note

It's strange to write a play that is so different from anything else I've written. I didn't sit down and say, "I want to write something different." It just came—I don't know from where.

The play and the title came from seeing the front of a house. It was in the Village (Greenwich Village), but as I was writing, I was indoors in Cuba with the characters seeing those old country houses, with those big, big rooms—big because of the heat. And I saw a living room.

I was working on the play with actors and had some scenes written but I wasn't finished and the theatre wanted a title for publicity. I was walking in the Village with the play in my hand and I saw a sign *Abingdon Square* and I said, "Yes!" The name Abingdon *sounds* so rich, so upper-class, perfect for the play. And then those houses, they looked very turn of the century, but just a little shabby.

I kept thinking of the change from 1910 to 1920 *(the play begins in 1908 and ends in 1917)*. It's only ten years but so different. I was thinking of the women and how much their clothing changed. Suddenly you have jazz, the Charleston, and women dancing with dresses above their knees by 1917.

———————————

The cast was so perfect. Ordinarily it would take months and months to find a group of actors—you would have to see people in New York and then go to California to find such actors. Madeleine Potter *(Marion)* was perfect. She had that kind of youth and innocence, but her voice sounded like she knows—like an adult but not tired.

A man like John Seitz *(Juster)*—you would think it would be disgusting for a man his age to be in love with this young woman, but his voice was so romantic. Beautiful diction and sweetness. He, too, had a kind of innocence. In auditions he first read with a kind of lasciviousness and I said to him, "No, the character is very innocent." And he said, "Oh you think so." I thought he was one of those smart aleck actors and he said, "May I try again?" Then he read and he sounded even more . . . almost debauched. So I stopped him and said, "No, he is even more pure than you read the first time, in fact he is the one in danger of having his innocence violated. He is intelligent but it doesn't interfere with his purity and goodness. He thinks the world is good." Then he read it again, so perfectly, and I thought, "This guy is a genius. It was a miracle."

Some people thought the scene when Marion lets the glazer—who she does not know—take her behind the sofa was today's morality not the early 1900s. But people were no more moral then than now. At the time people didn't talk about sex because they spoke more Puritanically and they didn't warn their daughters about men and the daughters were always chaperoned. Marion is in the house, she's not chaperoned. She's never been told if a man comes and throws you on the floor, what is the next move you should make. And Marion's no saint. She enjoys it. He's not violent. She thinks this is a nice game.

I remember the night before the first performance, probably previews, I said to Madeleine, "I have a new speech for you." And I tried to speak in my most innocent voice, 'I've been working on it and it is finished, I will make no changes." I said, "I have it in my pocket, if you don't want to see it, you don't have to. Or if you want to see it and don't want to do it, my heart is with you. I won't be angry or disappointed. It's up to you, don't do it for me." I knew she would be more open if I used these tactics. So she looked at it and she said, "I'll do it."

I said, "Does this mean that you like it?"

She did it wonderfully. I only brought it in because it was good for the character and necessary for the play. I don't remember which speech, but it was long, maybe fifteen lines. It was quite extraordinary.

I think that the lights were put together at the last minute because I was writing the play as we rehearsed—as usual—and there was no time for Donald *(Holder)* and I to go through the places in connection with the lights, with the placement of the actors.

There was something about the play that appealed to the people working on it. It was so perfect, the physical look of the actors, the sets, the lights. It was a very satisfying production.

—From a conversation between
María Irene Fornés and Suzanne Bennett,
July 24, 2002

An earlier version of *Abingdon Square* was given a workshop production at Seattle Repertory Theatre in 1984. Following a staged reading at New York's American Place Theatre in April, 1987, *Abingdon Square* opened there on October 8, 1987, produced by the Women's Project & Productions. The text published here is a revised version.

Abingdon Square was directed by the author, with set design by Donald Eastman, lighting design by Anne Militello, costume design by Sam Fleming. The production stage manager was Rebecca Green. The cast was as follows:

MARION	Madeleine Potter
MICHAEL	John David Cullum
JUSTER	John Seitz
MINNIE	Myra Carter
MARY	Anna Levine
FRANK	Michael Cerveris
THE GLAZIER	Mark Bagnall

CHARACTERS

MARION, from age 15 to 24
JUSTER, Marion's husband, from age 50 to 59
MICHAEL, Juster's son, the same age as Marion
FRANK, Marion's lover, one year older than Marion
MARY, Marion's cousin, the same age as Marion
MINNIE, Marion's great-aunt, from age 58 to 70
A GLAZIER, a very strong, tender man
THOMAS, Marion's son, eight-months old

TIME AND PLACE

Act One: 1908–1912.

In a house on 10th Street, New York City

Act Two: 1915–1917.

In the house on 10th Street; Mary's place, an apartment on Abingdon Square; a beer parlor; and Minnie's house

SETTINGS

The living room of a house on 10th Street. To the right is a double door which leads to the foyer and the main door. On the back wall there are two large French doors. On the right there are double doors that lead to other rooms. Up center, a few feet from the back wall are a sofa and two arm chairs. On each side of the sofa, there is a tall stand with a vase. Down left there is a chess table and two side chairs; down right there is a small desk. There is a chair on the upstage side of the desk and another on the right side. During intermission a telephone is placed on the desk.

The attic room or closet. A platform placed high against the back wall. On the upstage side of the attic there is a wall with a small door.

Mary's living room. An embroidered shawl is placed on the sofa.

The living room of an apartment on Abingdon Square. A back wall is placed behind the sofa. On the wall there is a fireplace; above the fireplace there is a large mirror.

The Beer Parlor. A square plain wood table and two chairs in a pool of red light, center stage.

Minnie's living room. A chair center stage in a pool of light.

Juster's bedroom. A platform on the right side of the stage. On the back wall there is a small door. Parallel to the back wall there is a narrow bed.

ACT ONE

Scene 1

10th Street. August 1908. It is dusk. Juster sits in the garden facing up left. He sings Handel's "Where'er You Walk." Marion hides behind the windows and listens.

JUSTER: *(Singing.)*
WHERE'ER YOU WALK
COOL GALES SHALL FAN THE GLADES

She moves to the left window and looks at him.

TREES WHERE YOU SIT,
SHALL CROWD INTO A SHADE.
TREES WHERE YOU SIT,
SHALL CROWD INTO A SHADE
MARION: Pst!

Juster leans over to see who has called. Marion moves her hand toward him.

Scene 2

Two weeks later. It is a sunny afternoon. Marion enters running from the left. Michael is chasing her. They run around the room laughing and screaming. He grabs her and takes a piece of chocolate from her hand. He unwraps the chocolate and puts it in his mouth. She chases him. She grabs him and they fall. He covers his mouth. She tries to pull his hand away.

MARION: Give it to me.

He swallows the chocolate, lets her remove his hand, and opens his mouth.

MICHAEL: It's gone. I swallowed it.
MARION: You're bad! *(She holds him tightly.)* I love you Mike! I love you.

He holds her.

MICHAEL: Me too! I love you too!
MARION: You are like a brother to me. I love you as a sister loves a brother. But I must love you as a mother loves her son since I will soon marry your father and you need a mother. I must be a mother to you. How could a boy like you grow up without a mother? You need a mother.
MICHAEL: I'd rather have you. You're more to me than any mother ever could be. You're my sister, my daughter, my cousin, my friend. The very best! You're my friend! My grandmother! You're everything.

MARION: You're joking and I'm serious.

MICHAEL: I'm serious. You're the best person I know or will ever know.

MARION: You need a guide, a teacher in life.

MICHAEL: I don't need a guide. I need a friend.

MARION: You need someone who'll guide you in your life.

MICHAEL: Oh no, I don't, I'm doing very well. I'm a good boy. A mother would say to me, "You're doing fine m'boy. You give me no trouble and you don't need a mother." When I need help I'll go to you and you'll help me.

As the following speech progresses, Marion speaks rapidly as if in an emotional trance.

MARION: You're sweet. You are the sweetest creature on earth. I wish I were sweet like you. I wish I had sweetness in my heart the way you do. Soon I will, officially, be your mother, and I say this in earnest, I hope I can make myself worthy of both you and your father. He brought solace to me when I knew nothing but grief and I experienced joy only when I was with him. His kindness brought me back to life. I am grateful to him and I love him. I would've died had he not come to save me. I love him more than my own life and I owe it to him. And I love you because you are his son, and you have a sweetness the same as his. I hope I can make myself worthy of the love you've bestowed upon me and I hope to be worthy of the honor of becoming one of this household which is blessed with a noble and pure spirit. I know I sound very formal, and that my words seem studied. But there is no other way I can express what I feel. In this house, light comes through the windows as if it delights in entering. I feel the same. I delight in entering here. I delight in walking through these rooms and I'm sad when I leave. I cannot wait for the day when my eyes open from a night's sleep and I find myself within these walls. Being here I feel blessed and I hope I never give you cause for regret. I hope you, as well as he, will always tell me if I have done something wrong—or I have done less than you expect, or if you have any reason to be disappointed in me. Would you promise me you will?

MICHAEL: I promise.

Scene 3

A few minutes later. Minnie and Juster are entering from the foyer. Marion stands left.

MINNIE: *(As she goes to sit, to Marion.)* Sit down, dear.

Minnie sits right. Juster sits left, Marion sits on the sofa.

MINNIE: I was just talking to Juster about the question of your obligations here. The questions you posed to me, and whether you will continue your studies, or what obligations you will have. And I thought you should ask the questions directly to him. Because I wasn't sure that I ever heard the answers to them. He doesn't seem to know the answer. I mean even if he doesn't know the answer he—Go ahead dear.

Marian takes a few steps toward Juster.

MARION: I wanted to know what are my obligations here. I believe when one marries one has obligations and I asked Aunt Minnie what may my obligations be. And she said she wasn't sure. But that she thought maybe sooner or later I will be running the house. And I told her that I have never run a house and I asked her and if it's something I could learn to do and if it is, where could I go to learn it. I asked and she said she'll inquire. I told her that. But that I should also do some inquiring.

JUSTER: I'm embarrassed to say that I have no idea what your obligations are, Marion. I never ran the house. As far as I know they are what my Mother did. Then, when I married, my wife Martha ran it. Then, Jenny, our house-keeper, took over the running of the house. And when my wife Martha died, Jenny continued running the house to this day. I never did. So, maybe Minnie can tell you how to run a house. *(To Minnie.)* Minnie, do you know how it's done?

MINNIE: Yes, I do. I run my house, Juster. But I don't think I run my house the way you run yours.

JUSTER: You should talk to Minnie, Marion, and decide what it is you should do.

MARION: I will.—Will my cousin Mary continue giving me classes? I would like to know if that is something she will continue doing, tutoring me.

JUSTER: Indeed Marion, nothing in your life should change—unless you want it to change.

MARION: Because of all the years I was not able to go to school, I feel I don't yet comprehend a great many things.

Scene 4

Two months later. October 1908. It is dusk. Juster stands center left. Michael stands up left. Mary stands up right. Marion and Minnie embrace center. Marion holds a white veil and a missal. Minnie sobs.

MARION: My dear aunt, I am happy. Believe me, I am happy. I will be very happy. *(Minnie sobs. Marion holds her. A few seconds pass.)*
MARION: Don't cry, my dear. *(Minnie sobs. Marion holds her. A few seconds pass.)* My dear aunt, don't cry.

Minnie goes on sobbing. Marion releases her slowly and takes a step away from her. Marion lowers her head. Mary puts her arm around Minnie and exits with her. Minnie mumbles and cries while she exits.

MARION: Why is she so unhappy?
JUSTER: Weddings make people cry, Marion.

Marion looks at him. Juster takes her hand and brings it to his lips. She kisses his cheek.

Scene 5

Six months later. April 1909. It is late afternoon. Marion and Mary sit on the couch. Mary whispers in Marion's ear. Marion goes to the desk and sits. She writes in a notebook. There is an open textbook in front of her.

MARY: That's what I heard.
MARION: Who told you!
MARY: My cousin. He knows the man. And he also knows his wife.—The man is married. And his wife has a sister. The sister came to visit. She lives in New Paltz. Both sisters are from New Paltz. *(Standing and taking a few steps center.)* The sister—the sister of the wife—came to visit but she stayed for months. And the three of them slept together. In the same bed. The man and the wife and the wife's sister slept together in the same bed.
MARION: *(Standing and taking a few steps toward Mary.)* The three of them?
MARY: Yes! The three of them in the same bed.
MARION: Why did they do that?
MARY: To do awful things!
MARION: What things!
MARY: Don't you know?
MARION: You do know?
MARY: I don't.
MARION: Yes, you do.
MARY: I do. I imagine he first makes love to one and then the other.
MARION: That's perverse!
MARY: It is! That's why I'm telling you.
MARION: You are!
MARY: Yes!
MARION: That's horrendous!
MARY: I know.
MARION: How did you find out?
MARY: He told me.
MARION: He!
MARY: My cousin.
MARION: How did he know?
MARY: Everyone knows.
MARION: How?
MARY: Noises in the bedroom. The servant heard them.
MARION: It couldn't be true.
MARY: Oh yes, if you see them you would know.

MARION: How?
MARY: The way they behave.
MARION: How?
MARY: Sinister, Marion, and sexual.
MARION: What!
MARY: Yes, Marion.
MARION: How did they do that?

Mary tries to create a sexual facial expression.

MARION: The wife is not jealous?
MARY: No.
MARION: And the sister is not jealous?
MARY: No.
MARION: He's with both of them?
MARY: Yes!
MARION: In the street?
MARY: Yes. Anywhere. He looks at one and then the other—passionately.
MARION: He's shameless.
MARY: They all are.
MARION: It's he who does it.
MARY: Not only he. They also look at him.
MARION: With passion?
MARY: Yes.
MARION: In front of the other?
MARY: They don't mind.
MARION: They don't!
MARY: Apparently not?
MARION: The wife's to blame then.
MARY: Yes it's her fault, not his.
MARION: It's his fault too.
MARY: The sister is pretty. Who can blame him?
MARION: Is she?
MARY: She's lovely. If she lets him—what is he to do?
MARION: He can say no.
MARY: If the wife doesn't mind, why should he?
MARION: Because it's sinful. It's a sin he's committing. He will go to hell. God won't forgive him. It's his soul. He is responsible for his own soul. He can't just say, "They don't mind." He should mind. It is his own soul he has to care for. He'll go to hell.
MARY: I know—they'll all go to hell.
MARION: And we will too.
MARY: Why!
MARION: For talking about it!
MARY: No, we won't!

MARION: Yes! We will! We must do penance!

MARY: We didn't do anything!

MARION: Yes, we did!

MARY: What!

MARION: We talked about it and we thought about it.

MARY: Did you!

MARION: Of course!

MARY: What did you think?

MARION: I thought about it. I imagined it! I did!

MARY: Marion, how could you?

MARION: Didn't you?

MARY: No!

MARION: Oh, God! I've sinned!

MARY: Oh, Marion! Repent.

MARION: I repent! Oh God! I repent! Oh God! How could I! Oh God! *(She falls on her knees. She is out of breath.)* Oh God! Forgive me! *(She begins to calm down.)*

MARY: *(Kneeling next to her.)* What did you think?

MARION: I imagined them in bed.

MARY: What did you imagine?

MARION: I can't tell you.

MARY: What?

MARION: He makes love to one while the other is there, very close. She looks and she listens. She watches their bodies move. She's very close.

MARY: How close?

MARION: Touching. She must.

MARY: That's just awful.

MARION: She must.

MARY: Oh. Marion. And then?

MARION: He kisses her too.

MARY: No!

MARION: He holds them both. And knows them both.

Mary gasps.

MARY: Oh, Marion. I too have sinned. Will God forgive us? *(They embrace.)*

Scene 6

One month later. May 1909. It is evening. Juster sits up left reading. Michael sits cross-legged on the floor in front of the sofa. He reads a book. Marion sits at the desk. She writes in a diary.

JUSTER: *(Reading*)* If you wish to see it for yourself, take a pencil and push the pointed end into the open mouth of the flower and downward to-

---

*From *My Garden in Autumn and Winter* by E. A. Bowles

ward the ovary and the honey, just as a bee would thrust in its tongue. If it is a young flower you have chosen you will see two anthers bend down as if they knew what they were doing, and touch the pencil about two inches from the point leaving a smudge of golden pollen on it. A day later, the stigma will have lengthened and, if you would, then push your pencil in again, you will find that it now hangs far enough to touch the pencil in the same place where the pollen was laid, while the empty anthers have shriveled.—Thus on its first day of opening the anthers rub their pollen on the back of visiting bees; and on the next the stigma hangs down far enough to receive pollen from a younger flower.—If you wish to see the mechanism by which the anthers are bent down, cut away the hood until you lay bare the stamens as far as the point where they are joined to the corolla. Here you will notice that they have slender white flying buttresses that keep them in place. Just in front, standing out into the passageway down the tube of the flower, are two white levers growing out from the filaments and blocking the mouth of the tube. Push your pencil in again and you can see what happens. It strikes against these levers and pushes them down with it. As the buttresses hold the filaments in place, their upper portion is bent over from that point until the anthers touch the pencil.

Scene 6a

The lights fade. Marion and Michael exit, Juster goes to a window and looks out.

Scene 7

The attic. Five months later. October 1909. It is morning. Marion stands on her toes with her arms outstretched, looking upward. She wears a white camisole and underskirt. Her whole body shakes with strain. She perspires heavily. On the floor there is a blanket and a large open book. She rapidly recites the following passage from Dante's "Purgatorio" from the nineteenth-century translation by Henry Frances Cary. (Minnie's words should not interrupt Marion's speech.)

MARION:
   He girt me in such manner as had pleased
   Him who instructed; and O strange to tell!
   As he selected every humble plant,
   Wherever one was pluck'd another there
   Resembling, straightway in its place arose.
   Canto II: They behold a vessel under conduct of an angel.
   Now had the sun to that horizon reach'd,
   That covers, with most exalted point
   Of its meridian circle, Salem's walls;
   And night, that opposite to him her orb

> Rounds, from the stream of Ganges issued forth,
> Holding the scales, that from her hands are dropt
> When she reigns highest: so that where I was
> Aurora's white and vermeil-tinctured cheek
> To orange turn'd as she in age increased.
> Meanwhile we linger'd by the waters brink,
> Like men, who musing on their road, in thought
> Journey, while motionless the body rests.
> When lo! as, near upon the hour of dawn,
> Through the thick vapors Mars with fiery beam
> Glares down in west, over the ocean floor;

MINNIE: *(Offstage.)* Marion . . .

MARION:

> So seem'd, what once again I hope to view,
> A light, so swiftly coming through the sea,
> No winged course might equal its career.
> From which when for a space I had withdrawn
> Mine eyes, to make inquiry of my guide,
> Again I look'd, and saw it grown in size

MINNIE: *(Offstage.)* Marion . . .

MARION:

> And brightness: then on either side appear'd
> Something, but what I knew not, of bright hue,
> And by degrees from underneath it came
> Another. My preceptor silent yet
> Stood, while the brightness, that we first discern'd,
> Open'd the form of wings: then when he knew

MINNIE: *(Offstage.)* Marion, are you there?

MARION:

> The pilot, cried aloud, "Down, down; bend low
> Thy knees; behold God's angel: fold thy hands:
> Now shall thou see true ministers indeed." *(She faints.)*

MINNIE: *(Offstage.)* Marion . . . *(A moment passes.)* . . . Marion . . .

MARION: *(Coming to.)* . . . Yes. Don't come up . . . I'll be right down.

Minnie enters.

MINNIE: Are you all right?

MARION: . . . Yes.

MINNIE: *(Kneeling and holding Marion in her arms.)* What are you doing?

MARION: I'm studying.

MINNIE: . . . You're drenched . . .

MARION: I know . . .

MINNIE: Why don't you study where it's cool?

MARION: I have to do it here.

MINNIE: You look so white. *(Drying Marion's perspiration.)* Look at how you are drenched. Why do you do this?

MARION: I wasn't aware of the heat.

MINNIE: Now you are cold. You're as cold as ice.

Marion moves to the left. She leans against the wall and covers herself with the blanket.

MARION: I feel sometimes that I am drowning in vagueness—that I have no character. I feel I don't know who I am. Mother deemed a person worthless if he didn't know his mind, if he didn't know who he was and what he wanted and why he wanted it, and if he didn't say what he wanted and speak clearly and firmly. She always said "a person must know what he ought to believe, what he ought to desire, what he ought to do."—I write letters to her.—I know she's dead. But I still write to her. I write to her when I'm confused about something. I write and I write until my thoughts become clear. I want my thoughts to be clear so she'll smile at me. I come to this room to study. I stand on my toes with my arms extended and I memorize the words till I collapse. I do this to strengthen my mind and body. I am trying to conquer this vagueness I have inside of me. This lack of character. This numbness. This weakness—I have inside of me.

Scene 8

A day later. Dusk. Juster walks from left to right in the garden. He wears a shirt with the sleeves rolled up. He carries a small tree, whose roots are wrapped in canvas, under one arm.

Scene 9

Five months later. March 1910. It is late afternoon. There is a phonograph on the table. Michael is placing the needle on a record. It plays a rag. Marion and Michael dance.

MICHAEL: That's it. You're doing well. That's good. Ta rah. Pa rah.

MARION: Teach me the words. Teach me how to sing it.

MICHAEL: Ta rah. Pa rah. Ta rah. Pa rah.

They sing these words to the whole song. The record comes to an end.

MARION: Again. . . . Let's do it again.

He starts the record again.

MARION: Hold me, Mike, and sing into my ear as they do in the dance halls.

Michael does. Juster appears in the vestibule. He hangs his hat on the hat rack. He takes off his coat and hangs it in the closet. He comes into the living room and watches them dance. Marion sees Juster and waves to him. He waves to her.

MARION: Look at me, I'm dancing. Look at this. *(They do a special step. Juster smiles.)*
MICHAEL: And this. *(He demonstrates another step.)*
JUSTER: That's wonderful.
MICHAEL: Come, learn how to do it, Father.
JUSTER: *(Smiling.)* Oh, I don't think I could.
MICHAEL: Yes, yes, you could. I'll teach you. I just taught Marion.
MARION: Oh, yes, it's easy. You just listen and the music and the words will tell you how to move. I learned. I am sure you could learn too. I never thought I could learn and I did. *(Marion dances toward Juster. Michael puts Juster's arms around Marion in dancing position.)*
MICHAEL: Do it.

Juster tries to move.

JUSTER: Oh, I don't think I can. I never was light on my feet.
MICHAEL: Yes you are. Father. You could do it. You could dance beautifully. You already have the stance.
JUSTER: Oh. I don't think I can.
MARION: Try again. Just listen to the music.
JUSTER: No, no I'm sure I can't. You dance. I'll watch you. I like to watch you. *(He leads Marion toward Michael, then sits and watches.)* I like to watch you do it. *(Juster claps while they dance.)*

Scene 10

Four months later. July 1910. It is late afternoon. Marion sits at the desk. She is writing in a diary. Michael appears in the doorway to the left. He holds flowers in his hand. He tiptoes up behind her and covers her eyes.

MARION: *(Pressing the diary against her chest.)* Oh!
MICHAEL: *(Taking his hand away.)* I didn't mean to scare you.—It's only me.—I brought you flowers. *(Marion sighs. She closes her diary.)* Don't worry. I didn't read any of it.
MARION: It's a diary. *(Michael sits.)* I was describing an event.
MICHAEL: What event? Is it a secret?
MARION: It's a secret. A meeting.
MICHAEL: What sort of meeting?

MARION: Something imagined. In my mind.

MICHAEL: Diaries are to write things that are true.

MARION: This diary is to write things that are not true. Things that are imagined. Each day I write things that are imagined.

MICHAEL: Could I read it?

MARION: No.

MICHAEL: Why not? If it's imagined.

MARION: It would embarrass me.

MICHAEL: Is it romantic?

MARION: Yes. It is the story of a love affair.

MICHAEL: Whose?

MARION: A young man's named F.

MICHAEL: With whom?

MARION: With a young girl.

MICHAEL: Who is she?

MARION: Me!

MICHAEL: You!

MARION: Yes! *(He gasps.)*

MICHAEL: You! *(Touching the diary.)* In this? How thrilling!

MARION: Yes.

MICHAEL: Do you write each day?

MARION: Yes.

MICHAEL: Since when?

MARION: Since August.

MICHAEL: Do you see him each day?

MARION: No.

MICHAEL: Why?

MARION: Because I can't.

MICHAEL: Why not?

MARION: Because I'm married.

MICHAEL: Really?

MARION: Yes. A married woman cannot see her lover often. *(She opens her mouth in amazement. They laugh.)*

MICHAEL: Where do you meet?

MARION: In the street. In a parlor.

MICHAEL: Does he come here?

MARION: No!

MICHAEL: And then?

MARION: We talk.

MICHAEL: Have you kissed?

MARION: No!

MICHAEL: Will you kiss him?

MARION: I think so. In the future.

MICHAEL: Is he real?

MARION: He is real, as real as someone who exists. I know every part of him. I know his fingernails—every lock of his hair.

MICHAEL: What does F. stand for?

MARION: I haven't found out yet.—Francis of course. What other name starts with an F?

MICHAEL: Franklin.

MARION: No. His name is not Franklin.

MICHAEL: Of course not. Floyd.

MARION: No.

MICHAEL: Felix.

MARION: No. Don't ask such questions.

MICHAEL: I'm sorry. I'm intruding. I'm sorry.

MARION: I'll tell you what you want but be discreet. You have to know how to enter another person's life.

MICHAEL: I know. I'm sorry. *(There is a pause.)* What does he look like? May I ask that?

MARION: He's handsome. He has a delicate face and delicate hands. His eyes are dark and his hair is dark. And his skin is white. He looks like a poet. He looks the way poets look. Soulful.

MICHAEL: Where did you first meet him?

MARION: In a shop.

MICHAEL: Where does he live?

MARION: I don't know yet. I don't know him that well.

MICHAEL: How long have you known him?

MARION: Three months.

MICHAEL: How often do you meet?

MARION: Once a week.

MICHAEL: Why not more often?

MARION: You have to be careful. *(They laugh.)*

MICHAEL: You're mad.

She laughs.

MARION: I know.

Scene 11

Three months later. October 1910. It is morning. Marion enters right, carrying a hooded cloak. She walks left, furtively and looks around. She puts on the cloak, lifting the hood over her head, covering her face. She looks around again and exits right hurriedly.

Scene 12

Three months later. January 1911. It is evening. It is Juster's birthday. Marion sits in the chair to the right. Minnie and Mary stand by her side. Michael sits on the floor to Marion's right. He holds a banjo. Juster sits in the chair to the left.

MARION: My dear husband, in honor of your birthday, we who are your devoted friends, son and wife, have prepared a small offering—an entertainment. May this, your birthday, be as happy an occasion for you as it is for us. *(Marion extends her hand toward Michael, who starts playing.)*

MARION, MINNIE, MARY and MICHAEL: *(Singing.)*
TRUE LOVE NEVER DOES RUN SMOOTH,
AT LEAST THAT'S WHAT I'M TOLD,
IF THAT'S TRUE THEN OUR LOVE SURELY MUST BE GOOD AS GOLD.
HOW WE BATTLE EVERY DAY AND WHEN I WANT A KISS,
I HAVE TO START EXPLAINING
AND IT SOUNDS ABOUT LIKE THIS:

"DEARIE, PLEASE DON'T BE ANGRY
'CAUSE I WAS ONLY TEASING YOU.
I WOULDN'T EVEN LET YOU THINK OF LEAVIN'—
DON'T YOU KNOW I LOVE YOU TRUE.

JUST BECAUSE I TOOK A LOOK AT SOMEBODY ELSE
THAT'S NO REASON YOU SHOULD PUT POOR ME ON THE SHELF.
DEARIE, PLEASE DON'T BE ANGRY
'CAUSE I WAS ONLY TEASING YOU."*

They repeat the song. Marion and Mary do a dance they have choreographed.

MARION: Dear husband, now it's your turn to sing.

They all gesture toward Juster.

JUSTER: *(Singing.)*
DEARIE, PLEASE DON'T BE ANGRY
'CAUSE I WAS ONLY TEASING YOU.
I WOULDN'T EVEN LET YOU THINK OF LEAVIN'
DON'T YOU KNOW I LOVE YOU TRUE.

JUST BECAUSE I TOOK A LOOK AT SOMEBODY ELSE
THAT'S NO REASON YOU SHOULD PUT POOR ME ON THE SHELF.
DEARIE, PLEASE DON'T BE ANGRY
'CAUSE I WAS ONLY TEASING YOU.

Marion kisses Juster on the cheek.

---

*Angry by Dudley Mecum, Jules Cassard, Henry Brunies, and Merrit Brunies.

Scene 13

One month later. February 1911. It is evening. Marion sits in the left chair. Michael lies on the floor. They are both still, stiff and somber.

MARION: It was he. There was no doubt in my mind. I saw him and I knew it was he.
MICHAEL: Did he see you?
MARION: No. I hid behind the stacks.
MICHAEL: Then?
MARION: I took a book and buried my head in it. I was afraid. I thought if he saw me he would know and I would die. He didn't. I saw him leave. For a moment I was relieved he hadn't seen me and I stayed behind the stacks. But then I was afraid I'd lose him. I went to the front and I watched him walk away through the glass windows. Then, I followed him . . . a while . . . but then I lost him because I didn't want to get too near him.—I went back there each day. To the bookstore and to the place where I had lost him. A few days later I saw him again and I followed him. Each time I saw him I followed him. I stood in corners and in doorways until I saw him pass. Then I followed him. I was cautious but he became aware of me. One day he turned a corner and I hurried behind him. He was there, around the corner, waiting for me. I screamed and he laughed. He grabbed me by the arm. And I ran. I ran desperately. I saw an open entranceway to a basement and I ran in. I hid there till it was dark. Not till then did I dare come out. When I saw that he wasn't there I came home.—I haven't been outside since then. I'll never go out again, not even to the corner. I don't want to see him. I don't want him to see me. I'm ashamed of myself. I'm a worthless person. I don't know how I could have done what I did. I have to do penance.

Scene 14

One year later. February 1912. It is evening. Michael and Juster play chess. Michael sits down center. He studies the board. Juster stands behind Michael and also studies the board. Marion stands up left. Juster turns to look at her.

JUSTER: You look beautiful. You look like a painting. *(She smiles with faint sadness.)* Play, Michael. Make up your mind.
MICHAEL: I don't know what move to make.
JUSTER: Make whatever move seems best to you.
MICHAEL: I get confused. I don't see one move being better than the next.
JUSTER: What do you think, Marion?
MARION: What do I think?

JUSTER: Yes what should Mike do? Should he scrutinize the board and imagine each move and its consequences, or should he just play and see what happens? I imagine both are good ways of learning. *(As he walks center.)* One way, I think, is a more Oriental way of learning—through meditation. The other is more Western. Reckless. We are reckless, we Westerners. Orientals meditate until they have arrived at a conclusion. Then they act. We Westerners act. Then, we look to see if what we did makes any sense. Which do you think is the best way to act?

MARION: I don't know. I think I'm like an Oriental. I don't think I take chances. I don't take any risks. I don't make any moves at all.

MICHAEL: *(As he moves a piece.)* Check. *(Juster looks at the board.)*

MARION: Does that mean you've won?

MICHAEL: No. It's exciting to check though. It's exciting to make a move and be reckless and create an upheaval and for a moment think that it's mate.

MARION: And if it isn't mate? Do you lose?

MICHAEL: I don't know.

JUSTER: *(Making a move.)* For now he just loses a bishop.

MARION: Maybe it's best to be like an Oriental.

MICHAEL: I don't know. When you reflect you have to know what you are reflecting about. When you move without reflecting—*(as he moves a piece)* you just move! Just do it!

Marion lifts her skirt to see her toes and takes six steps looking at her feet.

MARION: Six steps and the sky did not fall.

Scene 15

Seven months later. September 1912. It is late afternoon. There are some letters on the chess table. Marion sits in a chair facing the window. FRANK stands in the garden outside the window. Marion's manner of speaking reveals sexual excitement.

MARION: You're trespassing.—Where you are standing is private property. It's a private garden and when strangers come into it, we let the dogs out.

FRANK: Let them tear me up. I'll stay here and look at you.

Marion moves between the two windows. Frank walks to her. She moves to the stage left chair and sits. Frank follows her and sits at her feet. She starts to go. He grabs her ankle.

MARION: Let go.

FRANK: I'm chained to you. I'm your shackle.

MARION: You are? *(Pulling her foot toward him.)*

FRANK: Come. *(Pulling back.)*

MARION: No—Let go.

FRANK: Never. *(She jerks her foot.)* Never. *(She jerks her foot.)* Never. *(She jerks her foot.)* Never. *(She laughs.)*

MARION: What if someone sees you?

FRANK: I'll be arrested.

MARION: Let go of my foot. *(She touches his face. She is scared by her own action and withdraws her hand.)*

FRANK: I know every move you make. I've been watching you.—You spy on me. I spy on you.

MARION: Let go. Someone will see you.

FRANK: There's no one here but us.

MARION: How do you know?

FRANK: He won't be home for hours.

MARION: Who?

FRANK: Your father.

Marion is startled by his remark and becomes somber. She walks to the chair next to the desk and sits.

MARION: He's not my father.

FRANK: Who is he?

MARION: He's my husband. *(They are silent a moment.)* He's my husband and I don't want to see you ever again. I am married and you should not be here. *(Short pause.)* Leave now, please.

Frank is motionless for a moment. Then he walks away. Juster enters. He opens the closet in the foyer, puts his hat and cane in it, closes the door and walks into the living room. She is calm and absent as if something had just died inside her.

JUSTER: Good evening, dear.

MARION: Good evening.

Juster walks left, picks up the mail and looks through it. He looks at her.

JUSTER: Are you all right . . . ? You look pale.

MARION: Do I look pale?

He comes closer to her.

JUSTER: I think you do.

MARION: I'm fine.

He kisses her and walks left as he speaks, without turning.

JUSTER: Is Michael home?

MARION: He's in his room.

JUSTER: Will dinner be at six?

MARION: I believe so. *(Juster exits left.)* . . . I'm sorry . . .

Frank appears again.

FRANK: Did you speak to me?

MARION: I'm sorry.

FRANK: You've broken my heart.

MARION: I saw you and lost mine. And I also lost my mind. That's why I followed you. I had lost my mind.—I thought of nothing but you. Each day I looked for you in the streets. And if not, I dreamt of you. A few days ago I looked outside this window and I thought I saw you moving among the trees. I thought I was hallucinating. This happened a few times. Were you there? Was that you?

FRANK: Yes.

MARION: What madness. It's my fault. I know it's my fault. I've been married since I was fifteen and I've never done anything like this. I love my husband and I'll always be faithful to him. I won't hurt him. He doesn't deserve this. Please, leave or I'll start crying and they will hear me and they will come in and find me like this.

After a moment Frank runs off. Marion goes to the couch and sits. She sobs. The lights fade. They come up again. The room is dimly lit. Juster enters.

JUSTER: Have you been here all this time?

MARION: I was looking at the clouds. It seems it's going to rain.

He looks out.

JUSTER: I don't think so. Night is falling. That's why it's getting dark.—Dinner is served, dear. Will you come?

MARION: Yes.

JUSTER: Are you all right?

MARION: . . . No . . . I'm not feeling very well.

JUSTER: Should you have dinner?

MARION: . . . I think not . . .

JUSTER: Would you like to stay here?

MARION: I'll go up to my room.

JUSTER: May I help you up?

MARION: I'll be up in a moment . . . *(He sits next to her.)* What is today's date?

JUSTER: September twentieth.

MARION: Of course. It's the end of summer. The trees are beginning to turn.

JUSTER: Yes.

She leans on his chest. He puts his arms around her.

MARION: It's getting chilly.

He strokes her hair.

ACT II

Scene 16

10th Street. Two years, four months later. January 1915. It is early afternoon. The day is overcast. Marion stands by the window to the left. She looks out. She is motionless. An Adagio is heard.

Scene 17

10th Street. Three months later. April 1915. It is late morning. A glazier is standing on a ladder in the up left corner. He wears belted overalls. He hammers points on the upper part of the window. Marion enters right. She carries a vase with flowers. She stops to look at him. He continues working. She walks to the right stand. She looks at him again. She is transfixed. He turns to look at her. Their eyes lock. She cannot turn away.

GLAZIER: Could I have a drink of water?
MARION: Yes. *(She does not move. He comes half way down the ladder and waits.)*
GLAZIER: Well? *(He goes close to her. He puts the vase to his mouth and drinks water through the flowers. She stares. He lets out a long laugh.)*
GLAZIER: *(Referring to the drinking of the water.)* May I?

She does not answer. He laughs again. She stares at him. She is posessed. He picks her up and takes her upstage. They disappear behind the sofa. She emits a faint sound. The lights fade.

Scene 18

10th Street. Five months later. September 1915. It is evening. Michael sits left. Marion sits right. She looks pale and absent. She stares at the floor. Juster sits next to her.

JUSTER: I never thought I would have another child. I never thought Marion and I would have a child. I am so much older than she. I'm beside myself with joy. Marion is a little worried. She is fearful.—You're the first to know. I have suggested that she ask Aunt Minnie to come and stay with us. Marion needs a woman's companionship. But she hasn't decided if she'll ask her. Maybe you could persuade her.—She has missed you very much. I haven't heard any laughter in this house since you left. Marion has missed you. I hope you consider going to school in New York this year. Marion is desolate, Michael. Would you consider returning home? *(Juster looks at Marion. He then looks at Michael helplessly. Michael looks at Marion. He is pained.)*
MICHAEL: I will think about it. Father.

Scene 19

10th Street. One year later. September 1916. It is late morning. Center stage there is a playpen with a teddy bear sitting in it. Marion enters from left. She carries Thomas, eight months old. She takes the teddy bear. Frank appears outside the windows.

FRANK: Hello.
MARION: . . . Frank . . .
FRANK: My name's not Frank.
MARION: It isn't? *(He shakes his head.)* What is your name?
FRANK: Jonathan.
MARION: Jonathan?
FRANK: Yes.
MARION: Your name is not Frank? *(She laughs.)* That's not possible.
FRANK: My name is Jonathan. I was named after my father.

She laughs.

MARION: I'm so happy.
FRANK: Why?
MARION: I'm so glad to see you. *(She sighs.)* Where have you been?
FRANK: I was away.
MARION: Where were you?
FRANK: In Michigan.
MARION: What were you doing in Michigan?
FRANK: Working with my uncle.—Have you thought of me?
MARION: Oh, yes.
FRANK: What have you thought?
MARION: That I love you.
FRANK: What a pleasant surprise. May I come in?
MARION: *(Laughing.)* No.
FRANK: Come outside then.
MARION: Not now.
FRANK: When?
MARION: Tomorrow.
FRANK: At what time?
MARION: At one.
FRANK: Where?
MARION: In the square.
FRANK: Abingdon?
MARION: Yes.
FRANK: *(Moving his hand toward her.)* See you then.
MARION: *(Her fingers touching his.)* See you.

Scene 20

10th Street. Five months later. February 1917. It is evening. Marion sits to the left of the chess table. Michael sits down right.

MARION: He often speaks of closing the house and moving south, where the weather is temperate. He likes using that word. Temperate. It's quite clear why he does. He means moral balance. Evenness of character. He means that he knows what I do when I leave the house. That he knows about Frank and me. He's saying that he'll seek moderation at any cost. That he's ready to divorce me and put an end to our family life. I'm ready for it. I'm ready to face him with it. He's just making it easier for me. *(Michael looks down.)* What's the matter?

MICHAEL: When I'm with him, I care about nothing but him. *(They look at each other for a moment.)* I love him. He's my father and I love him. And I don't want to see him suffer. When I'm with you, I forget that he's my father and I take your side. He's my father and I love him and I respect him. And I feel terrible that I've been disloyal to him. And I feel worse to see that he's still gentle and kind to both you and me. I'm sorry because I love you too, and I know that you too need me. But I can't bear being divided, and I have to choose him. I'm leaving, Marion. I can't remain here any longer knowing what I know and feeling as I do about it. It's too painful and I'm demeaned by my betrayal of him. There are times when I want to tell him the whole truth. And if I don't, it's because I love you too and feel that there's no wrong in what you're doing. I really don't. I think you're right in what you're doing. You're young and you're in love and it's a person's right to love. I think so. Frank is handsome and I think he is honest. I mean, I think he loves you. He's not very strong, but he's young. No one is strong when he is young. I'm not. Only I'm still playing with soldiers and he has entered into the grown-up world. If I were in his place, it would terrify me to be the lover of a married woman. Good-bye, my sister. I must leave. I am constantly forced to act in a cowardly manner. I cannot be loyal to both, and I cannot choose one over the other, and I feel a coward when I look at you, and I feel a coward when I look at him. I am tearing out my heart and leaving it here, as half of it is yours and the other half is his. I hope I won't hurt you by leaving—beyond missing me, which I know you will. I mean beyond that. I mean that I hope my leaving has no consequences beyond our missing each other. Take care. *(He starts to go, then turns.)* What if you're discovered? Will he get a job, take on such responsibilities? Will he get a job and marry you?

MARION: . . . I don't know. I haven't thought about that . . .

JUSTER: *(Offstage right, in a disconnected manner.)* Are you leaving? *(A short pause.)* Are you staying for dinner?

MICHAEL: I have some studying to do.

JUSTER: Stay. We should be eating soon. You could leave after dinner. We should have dinner soon. *(He enters and walks to center without looking at them. He seems absent. He stops and looks at the floor as he speaks.)* How are you, my dear?

MARION: . . . Good evening . . .

JUSTER: You both look somber. I hope nothing's wrong.

MARION: . . . No, nothing's wrong.

JUSTER: *(Walking left as he speaks.)* I've had a bad day myself. Sit down, Michael. I'll be back in a moment. *(The volume of his voice does not change as he leaves the room.)* I'll be back in a moment. *(There is the sound of water running as he washes his hands.)* It was difficult at work today. Everyone seems to be constantly shirking responsibility. That seems to be the main problem in the world today. It's not possible to get things done properly, both in the house and at work. Will the person whose duty it is to prepare dinner be here in time to prepare it? Will that person be at the market early enough to ensure that the ingredients he gets are fresh and not wilted and sour? *(He enters drying his hands with a hand towel.)* Will my office staff appear to work properly dressed and properly shaven? It seems as if each day the lesson has to be taught again. The same lesson. Each day we have to restore mankind to a civilized state. Each night the savage takes over. We're entering the war. I'm sure we are.—In no time we will be in the middle of a war. Yes, you wash your face! Yes, you comb your hair.—Yes you wear clothes that are not soiled. Why can't people understand that if something is worth doing it's worth doing right! *(He sits down and puts the towel on his lap, he takes one of his shoes off.)* I take care of my feet. My socks are in a good state of repair. When they wear out I pass them on to someone who needs them *(taking off his other shoe)*. Others mend their socks. I don't. I don't mind wearing mended clothes. My underwear is mended. So are my shirts, but not my socks. *(With both feet on the floor.)* I have always wanted to give my feet maximum comfort. It is they who support the whole body yet they are fragile. Feet are small and fragile for the load they carry. I wear stockings that fit so they won't fold and create discomfort to my feet. If I treat my feet with respect, my brain functions with respect. It functions with more clarity and so does my stomach. I digest better. In the morning at the office, I look at my mail. Then I call my assistant. I discuss some matters with him. Then I call my secretary. She comes in with her stenographer's pad and sits down on the chair to my right. I collect my thoughts for a few moments. Then I stand on my feet, walk to the window at my left, and from there, standing on my feet, with my stomach properly digesting my breakfast and my brain as clear as the morning dew, I dictate my letters.

MARION: I will go see if dinner is ready. *(She exits left.)*

JUSTER: What is wrong with Marion? She's not herself.

MICHAEL: Nothing. Nothing I know of.

JUSTER: What is wrong with you? What is the matter with you?

MICHAEL: Nothing, Father.

JUSTER: Have you thought it over?

MICHAEL: What?

JUSTER: Are you coming home?

MICHAEL: Not yet.

JUSTER: Fine. You do as you must, Michael. *(There is a pause.)* It is hard to know whom to trust, whom to show your heart to.

MARION: *(Offstage.)* Dinner is ready.

JUSTER: Come, Michael. *(Michael walks up to Juster and waits for him.)* Let's have dinner.

Scene 21

10th Street. Two weeks later. March 1917. It is late afternoon. Marion and Frank are embracing in the space behind the sofa. She speaks with urgency.

MARION: I have been warned that this is a dream. That tomorrow you won't love me. I've been told I must prepare myself. That when you leave me my life will end. That my pain will be eternal. Hold me. Hold me in your arms. *(He does.)* Something terrible is happening. Something terrible happens each day. You're not touched by it.—but I am impure. I lie each day. I am rotten and deceitful. Except to you, each time I speak I tell a lie. Lies come out of my mouth. I am impure. How I wish I could spend my days with you and not have to lie. *(There is a pause.)* Frank, wouldn't you like it if we spent all our time together, day and night? If we traveled together? If we walked on the street together, holding hands? If we spent the whole evening together sleeping in each other's arms? How would you like that? *(There is a silence.)* Frank . . .

FRANK: We have to be careful.

Scene 22

10th Street. Two weeks later. Afternoon. Marion stands center left. Juster stands to her left. He holds a receipt in his hand. Juster's briefcase is on the floor next to the desk.

JUSTER: Do you know what this is? *(She lowers her eyes.)* This is a rent receipt! This is a receipt for the rental of a place on Abingdon Square. It's made out to you, do you know what this is? Do you know what this receipt is?

MARION: I've rented that place. I needed a place of my own. To be private. I needed to have my own place.

JUSTER: What for?

MARION: A place of my own.

JUSTER: A place to meet your lover? *(Taking her hand and crumpling the receipt against the palm.)* Take it! Take it! Take it! *(He goes to the desk and sits. As he as speaks, he opens the drawers, takes out papers and sorts them nervously. He speaks sharply.)* What are your plans?

MARION: In regard to what?

JUSTER: In regard to your life!

MARION: I've not made any plans.

JUSTER: Well, do. I'd like to know what you intend to do. How long would you need to decide? I would like to know what you plan to do as soon as possible. *(He starts putting papers, checkbooks and ledgers in the briefcase as he speaks.)* I expect you to leave as soon as possible. I expect you to move your things—what you can, today. A few things, what you need for immediate use. The rest I'll have sent to your own place. If you have a place of your own, you should move there. *(She starts to speak. He continues.)* Thomas will stay with me. Don't think you will take him with you. Don't bother to look for him. He's not in the house. I have taken him to a place where you won't find him and no one but I knows where he is. So don't bother to look for him. Don't try to find him. I am leaving now. I'll return later tonight. When I return I expect you'll be gone. Jenny will help you pack and she will take you and whatever things you want to take to that place or any other place you wish. If you don't leave, you'll never see Thomas again. You're an adulterous wife and I'll sue you for divorce. A court will grant me sole custody of the child. Do you have anything to say? *(There is a moment of silence.)*

MARION: I will not leave unless I take Thomas with me.

JUSTER: If you're still here when I return, you'll never see him again. *(Michael enters right.)* Marion is leaving tonight and she'll never enter this house again. She's not wanted here. She has debased this house. She will not be forgiven and her name will never be mentioned here again. And if you think other ever again, you'll never enter this house.

MICHAEL: Father, may I intercede?

JUSTER: In regard to what!

MICHAEL: Father—

JUSTER: *(Interrupting.)* No. I will not hear what you have to say. I don't want your advice. Marion will leave. You may escort her to wherever it is she is going if you wish.

Scene 23

Mary's place. One month later. April 1917. It is evening. Mary sits on the sofa. Juster sits left. He wears a hat and coat and holds his briefcase on his lap.

JUSTER: I never saw myself as deserving of her love. She was preciously beautiful, modest. She was thoughtful and respectful. There was no vanity in her.—When her mother died I don't believe she cried once but her spirit left her. She seemed absent. This was the way she grieved.—She was obedient. She did what was asked of her, but she had lost her sense of judgment and her desire to choose one thing over the other. She accepted what others chose for her. She sat for hours staring into space. I took her for walks. I took her to the park. We took boat rides on the lake. Our meetings became more frequent. We became natural companions. I loved her company, and I found myself always thinking of her. She was sad and still when I wasn't there. When she saw me, she smiled and came to life. Her aunt told me this too. That she only smiled when she saw me. I foolishly believed that this meant she loved me. I proposed marriage and she accepted. Her aunt, too, thought it natural when I asked for her hand in marriage. She gave us her blessing. There was no exuberant joy in our wedding, but there was the most profound tenderness. I was very happy and I thought Marion was also. There were times when she was taciturn, but I thought she was still grieving for her mother. She was a child and she needed a mother more than a husband. But a husband is all she had. I could not be a mother to her. Four years later Marion had a child. I was overwhelmed with joy, but Marion was not. She became more taciturn than ever. *(There is a pause.)* I began to feel she hated me. And she does hate me, and she has made me hate her. You see her. I know you see her. *(Pause.)* War has been declared, Mary, and I'm afraid Michael will be drafted. He too will be taken away from me.

Scene 23a

A beer parlor. That evening. Juster sits at a table. There is a glass of beer in front of him.

Scene 24

Abingdon Square. Two weeks later. May 1917. It is evening. Marion stands left. Mary sits right. They drink vermouth and smoke.

MARION: I am in a state of despair! Thanks to Frank. How could I not be. Have you ever lived with someone who speaks one way and acts another!— Someone for whom words mean nothing?—Or if they mean anything, they mean something different from what they mean to you? My life is a puzzle.—I don't know where I stand. I am constantly asking: What do you mean?—What is it you mean? What does that mean to you?- Why did you say that?—Why did you do that? Have you?
MARY: Me?

Marion sits left.

MARION: When I sinned against life because I was dead, I was not punished. Now that life has entered me I am destroyed and I destroy everything around me. May God save me. I have always trusted in his goodness and his divine understanding. May God have mercy on me.—I have never denied him.

Scene 25

A beer parlor. Two weeks later. Evening. Juster sits left. Michael sits right. There is a glass of beer in front of each. Juster speaks rapidly.

JUSTER: I have tried. I offered her some money. She didn't accept it. I knew she wouldn't. She stared at me and said nothing. We were in a public place. She stared and I waited for her to answer. After a while I knew she had no intention of answering. I said to her, "Do you have anything to say?" She still said nothing but I felt the hatred in her eyes. I said, "I suppose you are not accepting my offer?" She said nothing. I said, "For god's sake, say you don't accept it and if you don't let's get on to something else." Her hatred is such, it burns. Paper would burn if it were held up to her glance. When I reached the door, I saw her back reflected in the glass. She was so still that there was no life in her. She was still like a dead person. I regretted having offered her the money. I had no reason to think she would accept it. What do they live on? *(Short pause.)* Have you seen her?

MICHAEL: No.

JUSTER: She's gone berserk. She's gone wild like a mad woman. She's insane. You haven't seen her?

MICHAEL: No.

JUSTER: You haven't been in touch at all? Letters?

MICHAEL: No.

JUSTER: Last week I followed her to a dance parlor. *(Michael looks at him.)* Yes, Michael. You have not been here and you don't realize what's going on. Marion's behavior is irrational. She's not sane.—I followed her, outside, and yet people were already dancing—I took a table by the window. A man wearing a soldiers uniform greeted her. They started dancing. And moved to a dark corner. She knew I was there looking at her and that's why she did what she did. They kissed and caressed lewdly. I've never seen such behavior in public.—Never did I think I would see someone . . . I so cherished behave like that. She knew I was there. She knew I followed her there, and yet she did what she did. *(He takes a drink.)* One day, last week, she came to my office. I was standing by the window. I did not notice her at first. Then I heard her say, "Does this happen every afternoon?"—She had been standing at the door. And I said "Does what happen every afternoon?" She said,"Do you stand at the window every afternoon?" I said, "Yes." And she said, "What do you look at?" I said, "I look out. I don't look at anything in particular. I look out because that's how I concentrate on what I have to do." "And what is it you have to do?" "Right now I am in the middle of dictating my letters." Then she stood behind my secretary and leaned over to look at her writing pad. Then she said, "What is that? A secret code?" Shorthand! Then she said, "This is a love letter." Then, she came to where I was and looked out the window and said, "Do you use binoculars?" I told her that I could see quite well without binoculars and she said, "From where you are, can you see the house on Abingdon Square?" She thought I was spying on her. She's mad. She's capable of anything. *(He looks absently at the street. He takes a revolver from his pocket and puts it on the table.)* I carry this with me at all times. I don't know if I will shoot her or if I will shoot myself. I know that one of us will die soon.

MICHAEL: . . . Father . . . I must try to stop you.

Juster puts the revolver in his pocket. He takes a purse out of his pocket, takes money out and puts it on the table. He stands and starts to walk away. He stops.

JUSTER: Would you take care of the bill, Michael?
MICHAEL: . . . Yes . . . *(Juster starts to exit.)* Father . . . I've enlisted.

Juster stops, looks at Michael for a moment, turns away slowly and exits.

Scene 26

Abingdon Square. Two weeks later. June 1917. Marion stands up left. Mary sits right.

MARY: Juster?
MARION: Yes, Juster. I hate him. I will shoot him. I imagine I shoot him and I feel great satisfaction. A satisfaction equal to flushing a toilet, seeing the water flush out and vanish forever. I am crude. I know I am crude. I know I'm uncivilized. I know I am part of a civilized race but I am uncivilized. Thomas is not his!
MARY: Marion!
MARION: He's not.
MARY: Is he Frank's?
MARION: No.
MARY: Whose is he?
MARION: A stranger's . . . a stranger. Just someone. Someone who came in the house one day and never again. I never saw him again.—Just a man. A stranger. No one.—I have a bad destiny, Mary. I have an evil destiny. It constantly thwarts me.—Nothing comes to me at the right time or in the right way.

Scene 27

Minnie's living room. One week later. It is evening. Minnie sits on a chair, center stage. Marion is on her knees facing Minnie.

MARION: I need my child. I need my child, Minnie, I need that child in my arms and I don't see a way I could ever have him again. He has been irrevocably taken from me. There is nothing I could do that would bring him back to me. I have begged him to let me see him. I have gone on my knees, I have offered myself to him. I have offered my life to him. He won't listen. He won't forgive me. I am at his mercy. I wish for his death. I stalk the house. I stand on the corner and watch the house. I imagine the child inside playing in his room. When spring comes, I may be able to see him in the garden. I know he's not there, but that's how I can feel him near me. Looking at the house.

MINNIE: Why won't he let you see him?

MARION: He's gone mad! He's insane, Minnie.

MINNIE: He?

MARION: Yes! He's insane. He wants to destroy me. But I'll destroy him first.

MINNIE: Marion, I don't understand you. I forget things. I'm too old. I don't remember what you're talking about. It's no longer in my mind. The flesh is sore and swollen. *(Touching the other side of head.)*—This part of it is stretched and redder than the rest, as if it is hotter. As if it had a fever. As if it had hair.—It throbs.

Scene 28

10th Street. A few days later. It is late morning. Juster sits at the desk. He speaks to Michael on the phone. After a few moments Marion appears outside the left window looking in.

JUSTER: She follows me. She's insane. She's jealous, Michael. She's jealous of me. Her jealousy is irrational. As irrational as everything else she does.

Marion steps on a twig.

JUSTER: *(To Marion.)* What are you doing?

MARION: Who is here with you.

JUSTER: I'm alone.

She hears a sound and turns to the left.

MARION: What was that? Someone's in the back.

Juster does not answer. She exits left. He speaks on the phone.

JUSTER: She's outside. Doing who knows what in the garden. She just looked through the window and demanded to know who is here with me.— There is no one here with me. Not even Jenny is here. I have sent her away.— She is out of her mind.

Marion enters right.

MARION: Who are you with?

JUSTER: I am with no one.

MARION: Who are you talking to?
JUSTER: I am talking on the telephone.

She picks up the phone, listens for a moment and hangs up.

MARION: I had forgotten how I loved this house. I love this house. *(Pause.)* I have been ill. I have had fevers. *(Pause.)* I'll tell you a riddle. See if you can solve it: If a person owns an object, where is it? It's under his arm. If a person loves an object, where is it? It's in his arms. If a mother's baby is not in her arms, where is it? *(Pause.)* Where is it? Where is Thomas? Where have you taken him? Is there someone in your life? Someone influencing you? How can you do this? How can you put me through this? What do you gain?

Scene 29

Abingdon Square. Two weeks later. July 1917. It is evening. The stage is dark. There is the sound of a gunshot. The lights come up. Juster stands downstage facing up. He wears an overcoat and a bowler hat. His right arm hangs, holding a revolver. Marion is up center. She faces him. Her arms are halfway raised and her mouth and eyes are open in a state of shock. Mary enters running from the left. Marion turns to look at Mary. Both Juster and Marion go through the motions he describes.

JUSTER: I came in. I said nothing. I took the gun out and aimed at her. She stared at me. Her courage is true. She stared at death without flinching. My eye fell on the mirror behind her. I saw my reflection in it. I am much older than she. Much older. I looked very old and she looked very young. I felt ashamed to love her so. I thought, let her young lover kill her if she must die. I turned the gun to my head. She moved toward me calmly. She put her hand on mine and brought it down away from my head. She said, "Please." I was moved by her kindness. I turned to look at her. And again I was filled with rage. My finger pulled the trigger. *(He shoots again. Marion runs upstage and returns to her position at the start of the scene.)* That was the blast you heard, the gun was pointing at the floor. Everyone here is perfectly all right. *(Juster begins to choke. He turns front slowly. He starts to walk backwards gasping for air. He falls unconscious on the sofa. His eyes are wide open.)*

Scene 30

10th Street. A month later. August 1917. It is dusk. Marion sits right of the couch. Frank stands behind the sofa to the left.

FRANK: And if he doesn't come to, will you spend the rest of your life taking care of him?

MARION: When I reach out to touch him I don't know if I'm reaching outside of me or into me.—If he doesn't come out of the coma . . . ? I feed him. I bathe him. I change him. I wait for the day when I can speak to him. To speak to him at least once.

FRANK: I wanted to ask you if there is anything I can do.

MARION: . . . No . . . Thank you, Frank.

Frank sits on the right side of the couch.

FRANK: I may be leaving once again, Marion.

MARION: Oh . . . ?

FRANK: Yes, I may be moving on.

MARION: I know, Frank. I know you must go. *(They sit silently for a while.)*

Scene 31

Juster's bedroom. A day later. It is evening. Juster lies in his bed unconscious. His head is stage right. He is in a coma. He is unshaven. Marion stands on the upstage side of the bed. Juster begins to come to. His speech is impaired.

JUSTER: . . . It looks much nicer here than in the parlor . . .

MARION: What does?

JUSTER: . . . It feels bad.

MARION: What feels bad?

JUSTER: . . . It's happier here . . .

MARION: What?

JUSTER: It's happier. Don't you know it?

MARION: What?

His eyes open. They are bloodshot and swollen.

JUSTER: Who's here?

MARION: It's me.

JUSTER: Who?

MARION: Marion.

JUSTER: Marion?

MARION: Yes.

JUSTER: Why are you here?

MARION: Because you are ill.

JUSTER: What's wrong with me?

MARION: You had a stroke.

JUSTER: What have you done to me?

MARION: Nothing.

JUSTER: Yes, you have.

MARION: What have I done?
JUSTER: You've done harm to me.
MARION: No.

He looks at her suspiciously.

JUSTER: What have you done to me? Get out!
MARION: I've fed you.
JUSTER: What have you fed me?

She is silent.

JUSTER: Poison!
MARION: No.
JUSTER: You're repulsive to me. *(Pause.)* You've touched me!
MARION: Yes.
JUSTER: Do you enjoy seeing me like this? *(Pause.)* Where's Michael? *(Pause.)* Has he been here?
MARION: I sent for him.
JUSTER: I want to see him.
MARION: He's trying to get here.
JUSTER: Why can't he come?
MARION: He calls every day.
JUSTER: *(Starting to get out of bed.)* I want to get up. I want to be downstairs when he calls.
MARION: He won't call till later.
JUSTER: *(Still trying to get up.)* I'll call him.
MARION: He can't be reached.
JUSTER: Am I dying?
MARION: I don't know.
JUSTER: I don't want you here. *(She takes a step back.)* Get out! Get out! *(She starts to leave, then stops.)* Get out!
MARION: . . . May I come back later? *(He does not answer.)* I understand. *(She exits. He lifts himself to a sitting position, stands and stumbles to the living room.)*
JUSTER: . . . Marion . . . Marion! *(He starts to fall.)* . . . Marion . . . Marion . . . Marion . . .

Marion runs in. She holds Juster in her arms.

JUSTER: I love you.
MARION: . . . I love you too. *(She sobs. Michael enters, walks to them and stands behind them. He wears an army uniform. There is a bright light on them.)* Michael . . . ! Michael . . . ! He mustn't die! He mustn't die!

Juster's hand moves slowly toward Marion's face as music plays.

END OF PLAY

Jonelle Allen, Ebbe Roe Smith, and Deirdre O'Connell in *Etta Jenks* (Los Angeles performances) by Marlane Gomard Meyer, 1987. Photo © by Chris Gulker.

Author's Note

TWO NAKED PEOPLE

When I was asked to write an introduction to this play I knew I had to write about the interplay of biographical anecdote and inspiration and how they conspire to make you think you're a genius.

I believe, because I don't know for sure, that my play *Etta Jenks* began when I was a very small girl and I found a photograph of two naked people in an old suitcase under my bed. In this photo, the woman is lying on her back staring up at nothing, her face void of expression. The man is kneeling beside her, watching her, anxious, as if any minute she was going to start crying. I kept that photo hidden under my toy box and occasionally I'd take it out and study it. I felt there was something prophetic and mysterious about these two people. I wanted to know who they were and how they came to be naked with each other and what was going to happen next. I showed the photo to my friends, I became a big shot. The photo stayed under my toy box for a long time till one day it went missing. I immediately suspected my nemesis. My mother never mentioned finding the photo because it would give the lie to the carefully constructed myth of her tolerance. She was always overproud of "giving me my privacy," even at age five. We never spoke of the incident, but for several months I felt her watching me for signs of deviance and impurity.

Many years later, twelve to be exact, my friend and I moved to Hollywood to pursue our dream of becoming the girlfriends of famous men. The men were slow to respond, and we were forced to find jobs. I found work reading the Tarot for the patrons of an Armenian restaurant and my friend chose to earn money posing nude for gentlemen's magazines. We didn't think anything was wrong with this because it was during the time when sexual liberation and women's liberation seemed like the same thing. It took awhile to figure out it wasn't and an even longer time to do anything about it.

One more anecdote should be mentioned as a possible inspiration. My grandmother was dying in the hospital, slipping in and out of this kind of waking sleep. We were alone and she was quiet and I stepped out to get some coffee. When I returned, someone had drawn the curtain around her bed; I thought they'd taken her away, I could not feel her presence. But when I looked, her body was there but that energy that made her my grandmother and my savior had gone away.

I think the subconscious mind is like a great, kindly cook who takes our little stories, dreams, and old heartaches and makes something fresh and original and lets us take the credit, as I take the credit now for *Etta Jenks*.

—Marlane Gomard Meyer

Etta Jenks was presented in New York by the Women's Project on April 6, 1988, in a co-production with the Los Angeles Theatre Center, Bill Bushnell, Artistic Director. It was directed by Roberta Levitow, with sets by Rosario Provenza, lighting by Robert Wierzel, costumes by Ray C. Naylor, sound by Jon Gottlieb, dramaturgy by Mame Hunt, stage management by Joan Toggenburger, and the following cast:

SHERI	Sheila Dabney
CLYDE/SPENCER	Abdul Salaam El Razzac
DWIGHT/ALEC/	
DIRECTOR'S VOICE	Carmine Iannoccone
BEN	John Nesci
ETTA	Deirdre O'Connell
JAMES	John Pappas
BURT/SHERMAN/MAX	Ebbe Roe Smith
KITTY/SHELLY/	
WOMAN AT AUDITION	Dendrie Taylor
DOLLY	Ching Valdes/Aran

At the Los Angeles Theatre Center, the cast differed as follows:

SHERI	Jonelle Allen
DWIGHT/ALEC/	
DIRECTOR'S VOICE	Scott Burkholder
BEN	J.C. Quinn
DOLLY	Evelina Fernandez

CHARACTERS

ETTA JENKS, a woman in her early thirties
CLYDE, a man in his mid-thirties
BURT, a man in his late twenties, deaf
SHERMAN, Burt's twin brother, blind
BEN, a man in his forties
DOLLY, a woman in her forties
DWIGHT, a man in his late twenties
JAMES, a man in his late twenties
SPENCER, a man in his early fifties
SHERI, a woman in her mid-thirties
KITTY, a woman in her early twenties

ALEC, a man in his early twenties
MAX, a man in his late thirties
SHELLY, a young girl, eighteen

This cast can be doubled down to nine actors.

TIME

Present

PLACE

Los Angeles

PRODUCTION NOTE

With the exception of Etta, Burt, and Sherman, the characters should all be possessed of a certain animal quality, subtly suggested through makeup or gesture. The effect to be not cartoonish but queer. The landscape should suggest a kind of contained isolation that might be found in an empty aquarium at an abandoned sea park.

SCENE ONE

Darkness. A train whistle blows in the distance, the engine becomes audible. A covered light hangs down center stage. It comes up to reveal Etta standing on a small platform, she wears a long coat and carries a large suitcase. She seems to be leaning into the sound of the train, waiting, as the train approaches. The lights flicker, and turn flashing as the sound of the train roars by, Etta disappears in a blackout. The train sound recedes in the distance. The lights come up on a bare stage, we hear the sound of a busy train terminal; a voice announcing arrivals and departures, people milling, voices calling to each other.

Etta is center, she pulls a map from her purse. A young man enters with a load of luggage, a baggage handler, Burt. He glances at her briefly before unloading the luggage. A man approaches; his name is Clyde.

CLYDE: How you doin' . . . *(She moves away.)* Excuse me. *(She moves away.)* Miss? Excuse me . . . but . . . Miss? I can see you're from out of town . . .
ETTA: Please don't. *(She moves away.)*
CLYDE: I see you have what looks like a map?
ETTA: No.
CLYDE: Well, it sure looks like a map.

Etta approaches Burt.

ETTA: Could you help me?
CLYDE: I could help you.
ETTA: Please leave me alone.
BURT: I have to see your lips when you talk.

Clyde steps between Burt and Etta.

CLYDE: I'm insanely good with a map, like the army was havin' a hard time trainin' their guys to read a map? And they heard how good I was and they snapped me out of civilian life, bad knee, I had a metal plate in my head, they did not care 'cause I'm so good with a map, they flang me smack to the middle of Nam . . .
ETTA: *(To Burt.)* I fell asleep and I don't know where I am.
CLYDE: Angel city. *(She moves away.)*
BURT: Los Angeles.
ETTA: *(To B.)* I am looking for someplace to stay, someplace cheap.
CLYDE: I know just the place, let me help you with your bag. *(They struggle with the bag.)*
BURT: Like a motel.
ETTA: I'd like it to be cheap.

CLYDE: You can stay with me for nothin' . . .

BURT: You got any money?

ETTA: Not a lot.

CLYDE: I got a lot of money and I can show YOU how to get a lot of money . . .

BURT: Say again . . . ?

CLYDE: Meeting successful businessmen . . .

ETTA: I have some money.

CLYDE: Eating at expensive restaurants . . .

BURT: I have a brother might be able to rent you a place. You'd have to be out during the day.

ETTA: Out where?

CLYDE: Out on your ass.

BURT: Wherever it is people go when they're not home.

ETTA: Oh.

CLYDE: Oh. See? You don't even know where you're gonna be.

BURT: It's a sleeping room, jus' someplace t'sleep.

CLYDE: That means no visitors and suppose I want to visit?

ETTA: *(To B.)* Well, I'll probably be workin' in the movies.

BURT: *(Thinking.)* That's day work.

CLYDE: *(He stares at Burt, then at Etta.)* Oh shit . . .

ETTA: I can start anytime so there shouldn't be a problem . . .

BURT: *(Nods.)* Okay . . .

CLYDE: I see it now. I see the attraction.

ETTA: I imagine I'd be gone quite a bit . . .

CLYDE: Contract negotiations, celebrity luncheons.

BURT: My brother, Sherman, it's his house. He's a veteran and he's blind but he can hear if you stay in the room.

CLYDE: Hey, wait a minute . . . you don't even know this guy or his blind brother.

ETTA: Yeah and I don' t know you . . .

CLYDE: We could fix that.

ETTA: What's your job?

CLYDE: My job?

ETTA: *(She looks him over.)* What do you . . . get girls as they're comin' off the train?

CLYDE: Get? I don't have to get! They come!

ETTA: Why is that?

CLYDE: Why do you think?

ETTA: They're stupid.

BURT: You wanna call?

ETTA: Yes, let's call. *(She takes his arm and moves down and away from Clyde.)*

CLYDE: Oh yes, let's call . . .

BURT: I could take you there after work. I'm off in about thirteen minutes.
ETTA: That would be good. *(Looks back at Clyde.)* That would be real good.
(They move downstage, freeze; he looks at them, turns away.)
CLYDE: What's my job . . .? Shit, where do these bitches come from?

Lights fade on Clyde.

SCENE TWO

Burt watches T.V. Etta wears a slip. She sets her hair with hot rollers. Beat.

ETTA: I think my throat is closing up. Those french fries were so dry, I think
they're caught . . . like a lump in my throat. *(She nudges Burt.)* I think those fries
got caught in my throat.
BURT: Drink water.
ETTA: I wish I had a Coke. I saw this science experiment once, where they
put this tooth in Coke, and over a period of a few weeks or days . . . or maybe it
was just one day, it completely fell apart. Just disappeared. I guess that could
happen with a whole set of teeth if we were to sit around with a mouth full of
Coca-Cola day and night. I wonder how it would work, the teeth comin' out,
would you swallow and then what, would they come back in . . . somehow?
God, I'm stupid. What am I suppose to do? I thought by now I'd at least have
some kinda extra work, somethin' . . . I met this girl, Sheri, at the lunch
counter? I thought, she was pretty weird but she came out to be nice and she
said that one way to break into movies is to have a videotape of yourself made.
Performing a scene with someone or maybe doin' a monologue. But the problem is, it cost. I wonder how I could get five hundred dollars? I had four hundred, but that's just about gone. I wonder if I could find somebody with one of
those video cameras you use at home? *(She nudges Burt, he looks at her.)*
ETTA: Do you know anybody with a . . . home movie camera?
BURT: I know people with video equipment.
ETTA: You do? Video! Yeah, that's what I need!
BURT: It's very expensive equipment, I don't think they'd let you just use
it, just like that.
ETTA: I need an audition tape. *(Beat.)* This is great, I'll brush up on my
monologue or maybe get somebody to do a scene with me. When do you
think you could . . . *(She nudges him, he turns.)* When do you think we could
use the stuff.
BURT: What stuff?
ETTA: The videotape stuff.
BURT: I gotta ask.
ETTA: Do it.

BURT: I don't know.

ETTA: What do you mean?

BURT: This guy is not a very nice guy.

ETTA: Yeah.

BURT: He's a creep.

ETTA: What do you mean, a creep?

BURT: *(Beat.)* I don't really know.

ETTA: *(She touches him.)* You lie to me 'cause you think it's for my best good but all it does is make me not want to trust you. Don't lie to me, Burt. It makes me mad.

BURT: He's like, not a human being exactly.

ETTA: Go ask him.

BURT: He makes movies of women.

ETTA: Can you ask him now?

BURT: He's weird, Etta.

ETTA: I'll ask him.

BURT: *(He looks away. Beat.)* I'll ask him.

She kicks him, he looks up.

ETTA: Now. *(He stands.)* And while you're out . . . get me a Coke. Please. Okay? *(Beat.)* Okay?!

Burt moves upstage to Ben, the lights fade on Etta.

SCENE THREE

Ben is seated up left, he looks like a man mutating into a wolf. Dolly is standing down and right of him, she faces out with a drink. Burt enters.

BEN: *(Beat.)* Dolly, could you make our guest a drink?

DOLLY: *(Exaggerated.)* You want a drink?

BURT: Well, if you're gonna have one . . .

DOLLY: I've got one.

BEN: Get his drink! *(Dolly exits.)* What else?

BURT: Her name is Etta. She's got long arms and a big head.

BEN: *(Nods.)* A big-headed girl.

BURT: A natural blond.

BEN: Personality, or no.

BURT: *(Beat.)* It's very difficult for me to say, because I can't hear. I can read her words, but, since I can't hear how she says them, it's hard to say what she's like. You can tell a lot by how people sound, beyond what they tell you. If someone were to ask me, what's the worst part of losing my hearing,

I'd have to tell them that it's not being able to hear if someone is sincere. Like with you for instance? I have never heard your voice and it's hard for me to know what kind of man you are.

BEN: I'm an asshole.

BURT: I guessed that.

BEN: I'm not ashamed, I'm not proud, but I don't try and put it on like I'm anything but an asshole.

BURT: I'd have to say . . . she could be anything.

BEN: Anything at all.

BURT: She spends hours making up. Even when there's no place to go. She likes to look her best.

BEN: *(He stares in the direction of Dolly.)* Vain. They are all vain, and then when they get old and they look like shit, they get pissed off! *(Beat.)* So . . . she would like to be an actress?

BURT: She would like to be.

BEN: Is she any good?

BURT: I don't know. I do notice one thing. When she's talking, and she's excited, her face doesn't move. In my opinion, I'm not sure . . . that would make a very good actress. A wooden face.

BEN: Is she an easy lay?

BURT: Yes.

BEN: Details.

BURT: She came on to me the first night.

BEN: SHE came on to YOU?

BURT: She likes to have sex.

BEN: With a lot of white around the eyes?

BURT: Not at all.

BEN: She sounds like she has definite star quality.

BURT: *(Pause.)* How's Millie?

BEN: Millie . . . seems to have dropped out of sight.

BURT: Millie had star quality.

BEN: But she was unreliable.

BURT: She had a good sense of humor.

BEN: She was an addict.

BURT: After.

BEN: *(Cocks his head, shakes it.)* I don't know. I hate drugs myself. I don't even drink. *(Dolly enters with two drinks.)* My wife is a drunk.

DOLLY: I didn't drink at all when you first met me.

BEN: So what? What's that supposed to mean? That I made you a boozebag?

DOLLY: Maybe.

BEN: That's shit. You just need a way to sit still. 'Cause if you stopped drinking you'd probably have to get up and live! And the pressure's too much!

It's too damn much! Life scares the living shit out of you, and you're trying to blame me!

BURT: *(Facing away.)* I wish she wouldn't get involved with you, Ben.

BEN: *(To Dolly.)* Oh Christ! You piss me off!!!

Lights fade.

SCENE FOUR

Three Women stand downstage facing front. Etta and Sheri are among them. A Voice speaks to them from the dark.

VOICE: Hi. I'm the director, Thomas Schultz, and this is my A.D.Valerie. She'll be handling most of our problems and she'll be answering any questions you might have about your part. *(A Fourth Woman enters.)* Today we're casting for the role of the maid. It's a nonspeaking, nonpaying part, you'll plan to be here every night for rehearsal and provide your own costume. It would help if one of you were really a maid? *(Beat.)* All right. Who's first?

Sheri moves downstage.

SHERI: Hi Mr. Schultz, my name is Sheri Shineer and I'd like to do a monologue from the musical "Hair."

VOICE: That won't be necessary because you won't be talking. The deal is, and I want to be as honest as I can with you up front, your type is not the type I had in mind.

SHERI: What type did you have in mind?

VOICE: I don't know but you're not it.

SHERI: I am not my body . . .

VOICE: Maybe if you could all step up to the front of the stage and . . . yes.

Sheri watches the remaining women move forward and exits.

VOICE: That's right. *(Beat.)* Okay, you . . . second from the left, what's your name?

ETTA: Uh . . . Lana?

VOICE: Don't you know?

ETTA: I'm changing it.

VOICE: Okay, the rest of you can go. Thanks so much. *(The other girls exit.)* Have you ever worked in the theatre before Lana?

ETTA: Oh yes I have, yes, I worked as an usherette for two-and-a-half years at the Rialto . . .

VOICE: Wait a minute . . .

ETTA: Uh, Mr. Schultz? Did I understand you to say that nobody was gettin' paid here?

VOICE: Yes. We work for free. I mean, most of us work for free, and some of us work for a token salary . . . Valerie?

ETTA: Well . . . *(chuckles)*, how can that be?

VOICE: Lana, this is an Equity Waiver theatre, I told you at the beginning the part was nonpaying.

ETTA: It took a minute to sink in.

VOICE: Yes well . . .

ETTA: I guess I could do it for the practice?

VOICE: Make up your mind.

ETTA: I haven't really worked in two months.

VOICE: That's not my problem.

ETTA: I used to work at the Thrifty lunch counter but I burned my hand and they had to let me go and I was hopin' to begin to pursue my professional career now that I was between jobs.

VOICE: Do you want the part or not?

ETTA: No money at all?

VOICE: And you have to provide your own costume.

ETTA: Are you getting paid?

VOICE: *(Calling.)* Valerie?

ETTA: I really think I should have some money.

VOICE: The people producing this show can't afford to pay everyone. I'm not making that much myself.

ETTA: Like how much do you make?

VOICE: *(Beat.)* I make ten dollars every night the show is up.

ETTA: Ten dollars? How do you live on ten dollars? You know in a movie you get paid no matter if you're just standin' around in the background . . . ?

VOICE: Lana . . .

ETTA: It's evil not to pay people for work they do. That's the time of their life.

VOICE: That's their choice.

ETTA: This can't be right. Man. I hate theatre.

Lights fade out around her, Etta remains lit, she turns as lights come up on Sherman and Sheri.

SCENE FIVE

Sherman is cleaning his M-16 at a kitchen table and listening to the ballgame. Sheri and Etta enter and sit.

ETTA: Sherman.

SHERMAN: Home so early AGAIN, Etta?

ETTA: I don't know what to do. *(Beat.)* I could take a job typing. I'm a pretty bad typist.

SHERMAN: You'd improve.

SHERI: I hate office work.

ETTA: It makes me feel like I'm in a box.

SHERI: That's real.

ETTA: What would you do, Sherman.

SHERMAN: It doesn't matter. You and I have nothing in common. What do you want to do?

ETTA: Be a movie star.

SHERMAN: What's that?

ETTA: You know, like . . . be an actress.

SHERMAN: And what's that?

SHERI: Sherman . . . ?

SHERMAN: Like, what does SHE think it is?

ETTA: It's like . . . people are giving me money . . . 'cause of who I am.

SHERMAN: And who's that?

ETTA: *(Beat.)* I don't know.

SHERMAN: Maybe that's why you're not making much money.

ETTA: I'm not making anything.

SHERMAN: Maybe that's why. This is what stops most people, not knowing who they are or where they fit in the marketplace.

ETTA: Where do you think I fit?

SHERMAN: Well, let me just say this, I imagine that you are pretty, even when you lie or steal my cigarettes or when you stay for days on end in a room I specifically told you was for sleeping only! *(Sheri and Etta giggle silently.)* I still IMAGINE you're a good-looking girl.

SHERI: She takes a good picture . . .

ETTA: You think so?

SHERI: Oh yeah, definitely.

SHERMAN: But that's not all, see what I'm saying?

SHERI: No.

SHERMAN: People can imagine what they want about her. Tabula rasa.

SHERI: People can project what they want . . .

SHERMAN: She's like an archetype.

ETTA: Is that good?

SHERI: I think so. *(Nods.)*

SHERMAN: *(Emphatic.)* No.

SHERI: Like Monroe? *(Beat.)* Oh yeah.

SHERMAN: Icons who ascend to a level of worship and perish. It's a cliché.

SHERI: Maybe you shouldn't be in the movies.

ETTA: It's my only dream, Sheri.

SHERMAN: You've had no interest?

ETTA: Burt has a friend. I don't know though. I don't know about that. I'm suppose to go talk to him. But, I don't know.

SHERI: He said she could make three hundred dollars a day.

SHERMAN: Burt's friend.

ETTA: Ben.

SHERMAN: Primordial ooze.

SHERI: He makes movies.

SHERMAN: Pornography.

SHERI: It's a service industry, Sherman.

ETTA: I could use a hundred dollars a day.

SHERMAN: Pornography in its focus on the genital experience creates an ultimately carnal mind that is necessarily death-oriented since the body is always in a progressive state of decay. The earth begins to crawl up inside you . . .

SHERI: Ugh.

ETTA: We're dying anyway, who cares?

SHERMAN: The day you wake up with a mouth full of dirt, you'll care.

SHERI: I don't think it's like that.

SHERMAN: You start thinking you're a body; you're not a body.

ETTA: Then why did I get a tattoo?

SHERMAN: It's macho.

SHERI: I got one when I first moved here, a snake on my shoulder blade. I hate it.

SHERMAN: It made you feel like you had some control over your life.

ETTA: I think I should have had something by now, don't you? I mean, maybe this guy Ben is a break and I don't know it. I mean, how WOULD I know it? I have never had a break. I don't even know what a break looks like, do you?

SHERMAN: You can't know.

ETTA: Well, see there?

SHERI: I just do what's up next, and it seems to work out.

ETTA: And you know it could be these films are artistic.

SHERI: Yeah, Sherman.

SHERMAN: The difference between erotic art and Ben's business, is the difference between gourmet dining and eating fifty pounds of raw sewage in one sitting.

Etta sneaks a cigarette.

ETTA: What do you think of the name Lana, Sherman.

He catches her hand, takes the cigarette back.

SHERMAN: It sounds like a fat girl trying to be thin.

Sheri lifts her skirt, flashes him.

SHERI: I bet he's not really blind.

Sherman slowly points his gun at Sheri; Etta laughs.

BLACKOUT.

SCENE SIX

Ben and Spencer sit downstage. Lights flicker across their bodies, they are watching a movie.

SPENCER: *(Pause, disgusted.)* I hate dogs.

BEN: *(Absorbed.)* How can you hate a dog? Dogs have some of the best qualities of men.

SPENCER: How old is the girl in the doghouse?

BEN: Old enough . . .

SPENCER: How old?

BEN: These children are ancient sexual beings. They teach me.

SPENCER: God . . .

BEN: Don't God me Spencer, I built the pyramids, don't use that superior tone with me, I'm you.

SPENCER: *(Beat.)* Remember décolletage, Benjamin?

BEN: What's that suppose to mean?

SPENCER: A flash of thigh, a bare shoulder. Evening gowns, Grace Kelly, a single strand of pearls. Teeth. A slight overbite?

BEN: *(Sighs.)* God Spencer, you are so romantic. *(Etta knocks and enters.)*

SPENCER: *(To Etta.)* Welcome to the glue factory. *(Spencer exits, Ben looks at Etta.)*

BEN: *(Beat.)* I've heard very good things about you, high praise from my friend Burt. He thinks you have talent. And after meeting you, I have to admit, I'm impressed.

ETTA: Thank you.

BEN: I met Burt when I started out in this business but not many people make it the way I have. Most lose their stuff, like Burt, he couldn't handle the pressure.

ETTA: What pressure?

BEN: I personally don't know. Just, when people get out of the business they say it's 'cause of the pressure.

ETTA: Burt thinks this is a mistake.

BEN: Burt thinks. Yes. Burt is a big star.

ETTA: He says it's the quickest way to ruin your chances.

BEN: I have footage on Burt. He's a lame dog.

ETTA: He never said anything about that.

BEN: Burt is a loser. I think you know that already. Am I wrong? Okay. Good. Now, let's talk about you. I know you want to make a short video, is that right?

ETTA: I want to make a tape of myself doing a monologue or a scene so I can send it to casting directors or producers . . .

BEN: Okay. Back up. Has Burt told you I'm a producer?

ETTA: Not exactly.

BEN: I am. I make movies.

ETTA: Yeah, but . . . what kind?

BEN: Okay, let's not fool around. You know that.

ETTA: Yeah, I guess I do.

BEN: It's a business Etta. That's all it is. Business. And I want to tell you one more thing here Etta. Maybe you know this maybe you don't, but many of our finest stars made their debut in a skin flick. Okay? That's number one.

ETTA: Like who.

BEN: I beg your pardon?

ETTA: Like what stars made their debut in a skin flick.

BEN: The world of cinema is like a secret society, Etta. I myself would be happy to tell you the names of the other members, but these stars, these very rich and influential people consider discretion to be the first responsibility of art. When and if you decide that this business opportunity is one that suits your needs and if we find that you suit ours, within a very short time these names will be as familiar as your own. And believe me Etta, you will be surprised and flattered to be among these elite. Now where was I, number two?

ETTA: Number two.

BEN: Number two, you could make a shit load of dough doin' one film or maybe two films and use that money to start your acting career. Use that to finance your audition tape instead of coming in here and expecting me to bankroll your ass for no reason whatsoever. Did you stop to ask yourself that Etta? Why should I do this tape for you?

ETTA: I thought maybe as a favor.

BEN: I hate doing favors Etta, and you know why? Because in the long run you will resent me. That's right, you should always pay your way, Etta, and I'm speaking to you as a friend would. Owe nobody!

ETTA: How much money could I make?

BEN: How much could you make. *(Nods.)* I see. Cut to the chase. Okay. Let's just say this. It depends.

ETTA: On what?

BEN: Well . . . we'd naturally have to talk about that. We'd have to see.

ETTA: See what? See what I look like without my clothes?

BEN: That's not the only consideration.

ETTA: I look fine.

BEN: Show me.

ETTA: *(Beat.)* Just like that?

BEN: Exactly.

Etta removes her blouse, cross fade to Kitty. Kitty is facing upstage, she is nude from the waist up.

SCENE SEVEN

Lights come up on Sheri and Kitty. Sheri is dipping a big sponge in a bucket of makeup and wiping down Kitty's back.

SHERI: Like my dad was dying of cirrhosis, okay? Depressed, I mean, very. And he locked himself in his room with the windows closed and the gas going full blast and like that gas eats the oxygen in your body, so that when the cops opened the door he exploded.

VOICE: *(Off.)* Lana?!

KITTY: That's sad.

SHERI: It was a mess more than a feeling, Kitty, he was desperate. But like I started thinking about his . . . body idea. Suppose you're not desperate, I mean, there should be a way to scramble your protoplasm and . . . vamoose, you know? I mean, it would be like building a car without doors, you see what I'm saying? *(Etta enters wearing a robe and wig, she drops the wig on the floor.)*

KITTY: No.

VOICE: *(Off.)* You have five minutes Lana!

SHERI: I was just telling Kitty about disappearing the body.

ETTA: My hands smell like feet.

SHERI: I read about this yogi in India.

ETTA: *(She starts to sit down, grimaces.)* God, does anyone else have this infection . . . ?

KITTY: It's a fungus, everybody has it.

SHERI: This yogi had mastered dematerialization to such a degree that he could vanish at will.

ETTA: Sheri will you shut up? *(They trade, Kitty wipes down Sheri.)*

SHERI: So like that information is in race memory, Kitty.

KITTY: What information?

ETTA: Dematerializing . . .

SHERI: That means, it's available to anyone, through the subconscious.

KITTY: I don't get it.

SHERI: 'Cause we are one mind.

KITTY: What's the point of being able to disappear, anyway?

SHERI: You're walking down the street and a man comes out of nowhere waving a gun. . . . He feels like he's dead inside, misery loves company, he sees you. What happens?

KITTY: Get shot.

ETTA: Dematerialize, Kitty.

KITTY: I never heard of that happening.

SHERI: I'm just saying we should have that option.

ETTA: You know, I used to really enjoy sex? *(Beat.)* Now every time I make love even if it's somebody I like, I get this terrible urge that seems to come out of nowhere and it's all I can do to keep from gouging his eyes out or slitting his throat . . .

KITTY: Or hitting him over the head with a crystal ashtray you had to work two days to pay for.

ETTA: *(Curious.)* Yeah, yeah . . . what is that?

KITTY: *(Pause, thoughtfully.)* It's like some kind of rage.

SHERI: I'm not angry.

KITTY: Me either.

ETTA: I don't think I'm angry.

VOICE: *(Off.)* Lana?! Where's Lana?

ETTA: Shit . . .

VOICE: LANA!!?

ETTA: *(Standing slowly as she speaks.)* I AM NOT WEARING THAT STINKING COSTUME YOU STUPID SON OF A BITCH, WHERE'S BEN!!!! *(Etta exits, they watch her.)*

KITTY: *(Beat.)* She hasn't been in the business very long to complain about a dirty rig.

Cross fade to Burt.

SCENE EIGHT

Burt sits alone watching T.V., a suitcase is near his feet. Clothes are being flung into it from the shadows. Etta enters a moment later. She's packing.

BURT: He's married.

ETTA: Grow up.

BURT: What happened to just doing one film?

ETTA: What about it?

BURT: I thought that was the idea.

ETTA: What's your idea Burt?

BURT: I don't know.

ETTA: If you don't have any ideas, you can't play.

BURT: What are you mad at me for?

ETTA: You can't be me and make my decisions.

BURT: I don't know what you're talking about.

ETTA: It's degrading.

BURT: What does that mean?

ETTA: You can't be anything to me, you can't be me, you can't do anything for me, what is it you want?

BURT: I don't want you to go.

ETTA: If I keep working like this, I'll make more money than my lawyer.
BURT: Well, is that the point? Money?
ETTA: Yes.
BURT: I think the point is not to screw your life up.
ETTA: Are you in love with me?
BURT: I used to think I was.
ETTA: Okay, so what do you want to have happen?
BURT: Get married?
ETTA: Oh, get married.
BURT: Yes.
ETTA: And what? Have a kid, have a child?
BURT: I like kids, I mean . . . yeah, kids would be fine by me.
ETTA: Right, kids . . . and what else? A house?!
BURT: Yes, yes!
ETTA: Jesus!
BURT: What?
ETTA: I don't want that, that's not what I want. House, kids, husband, prison, *National Inquirer,* sour milk, cheese every day, it makes me feel sick!
BURT: Marriage is a woman's destiny.
ETTA: What?
BURT: Nothing.
ETTA: If something is your destiny, it shouldn't make you feel like puking your guts out!!
BURT: What about our sex? What about that?
ETTA: I hate sex.
BURT: Our sex is a comingling of spirits. It's the kind of sex married people have Etta.
ETTA: I can have sex with anything and make it look like I enjoy it. I'm a pro.
BURT: You're just being mean now. You're just trying to make me feel bad for complaining. All right. You don't want to be with me. Okay. But you know it's not a good idea to do things for money, money is never good motivation. It turns you hard.
ETTA: I don't do it for the money.
BURT: Are you on something?
ETTA: No!
BURT: 'Cause my brother hates drugs. He'd shit if he thought you were on something . . .
ETTA: Did you hear what I said?
BURT: You don't do it for the money. *(Beat.)* You don't?
ETTA: No.
BURT: What for then?

ETTA: I'm good at it.

BURT: Etta. That's disgusting.

ETTA: What's disgusting.

BURT: Don't you think I know what you're talking about?

ETTA: No, I don't think you do.

BURT: I've seen those movies, Etta.

ETTA: What am I talking about?

BURT: Screwing.

ETTA: What I'm talking about Burt is business.

BURT: Bullshit.

ETTA: Have it your way.

BURT: What about it do you like?

ETTA: I want to thank you for all the help you've given me Burt, I really appreciate it.

BURT: What do you think, you can just brush me off, just kiss me off, just like that?! You think you need an excuse to be a whore, you don't need an excuse. Money, no money, good, no good. I don't know what you're talking about anymore, I can't see into your face, how you're talking to me . . . it doesn't respect anything, Etta. I could be something to you. I could. But you won't have it. *(He sits down, rubs his ears. Pause. She takes a box out of her valise.)*

She nudges him with the box.

ETTA: It's a gift. *(Beat.)* It's a white silk shirt.

BURT: Where am I suppose to wear this, the Academy Awards?

ETTA: Good-bye Burt. *(She takes the T.V., crosses away.)*

BURT: WHY CAN'T YOU JUST TELL ME WHAT IT DOES FOR YOU??!

ETTA: *(Stops, beat.)* It makes me feel like I'm really here.

BURT: But what about me. *(He turns away. She exits.)* When you leave, where will I be? Who's going to see me? Sherman can't see me. My job can't see me. Somebody needs to see me for me to be okay, I can't say I'm gonna be okay if I don't have that, Etta!

Lights fade out on Burt.

SCENE NINE

Cancun, a beach in Mexico, beach sounds are heard. A light comes up on Ben, he is ly-ing on a reclining lounge chair in Speedos and sunglasses. Etta sits beside him sipping a drink. She wears a caftan. She watches him a long beat.

ETTA: You have so many moles, Ben. Aren't you worried about getting skin cancer?

BEN: I can't *stop* thinking about it.

ETTA: You should wear sunscreen.

BEN: I'm trying to remember the color of the room I grew up in. *(Beat.)* I think it was . . . blue. *(Pause.)* My bed was under a window, I would leave the shade up, moonlight made the walls of my room look white. Sometimes I would wake up, and there he would be, sitting on the edge of my bed, staring at me . . . and I would ask him . . . what was wrong. But he'd just sit, and stare, and not say a word. *(Beat.)* He was a drunk.

ETTA: Who?

BEN: My father.

ETTA: *(Beat.)* My dad and my mom's dad were the same person.

BEN: *(Sits up, slowly turns.)* Are you shittin' me?

ETTA: No . . .

BEN: That's freakish. *(Still staring.)* Aren't you suppose to be dead?

ETTA: No.

BEN: It's a good thing you're not going to have a baby.

ETTA: Yeah.

BEN: It'd be a turnip. *(He lies back down, pause.)*

ETTA: He used to wrap himself up in a blanket and chase me around the house. One day my mom saw that and started screaming at him. And right after that we moved. We didn't see him again for a long time and then one day he showed up. We were watching the moonshot and he came to the screendoor and looked in. I unlocked the door and he came in and the three of us sat there without speaking, watching this guy walk on the moon, till finally . . . he just got up and left. I looked at my mom but she wouldn't look at me. I told her she should go out and say good-bye but she wouldn't answer. She was always quiet but she hardly ever spoke after that. *(Beat. She sits up, takes off her glasses.)* I don't like Mexico, Ben, it's too hot. I want to go home.

BEN: Go.

ETTA: What about you?

BEN: I made some bad deals. Spencer wants to pay me back. Screw him.

ETTA: You're not going back.

BEN: Correctamente bien.

ETTA: What about me?

BEN: Screw you.

He laughs a short convulsive laugh. She watches him. Etta remains lit, as the lights fade on Ben and the beach.

SCENE TEN

A dance hall. Music. Couples dance. Sheri is standing downstage fixing her hair. She speaks to Etta who is off.

SHERI: Have you ever noticed how some people just can't seem to hang onto their money? *(Etta appears. She stares at her.) (Flatly.)* No. I never have.

SHERI: It's like they got this hole in their life and the money just sort of leaks out.

ETTA: I don't want to talk about this . . .

SHERI: I just thought you made a lot of money.

ETTA: I did.

SHERI: So what happened to all that money?

ETTA: I spent it.

SHERI: On what?

ETTA: I don't remember.

SHERI: Think.

ETTA: Sheri . . . ?

SHERI: Clothes?

ETTA: I bought a lot of clothes . . . and a fur coat.

SHERI: In California . . . ?

ETTA: I got cold.

SHERI: Shoes?

ETTA: I could never afford to buy good shoes before . . .

SHERI: You probably had about thirty pairs of shoes . . .

ETTA: I bought a car.

SHERI: Too bad about the car . . .

ETTA: You know those finance companies never even tell you they're gonna snatch the car, they just come and take it.

SHERI: You musta sent money home.

ETTA: Oh, yeah . . .

SHERI: How much?

ETTA: *(Beat.)* Not that much.

SHERI: I think if you don't like the way you make money that you blow it trying to make yourself feel better.

ETTA: Ben screwed me over.

SHERI: You let it happen.

ETTA: Bullshit, Sheri.

SHERI: Etta, life has ways of teaching us what we need to know, intuition is one and disaster is another. Ladies' choice, Etta.

ETTA: Look at this guy coming in. *(Dwight enters.)*

SHERI: Psycho.

ETTA: His name is Dwight.

SHERI: Dwight, like Norman, strictly from the Bates Motel.

ETTA: He seems like he's got a lot of money.

SHERI: He's a good-looking white guy. He could date anybody. I mean, except for his eyes he's handsome.

ETTA: He has a funny arm.

SHERI: Look at his shoes, patent-leather evening pumps, two hundred and sixty dollars. He's wearing an eight hundred dollar suit. You have to ask yourself, what's this guy doing paying you twenty-five cents a minute to dance.

ETTA: He talks.

SHERI: To talk then.

ETTA: He seems like he's lonely.

SHERI: They're always lonely because all their friends are dead. Oh here comes my dreamboat. He's looking for me. He's waving . . . *(She waves.)* 'Ola Carlos! *(Quietly.)* You fat pig. *(To Etta.)* See you later. *(Sheri moves off, Dwight steps up to Etta.)*

DWIGHT: Hello there, Lana.

ETTA: Hi, Dwight.

DWIGHT: Business is slow tonight.

ETTA: Yeah.

DWIGHT: You're looking especially pretty this evening.

ETTA: This is the same dress I always wear.

DWIGHT: *(Beat. He sighs.)* I would like it if you wouldn't use that tone of voice when you accept a compliment. As if I was insulting your intelligence.

ETTA: Well?

DWIGHT: If I think you look nice, I say so. That's all.

ETTA: You want to dance?

DWIGHT: Not really.

ETTA: I have to take your tickets even if we just talk.

DWIGHT: I came over to ask you if you'd like to go out with me. Since it's a slow night, maybe they'll let you off. We could go someplace.

ETTA: Like where?

DWIGHT: Ladies' choice.

ETTA: The health department closed the coffee shop, if that's what you're talking about.

DWIGHT: No. I was thinking we could have dinner someplace, a nice place, then maybe . . .

ETTA: We could stop off at your house.

DWIGHT: My mother's away for a few days. I'd like to show you our collection of porcelain figurines. There's one that looks just like you.

ETTA: *(Beat. She looks away.)* I don't think so.

DWIGHT: Why not? *(James appears upstage. He lights a cigarette before making his way over.)*

ETTA: I don't date the customers.

DWIGHT: I thought by now we were friends.

ETTA: The manager is watching us, you'll have to give me some tickets.

JAMES: *(To Etta.)* Hi ugly.

ETTA: What are you doin' here, James.

JAMES: Spencer's been lookin' for you.

ETTA: So what?

JAMES: So he wants to see you.

ETTA: What for?

JAMES: How should I know. *(To Dwight.)* What are you lookin' at?

DWIGHT: Nothing.

JAMES: What are you tryin' to date my sister here?

DWIGHT: We were talking about having some dinner, yes.

JAMES: Oh, some dinner? I see, dinner. Are you eating these days Etta?

ETTA: Get lost.

JAMES: *(To Dwight.)* I think she wants you to get lost.

ETTA: Not him . . .

JAMES: This is a strange place to find a girlfriend, pal, you plug one of these and your dick falls off . . .

ETTA: I'm calling the manager.

JAMES: *(To Dwight, grimacing.)* What's wrong with your arm?!

ETTA: You're an asshole . . .

DWIGHT: I had a muscle disease as a child.

JAMES: So now you're gimpified, is that right?

ETTA: Get the fuck out of here!

JAMES: Must have been something I said, shit, I'm such a jerk. *(Sheri enters as James starts to leave.)*

JAMES: Hi Sheri . . . how you doin'? What time you off?

SHERI: Two.

JAMES: Maybe I'll let you read my cards?

SHERI: I can't wait.

JAMES: We'll see you tomorrow, Etta. *(He exits. Sheri exits in the opposite direction.)*

ETTA: *(Thinking, she shakes her head.)* Great!

Dwight takes her arm, squeezes; she pulls away, he holds on. They freeze.

DWIGHT: What about if I pay you?

BLACKOUT.

SCENE ELEVEN

The lights come up on Spencer as he watches James light a cigarette.

SPENCER: *(Beat.)* GONE! Just like that, just like that! Shit.

JAMES: If you're so sensitive, maybe you should get out of the business.

SPENCER: You make me sick. You know that? You sicken me! *(A knock on the door. Both men watch the door. The knock comes again.)* Try and keep your mouth shut.

JAMES: Come in.

Spencer glares at James. Etta enters. A bandage covers her left eye, her right cheek is bruised, her arm is in a sling.

SPENCER: Good to see you Etta. *(Beat.)* You're looking well.

ETTA: I feel good.

SPENCER: Did you fall down a manhole?

JAMES: She's been bangin' freaks two at a time and she's getting what she deserves, isn't that right?

SPENCER: Shut up.

ETTA: Spencer. If the question is Ben, I have no idea where he is. He left me in Cancun with five hundred pesos and I haven't seen him since.

SPENCER: Ben is too slimy not to leave a trail, Etta. Ben is handled. *(James begins to laugh.)*

SPENCER: James doesn't know why he's laughing. Do you?

JAMES: I think something's funny.

SPENCER: And he can't shut up, can you?

JAMES: Why should I?

SPENCER: *(Beat. He turns back to Etta.)* What are you doing for work these days, Etta?

ETTA: I work at a dance place.

SPENCER: Like Arthur Murray?

James laughs; Etta laughs a beat later.

ETTA: Like taxi dancers.

JAMES: Like hookers dancing with scumballs . . .

ETTA: James is a regular.

JAMES: Eat shit.

SPENCER: So you're making a living wage?

ETTA: I do alright. I work part time and I go to school. *(James laughs.)* I'm taking a class in court reporting. . . . *(James laughs harder.)* *(To James.)* Screw you!

SPENCER: Etta, I have a little business proposition for you. Do you know what a talent scout is?

ETTA: Yes.

SPENCER: It's self-evident.

ETTA: It's somebody that scouts talent.

JAMES: Brilliant.

SPENCER: You come into contact with a lot of young women. They are needy . . . they need things . . . money, a job, a place, but mostly they need money.

ETTA: Oh brother . . .

SPENCER: Maybe movies wouldn't be an option but you present it in such a way as to persuade . . .

ETTA: For Ben's business?

JAMES: No, for MGM.

SPENCER: It's not Ben's business anymore. It's mine and I'm asking you to come in as talent coordinator.

ETTA: What's that?

JAMES: It's a hawk, idiot head.

SPENCER: You've made movies.

ETTA: That's right.

SPENCER: I want to make better movies.

ETTA: You want a class movie with class action.

SPENCER: I knew she was smart.

JAMES: Shit.

ETTA: Good-looking women with no problems, no junkies, no freaks, and they want to make a pornographic movie that has the potential of coming back at them years from now when they want to marry a minister or run for Supreme Court.

SPENCER: This is business, Etta.

ETTA: I don't want to hustle anybody.

SPENCER: You don't have to, the dollar sign is the bottom line. Better pay, better working conditions equal better product, it's a whole different operation.

JAMES: You are making a big mistake here, Spencer.

SPENCER: Shut up!

JAMES: *(To Etta.)* Stupid.

ETTA: Why don't you go home and eat a cockroach.

JAMES: I don't do that anymore!

SPENCER: James had this job, isn't that right James? *(James looks away.)* But James cannot keep track of the women. They vanish, sometimes the day of shooting, sometimes in the middle of a film, or one or two movies later. You never know what becomes of them, they just disappear!

JAMES: Screw you.

SPENCER: Screw you! *(James moves away.)* So. I am prepared to pay you three a week and fifty for every warm body you scare up. There's the deal.

ETTA: Is that what James was making?

JAMES: No way, bitch . . . *(To Spencer.)* Can you feature this?

ETTA: You want me to do a better job than James and you want to pay me less.

SPENCER: I'll pay you four a week and a hundred for every girl that completes an assignment.

JAMES: You're pissing me off, Spencer.

SPENCER: Why don't you get lost for a while.

James and Spencer exchange looks; James looks at Etta.

JAMES: Yeah, okay. *(Laughing, he exits.)*

SPENCER: James is walking out to his car right now imagining that you and I are having it off. *(Sighs.)* James is a victim of this business. When he's not dreaming of latex mini skirts he's sitting in a quarter booth. Images of comfort and security. *(Spencer pulls three hundred dollars from his wallet.)* One week's salary.

She starts to take the money, stops, moves away.

ETTA: *(Beat.)* I don't think so, Spencer. *(She gathers her things to leave.)*

SPENCER: It's really not about thinking Etta, it's about instinct, survival of the fittest, adaptation to environmental demands. Many women don't like business, they find it dull, or too competitive, or their priorities shift and they lose interest, but I don't think you're that kind of woman.

ETTA: What kind?

SPENCER: You ever been married?

ETTA: Once. *(Beat.)* Look Spencer, the deal is I'm gonna take acting classes and get my SAG card. I mean that's why I came out here and with court reporting, I mean it pays real well and you can work around auditions so . . .

SPENCER: You know, Etta, not everyone is Grace Kelly.

ETTA: Nobody is, Spencer, she's dead.

SPENCER: What I'm trying to tell you is, you're no actress. I think we both know that.

ETTA: Well, I'm better than I was.

SPENCER: But you're not good enough to overcome having done skin flicks.

ETTA: Overcome.

SPENCER: Yes.

ETTA: *(Beat.)* Ben said a lot of stars did movies to finance their careers.

SPENCER: He lied.

ETTA: Ben said that since they all did it, it was acceptable, and that nobody thought anything about it.

SPENCER: What world do you live in, Etta? What do you think legitimate actors and actresses risk their credibility to make porno, for what? For money? You meet actors waiting tables, tending bar, they could make better money here, why don't they?

ETTA: *(Beat.)* 'Cause it ruins your chances?

SPENCER: 'Cause people are hypocrites, Etta. If you and another actress are up for the part of the Virgin Mary and both of you are equally awful, who do you think they're going to give it to? You? With your spread shots from here to Timbuktu. It's a high-profile industry, somebody is bound to recognize you. Especially with your circulation. You're a star.

ETTA: *(Pause.)* It's my only dream, Spencer.

SPENCER: Dreams are a lot like movies, they function to keep you from seeing how shitty life is. But once you know that, you're free of those stupid expectations that drive people crazy.

ETTA: I feel like somebody slipped the bones out of my body. *(Pause.)* I don't know what I'm suppose to want if I don't want that, I mean, if I can't have that, what am I suppose to want?

SPENCER: Money is a good place to start, you have a little feeling for it, otherwise you would never have made your first reel, am I wrong?

ETTA: No.

SPENCER: Think about buying a fur coat and a closet to put it in . . . think about a car the color of your eyes built in the country your ancestors came from. Think about getting into that car and driving home to visit those people who checked their ambition years ago. You're still gonna be in the movies, Etta.

ETTA: My friend Sherman says that the way to get what you want is to keep a picture of it in your heart. That any image you can hold on to, you can make it happen in your life.

SPENCER: *(Beat.)* You go to the movies?

ETTA: I haven't been going much lately.

SPENCER: When you imagine yourself up there on the wide screen, with the big stars, what do you see?

ETTA: When?

SPENCER: In your head, in your heart, in your imagination, think. People are sitting in the dark, eating popcorn, watching you, what do they see?

Etta takes a long beat to see what she actually thinks.

ETTA: Lana. They see Lana. Her body makeup streaked with sweat 'cause she's running a temperature from an infection she can't seem to get rid of. She's smiling at a man she hates, and giving herself to him, 'cause it's what he wants. It's what everybody in the audience wants.

SPENCER: And what does she want?

ETTA: *(Beat.)* Bigger tits.

SPENCER: And what do you want?

Pause. She looks at him, holds out her hand.

ETTA: A raise.

BEAT. BLACKOUT.

SCENE TWELVE

Music, lights up, dance hall. Sheri is standing downstage looking out. James enters, he lights a cigarette before crossing to where she is.

SHERI: Do you have to smoke so much? Christ . . . !

JAMES: How you doin' Sheri? *(She turns away.)* What? Are you mad about the other night? I had to work.

SHERI: Yeah . . .

JAMES: So it's all the same, right? We both made money, except you came here.

SHERI: I came here, what's that suppose to mean?

JAMES: Just that you came here and picked up a few bucks, right?

SHERI: Yeah.

JAMES: I bet you can barely get high on what you make here.

SHERI: I'm not getting high like I used to. I'm changed.

JAMES: All I'm saying is you could do better.

SHERI: *(Beat.)* So, what are you doin' later on?

JAMES: I have some people I gotta see.

SHERI: Business again?

JAMES: For people like us, business is ninety percent of our lives.

SHERI: You and I are not the same kind of people, James.

JAMES: Well anyway, my business involves one other person.

SHERI: I'm not loaning you any money.

JAMES: Sheri, you are so paranoid.

SHERI: I am not a savings and loan.

JAMES: And here it is, I used to get you high . . .

SHERI: Please . . . that shit you SOLD me?

JAMES: I just thought you might want to make some easy money, that's all.

SHERI: Nothing you do is easy James, that's you.

JAMES: That's me, what's that suppose to mean?

SHERI: How much.

JAMES: Five big ones.

SHERI: What's a big one to you James, a buck?

JAMES: A hundred is a big one, and five big ones is five hundred dollars.

SHERI: Who do I have to kill?

JAMES: God, you know, you really have a good sense of humor?

SHERI: Eat me.

JAMES: Seriously, like . . . Joan Rivers.

SHERI: What's the deal.

JAMES: It's a movie.

SHERI: Why are they paying so much?

JAMES: Part of it's travel money.

SHERI: Where do I have to go, Mars?

JAMES: *(Laughs.)* Uranus.

SHERI: Where do I have to go?!

JAMES: Mexico.

SHERI: Mexico? *(Uncertain.)* No, *(Firm.)* no, forget it.

JAMES: Forget five hundred dollars?

SHERI: Don't you think I know what kind of movie they make in Mexico?

JAMES: What kind?

SHERI: You know.

JAMES: No, I'm stupid, you're smart. You tell me.

SHERI: *(Beat.)* You have to do it with a donkey.

JAMES: *(Bursts out laughing.)* Donkey?! *(Laughs again.)* I'm so sure! *(Calms.)* You don't have to do it with a donkey. No.

SHERI: So then what do I have to do.

JAMES: Although, it's not a bad idea.

SHERI: James . . . !

JAMES: Lay there and cooperate.

SHERI: Five hundred dollars.

JAMES: And I can get you high.

SHERI: Straight sex.

JAMES: And I'm driving your ass down there, we have a party in the car, I got some smack, some blow, I got a bottle of Chivas and some whites if we need them.

SHERI: Five hundred dollars.

JAMES: You wear some rubber is all.

SHERI: That's not straight sex!

JAMES: *(Surprised.)* It's not?

SHERI: No!

JAMES: *(Beat.)* Okay, screw it, I'll catch you later.

SHERI: Hey! *(Beat.)* Are you going to be there or what?

JAMES: Yes I am.

SHERI: 'Cause like I wouldn't mind a trip to Mexico but like I don't want to get stranded, you know?

JAMES: *(Smiles.)* What do you think, I'm gonna leave your ass in Mexico, I'm so sure.

They freeze.

BLACKOUT.

SCENE THIRTEEN

Lights up, Kitty and Etta are seated in the office. Etta is well-dressed, upscale, in a business suit.

ETTA: So tell me Kitty, how's Moe?

KITTY: Moe's good, yeah . . . he's real good. He's been clean like what, three weeks?

ETTA: Three weeks.

KITTY: Pretty clean. Chipping on the weekends is all. Recreational. *(Beat.)* So what do you think, Etta?

ETTA: Let me see.

Kitty stands. She is pregnant.

KITTY: I wouldn't want anything to happen to the baby.

ETTA: It's not a baby yet.

KITTY: Moe wanted me to get rid of it.

ETTA: Moe is not as stupid as he looks.

KITTY: I'm two months.

ETTA: You look four.

KITTY: I can't remember.

ETTA: Okay Kitty, look. I have a good doctor in Century City, a thousand dollars.

KITTY: A thousand dollars.

ETTA: You could make that in two days, plus five hundred extra 'cause you're pregnant.

KITTY: Five hundred extra.

ETTA: And you still have time to get rid of your problem.

KITTY: It's not a problem.

ETTA: It's going to be.

KITTY: You don't like kids.

ETTA: Don't pretend to know anything. What are you, twelve years old? You know something, you don't know shit.

KITTY: I know you don't like kids.

ETTA: I have a kid. She lives with people she calls Mom and Dad and when she gets sick, she goes to a doctor and when she needs discipline, she will understand why she's being punished. The element of random violence will not be present in her life.

KITTY: I want to keep my baby.

ETTA: And teach it what? How to be you, how to be Moe?

KITTY: What's wrong with Moe?

ETTA: Kitty, I'm sure you've noticed how a baby can scream? Did you know they're suppose to be allowed to do that? It's good for them? Because they're pissed off. They're pissed off about being in the world, and so they scream.

KITTY: *(Pause.)* One time, I saw Moe rip a faucet out of a wall when he couldn't get it to stop dripping. He hates noise. *(Kitty gets a cigarette out of her bag, Etta lights it for her.)*

ETTA: Sheri used to work for Moe.

KITTY: Sheri did?

ETTA: She popped, he had her back on the street in two weeks.

KITTY: Moe said I didn't have to work anymore.

ETTA: That's what he told Sheri.

KITTY: I didn't know Sheri had a kid.

ETTA: She doesn't. He's a memory.

KITTY: *(Beat.)* I don't believe you.

ETTA: *(Holds the phone out.)* Call Sheri, ask her. *(James enters. He's nervous, smoking. He sits down, stares away from the women.)*

KITTY: No.

ETTA: It's a simple solution to a complex problem, Kitty, think about it and let me know today.

KITTY: I'm gonna see Moe and see what he says. 'Cause like, he seems happy about the baby and everything and I could see a baby making a big difference in our lives, a good difference, you know? We'd have a reason to get straight? For the sake of the baby? I'll call you, Etta, okay? I'll call you. *(To James.)* Bye, Bug.

JAMES: Bitch. *(Kitty exits, James lights a cigarette from one in the ashtray. Etta makes a phone call.)* Isn't it fucked how sometimes you want things to work out a certain way but they never do, they just keep . . . you know, screwing up and I wonder, like, do you think that's genetic?

ETTA: Shut up.

JAMES: Like with me and Dixie. We were gonna get married and like have a house, this and that.

ETTA: But you had to kill your parents.

JAMES: Just my mother. *(Beat.)* She made me kill her.

ETTA: *(She hangs up.)* Have you seen Sheri?

JAMES: WHAT DO I LOOK LIKE, PUBLIC INFORMATION, HOW SHOULD I KNOW WHERE SHE IS??

ETTA: Stop yelling.

JAMES: My parole officer says that every time a person commits a crime it's because they're reaching for a better life. What do you think? Do you think that's evolution expressing itself?

ETTA: Why don't you take a bath once in awhile?

JAMES: You got any money, Etta?

ETTA: This is a loan . . . do you know what a loan is? *(She digs in her purse, hands him twenty.)*

JAMES: What am I suppose to do with twenty dollars? I can't even get laid for twenty dollars. I mean I could, not that I ever pay for it . . . I mean, I like to pay for it 'cause . . . you know . . . you can do what you want . . . but not for twenty dollars Etta, I need at least fifty.

ETTA: I'm not giving you fifty dollars to get laid.

James has two cigarettes going; he lights a third cigarette.

JAMES: How about you and me go someplace for a drink?

ETTA: No.

JAMES: You think you're too good to go out with me?

ETTA: Yes.

JAMES: Don't you think I know that? I'm offering to buy you a drink, I'd like to buy you dinner but I'm short, I mean, I'm not short, I'm average height for a man with my build, but I look that way 'cause I work out.

ETTA: What are you on?

JAMES: Speed.

ETTA: You're talking like a jerk.

JAMES: Etta, I take it everyday, it helps me think.

She pulls more money from her purse and hands it to him.

ETTA: Here. Now get lost.

He looks at it. Beat.

JAMES: I don't want to go home right now. I don't really feel like being by myself and I don't feel like being with strangers and you and Spencer are the only friends I have. You don't have to loan me any money, here . . . *(He lays the money on the desk; he takes a chair, straddles it.)* You don't even have to go out in public with me, I'll just sit here awhile, I won't talk. If I could just stay here for awhile, I think I could be okay, if I could just get my breath, and cool out I won't even talk and you can just do your work. Okay? Okay? *(Pause. Etta watches him, James lays his arms across the back of the chair and puts his head on his arms. Freeze.)*

Etta moves around her desk. Spencer enters, they watch him.

SCENE FOURTEEN

JAMES: *(Explodes.)* YOU ARE NOT MY BOSS!!

ETTA: I've been waiting a long time for this talk, James.

JAMES: Sheri could have been gone for months without a soul in the world being any the wiser except for YOU now have to be the big EYE.

ETTA: I love this, it's my fault, right?

JAMES: Yes! Because women don't belong in business.

ETTA: Did you know she was expected for dinner?

JAMES: How would I?

ETTA: Sunday night?

JAMES: Oh Christ, Spencer . . . !

ETTA: Her mother called me.

JAMES: So what?!

ETTA: She said Sheri left town with you.

JAMES: She's lying.

ETTA: She also said she called the police and they might be showing up pretty soon . . .

SPENCER: What happened, James?

JAMES: How should I know . . . ?

SPENCER: James?!

JAMES: I DON'T KNOW!

ETTA: *(Kinder.)* You know something, James.

JAMES: *(Beat.)* I heard . . . don't ask me where, that somebody thinks she might have gone to Mexico to do a movie.

ETTA: Mexico.

SPENCER: Oh shit.

ETTA: What in the hell did you take her down there for?!

JAMES: I don't know!

ETTA: *(Rage.)* GOD DAMN YOU, I KNEW HER.

JAMES: *(Cowed.)* So you knew her? Big deal. Know somebody, it makes a difference.

ETTA: She was my friend!

JAMES: She was my friend too . . . I don't know what happened, she was supposed to meet me and I waited and waited and finally I just said . . . fuck it. What am I suppose to do Spencer *(giggles)*, hang around, waiting for a . . . a . . . woman?

SPENCER: Where did you take her?

JAMES: Just a house.

SPENCER: JAMES!

JAMES: I took her to Ben.

SPENCER: Ben.

ETTA: I didn't know he was doing business.

JAMES: I dropped her off, she wanted to go. She asked me for a ride, that's all.

SPENCER: And then what?

JAMES: I went back to pick her up. Nobody was there, the house was empty. Nothing.

ETTA: Did you call Ben . . .

JAMES: I don't know where he is.

ETTA: Bullshit!

JAMES: I don't know, he calls me, that's all . . . I never know where he is.

SPENCER: You haven't talked to him since?

JAMES: *(Beat.)* Once.

SPENCER: And what did he say?!

JAMES: He says she disappeared.

ETTA: You mean like vanished?

JAMES: Like that's all he said!!

ETTA: He's lying!

SPENCER: I think you should vanish as well.

JAMES: Absolutely . . .

SPENCER: *(He hands him some money.)* Now.

ETTA: We're just gonna let him go?

JAMES: I can't split without my stash.

SPENCER: If you are determined to risk it, fine.

JAMES: Risk what?

ETTA: Spencer!

SPENCER: If you want to stay outside, I assume you do.

JAMES: You would give me up.

SPENCER: In a nanosecond.

ETTA: Shit.

SPENCER: *(To James.)* What are you waiting for?

JAMES: *(Astonished.)* This is my home, all my friends are here. How long do I have to stay gone?

SPENCER: Forever.

JAMES: Is that necessary?

SPENCER: Get out of here you scum-sucking leach before I put the police on you myself.

JAMES: *(Beat, to Etta.)* I'll get you for this. *(James exits.)*

SPENCER: *(Pause.)* Etta.

ETTA: Don't say it.

SPENCER: Sheri was a big girl, she knew what she was doing.

ETTA: Spencer . . . ?

SPENCER: I didn't kill her. *(She stares at him a beat.)* What do you want to do, get mad?

ETTA: I want to get even.

SPENCER: Oh shit Etta, grow up.

He moves off. Etta looks out, she remains lit while the lights fade around her. She moves downstage. A light comes up on Dolly.

SCENE FIFTEEN

Dolly is wearing a loose wrapper. She holds a drink in one hand and a fan in the other. She's drunk.

ETTA: You hear about Sheri?

DOLLY: Oh Christ, is that what you came to talk about?

ETTA: I want to know where Ben is, Dolly.

DOLLY: Like, what? I'm supposed to help you? Screw off, Etta.

ETTA: What's the matter, Dolly, you getting old?

DOLLY: Maybe I think about the past a lot, things that happened, things that didn't work out. But I hold a grudge for you. Maybe that's not right, but I do.

ETTA: About Ben.

DOLLY: Ben and me had a good thing going.

ETTA: Ben was chewing you up and spitting you out a piece at a time.

DOLLY: Well . . . it was good in the beginning.

ETTA: Everything is good in the beginning. It's only when they start to change, when repulsive personal habits start to show up, that you have to wonder what you were thinking in the first place.

DOLLY: Yeah, we all change, but I don't like the way you've changed, so get out.

ETTA: They ever find your sister, Dolly?

DOLLY: Shut up . . .

ETTA: She was dating James for awhile, and then all of a sudden she was nowhere to be found.

DOLLY: *(Beat.)* Ben says she's in Texas . . . but . . . I don't think she's anywhere, you know . . . I just have that feeling. I can always tell when he's lying, that son of a bitch. You know, in my business, you would have thought I'd meet a lot of men and that one of them would have meant something to me . . . *(Beat.)* I get lonely. I brood. It's probably because of this that Ben begins to look good. I went down to see him a few months ago. To see, you know, if there was anything there. He wanted it too. *(Beat.)* I couldn't recognize him. I'm Mexican and in Mexico, I'm very psychic. When he met me at the airport and kissed me hello, I got this taste of dirt in my mouth. He hugged me, I heard my bones crack and turn to dust and I saw us become this cloud of white powder blowing down the runway. I took a plane out of there so fast. He's in Mexico City, Etta, he has a house near Chapultepec Park, he does business out of the hotel there. But don't go yourself. Send a man. I know somebody. I'll give you his name.

LIGHTS FADE.

SCENE SIXTEEN

Lights come up on Max. He sits downstage at a small table. Alec sits upstage on a barstool.

Etta moves to Max. Bar sounds come up. She takes the check from in front of him and puts it on her side of the table, sits down.

MAX: Have you ever been to a funeral for a baby?

ETTA: I never have, no.

MAX: The box is so small. You wouldn't believe it. My sister's baby died. It tweaked her. She couldn't stop talking about it. What she'd be doing if she were alive . . . You know, learning to crawl, teething . . . all that.

ETTA: Interesting.

MAX: What about you, you want to have kids?

ETTA: I don't think about it. So maybe I don't.

MAX: You married?

ETTA: I didn't come to talk about myself.

MAX: You're not married. I know all about you, you're not even engaged.

ETTA: Nobody engages me.

MAX: *(Laughs.)* God, I love a woman who can make me laugh. You have no idea how many broads can't crack a joke.

ETTA: It's passive humor. I made a joke off of what you said, it's not like I'm funny, it's more like I'm quick.

MAX: It was a compliment.

ETTA: It was bullshit.

MAX: Have it your way.

ETTA: Twenty is your price.

MAX: Correct.

ETTA: That's high.

MAX: It's mid-range. Plus I have a partner. Safety in numbers, that's why policemen have partners, even if it's a dog. You like dogs?

ETTA: Not really.

MAX: That's too bad 'cause I knew a place in Hong Kong serves a very nice dog . . . ever been to Hong Kong?

ETTA: No.

MAX: You want to go?

ETTA: I hate to fly.

MAX: We could take a boat.

ETTA: Look, I'm sure you're a very nice person but . . .

MAX: Wait a minute. Are you turning me down?

ETTA: Jesus . . . look . . . okay . . . Forget it . . . *(She stands.)*

MAX: No no no no wait . . . sit down. *(He takes her hand, pulls her down.)* Your hands are freezing . . . *(He rubs her hands in his.)* You want me to take this job?

ETTA: If you think you can do it.

MAX: If I think . . . I'm taking it, okay?

ETTA: Fine.

MAX: Your hands aren't getting any warmer.

ETTA: I'll check my pulse . . .

MAX: You should try a massage . . .

ETTA: I have to go . . .

MAX: What do you . . . wait . . . what do you want, dating?

ETTA: Look Max, I'm not interested.

MAX: *(He lets go.)* What are you, queer?

ETTA: Yeah, I'm queer Max, okay?

MAX: No, you're not queer . . . but I love a woman who lies . . . they could get their stupid face slapped off lying to me but they don't care. Okay . . . go. You want to go, go. I happen to know that I am a very attractive and interesting person . . . I can talk to anybody.

ETTA: *(Beat.)* You know my business?

MAX: Frankly, it makes me uncomfortable. You're providing a public service for what I term nuisance individuals, lonely men who can't stop thinking about their cocks and also I'm a Catholic and I believe it undermines the stability of the family, I mean, these men are searching for some lost part of themselves, i.e. the erotic, the animal, the beast, the devil, instead of spending the time with their wives and making sure their children are home instead of ripping off my fucking radio out of my brand new Porsche and ruining the console it'll probably cost me two, three thousand dollars to replace it . . .

ETTA: I don't date people outside my business because they expect something that's not there.

MAX: Like what is it?

ETTA: A fantasy.

MAX: About sex?

ETTA: About people.

MAX: Maybe it was never there.

ETTA: It was. That's how I know it's gone.

MAX: Maybe that's why you got in the business.

ETTA: Max, when I look at you . . . I don't see a human being anymore. I see meat.

MAX: That's what I see when I look at everybody. I mean, if you think about it, that's good for me. Not that I had anything to do with it. I mean . . . you know, I don't have a full set of human emotions. Poor parenting during the years between two and four? I'm not a psycho, like my partner, he really likes the work, but not me, I'm just sociopathic. I can still have a good time doing business, but it's an avocation rather than a calling, you see the difference?

ETTA: I hate sex.

MAX: Me too, it's dirty.

ETTA: I don't want to have sex with you is what I'm saying.

MAX: I don't blame you, I have a disease.

ETTA: Okay Max. You want to fall in love with me, do it, you probably deserve it.

MAX: Who said anything about love?

ETTA: I'll be in touch. *(She moves down right and stands staring out. A moment later Alec enters, he sits down, finishes Max's drink.)*

MAX: *(Chuckles.)* These bitches, they think they're so tough.

ALEC: Is it on or is it off?

MAX: People crave love Alec . . . everywhere you look, hunger, yearning, people are starving for love.

ALEC: Is it on or is it off?

MAX: And yet when it's presented to them, boom, straight forward they duck, quack quack, they wag their head, they say . . . why me? Suspicious. Why is that?

ALEC: How would I know?

MAX: You ever been in love?

ALEC: Why should I?

MAX: Never mind . . . Waiter?

They freeze.

BLACKOUT.

SCENE SEVENTEEN

Lights flicker across Etta. Ben enters a moment later. They are watching a movie. Etta moves away, the movie ends. Lights up. Ben is a weird shade of green and is deadly calm.

BEN: It is possible, but not probable. Because it's a particular type of commodity. The price, exorbitant. And you get what you pay for. People, clients, say they can tell the difference. You can't fake it, that moment the spirit departs the flesh, you could see for yourself, how intimate. It makes straight sex look like a kiss on the cheek.

ETTA: Jesus.

BEN: *(Sweetly.)* Don't use that tone of voice, I mean it.

ETTA: I don't like to think you're this kind of human being.

BEN: It's a market Etta. You can't begrudge the market. You can't wage war on entrepreneurs, can you? You live by the sword and you die by the same sword Etta. Wise up. *(He hands her a drink.)* You look green.

ETTA: I feel sick.

BEN: Wait till you get used to the water.

ETTA: I don't think that's it, water.

BEN: I myself hate philosophy, but if I were you, I'd either put up or shut up.

ETTA: I don't like myself.

BEN: I have felt that way for years, believe me, you will in time adjust.

ETTA: You did.

BEN: Yes.

ETTA: And you're happy.

BEN: *(Thoughtfully.)* Happiness is not destiny. You must be happy, no. Even the Founding Fathers wrote, "The pursuit of happiness." 'Cause they knew it was a crock. *(Smiles.)* They were not stupid like most people.

ETTA: If it weren't for you, I wouldn't be in this business.

BEN: Oh I don't know. All I did was exploit a situation to the mutual advantage of us both.

ETTA: You lied.

BEN: Lying is a tricky accusation, Etta. You can say I lied. I can say you believed the lie. Because deep down inside you didn't think you could make it. You see what I'm saying, Etta? It wasn't me that sold you out, it was you.

ETTA: No. It was you.

BEN: Think about it, Etta.

ETTA: No.

BEN: *(Smiles.)* See, it doesn't pay to become circumspect.

ETTA: *(Beat.)* I think you used a friend of mine in a movie.

BEN: We've been using mainly Brazilian prostitutes we buy in bulk.

ETTA: James brought her in. She had a tattoo of a snake on her back.

BEN: A snake. With its shedding skin . . .

ETTA: Her name was Sheri . . .

BEN: I know Sheri.

ETTA: What happened to her?

BEN: We were making a movie. When what is visible, becomes invisible. Her hair, skin, her eyes go transparent and she vanishes. Freaked my fucking film crew out of their gourds. I kept waiting for her come back. But she never did. And then I noticed this smell, like gardenias, overpowering . . . it seemed to hang in the air for hours. *(He takes the flower from his lapel.)*

ETTA: Gardenias, Ben?

BEN: Yes.

ETTA: You like gardenias.

BEN: They're my favorite flower.

Beat. She lights a cigarette.

ETTA: I'll try and remember. The next time I see you I'll be sure to bring flowers. *(Beat.)* I have some vendors coming in from Seattle I want you to meet.
BEN: What are they vending?
ETTA: Runaways.
BEN: I have all I can use.
ETTA: We can talk.
BEN: I love to talk.
ETTA: They're very well-educated, one of them studied at Yale. We'll have a nice dinner. You feel like eating Ben?
BEN: Don't push me, Etta.
ETTA: Good. I'll see you at eight o'clock then.
BEN: Should I dress up or what?
ETTA: I think you should.
BEN: You do.
ETTA: Try and look your best.
BEN: *(Beat.)* All right, eight o'clock. I'll see you.

Freeze. Etta exits, Ben moves right, Max and Alec move down. Max sits, Alec stands up. Ben picks up a telephone and listens.

SCENE EIGHTEEN

MAX: First they had to tear the fence out to get the bulldozer in to dig the hole, right? The fucking idiots dug the hole so close to the property line they couldn't drive the dozer out again, can you believe the intelligence? So these guys put boards, like plywood, over the hole? Then they try and drive it out . . .
ALEC: Max, will you shut up.
MAX: They try and drive it out, right? The bulldozer weighs a million tons or something on these matchstick boards, of course it falls in the hole, and they have to get a crane, coming over my house, it's twenty stories high and arrives in the middle of the night.
ALEC: Nobody's listening to you. *(Ben hangs up, stares at the phone.)* They take this fucking bulldozer up into the air and then suddenly it drops, straight down on my neighbor's car, a fucking Bentley, right? Antique? He just finished restoring the leather? We're talking about a hundred-thousand-dollar automobile, for Chrissakes! *(Max is doubled up laughing. The two men watch him, his laughter subsides.)*
BEN: I don't know where she could be.
ALEC: Is she always late?
BEN: No.
ALEC: I am starving.
BEN: Can I offer you a drink?

ALEC: I'm not drinking.

MAX: I don't trust a man who doesn't drink, do you Ben?

BEN: I don't think about it.

MAX: Ben, why don't you have a drink, you need to relax.

BEN: It's eight-thirty, she should have been here.

MAX: She didn't call . . . ?

BEN: Maybe I should check her room.

ALEC: I don't think so.

MAX: I'll check . . . oh, wait a minute.

ALEC: I wouldn't.

MAX: Yeah, absolutely. I don't think we should get involved with this . . . missing person.

BEN: You don't think I should?

ALEC: I wouldn't.

Ben watches them, Max and Alec exchange looks.

MAX: Hey, you know . . . I'm curious. Why don't you go ahead and check.

BEN: She could be sick, or something, it's better to know than not know. *(Ben crosses to the door.)* I'll be right back. *(He exits.)*

MAX: Jesus, he's ugly.

ALEC: So where is she?

MAX: She's gone home.

ALEC: Oh.

MAX: She came down to make sure. She's very fair. She's a natural blond.

ALEC: What, are you thinking of selling her?

MAX: Weren't you?

ALEC: No. She's a very nice woman, a little stiff . . . but . . .

MAX: It was a joke. Fair, blond.

ALEC: God.

MAX: So . . . you want to wait, eat first . . .

ALEC: No, we don't wait! Eat, Jesus.

Max moves around the room, he stares out downstage.

MAX: Gee, I'd love to see the museum while I'm here, you know? I've read they have this incredible archeological museum?

ALEC: I'm getting a headache.

MAX: You know the trouble with you? You can't relax, you can't talk, like normal people. Chit chat.

ALEC: Please Max.

MAX: It's civilizing to be able to make small talk, Alec.

Ben enters.

BEN: She's gone.

MAX: How do you mean?

BEN: Like she was never there. The room is open, the bed is smooth, nothing.

MAX: Amazing. Alec, did you hear what Ben just said?

BEN: It's not like her. She says yes, she says no, it means something.

MAX: So she turned, what are you gonna do, let it ruin your weekend? Shit Ben, grow up.

BEN: I'm disappointed, that's all, to have poured so much of my time and talent into one individual and to be repaid in this way . . .

MAX: I think we know.

BEN: This is weird.

ALEC: What do you say we go get something to eat?

MAX: Yeah, let's go get some grub and do some business.

ALEC: A little food, you'll feel like a new man.

MAX: We thought we'd drive out to La Casita.

BEN: That's a long way to go.

ALEC: I only eat seafood.

BEN: They have a very good turbot right here at the hotel.

ALEC: I only eat shellfish.

BEN: I'm not very hungry.

ALEC: Why don't you just come along to keep us company?

BEN: No.

MAX: I wish you would Ben, I sincerely do. I think it would do you a world of good. You don't have to eat, just come out to be social. Alec is no company at all, and I myself like to enjoy a good conversation with my meal. What do you say Ben? Why don't you come with.

BEN: Why don't you go fuck yourself.

MAX: *(To Alec.)* That's not very nice, is it?

ALEC: No, it's not. *(Ben makes a grab for the phone. Alec intercepts him.)*

BEN: I swear to God, if you touch me I'm gonna scream my fucking head off! *(Alec rips the receiver from the base of the phone.)*

MAX: Touch you, why would we touch you? What are we, queers? I mean, Alec is queer, but so what . . . He never forces himself on people, at least not ugly slobs like you, you're too old. *(Alec tosses the cord to Max.)* You have nothing to fear from Alec.

BLACKOUT.

SCENE NINETEEN

Lights up on Etta downstage. She is cleaning out her briefcase in a deserted office. Spencer stands watching her. He is very tense.

SPENCER: Sheri was a zero, she was a thing.

ETTA: So was Ben.

SPENCER: Ben?! *(Snorts.)* I KNEW Ben. We went to school . . . okay? I mean . . . his mother knew my mother, we used to piss in the same toilet for Chrissake! *(Beat.)* Where are we when women decide it's time to get even. We're talking chaos, extreme situations, danger, danger . . . danger!

ETTA: You can trust me.

SPENCER: Ben was my friend, Etta.

ETTA: I saw the films he made.

SPENCER: What are you, a critic? Nobody takes those films seriously, they're pictures.

ETTA: They're people.

SPENCER: They're self-hating greedbags who'll do anything for money.

ETTA: Like me.

SPENCER: Did I say you?

ETTA: You meant me . . .

SPENCER: I meant other women . . .

ETTA: I am other women.

SPENCER: It's in your heads, if it weren't we'd be out of business.

ETTA: I'm out.

SPENCER: Just like that?

ETTA: Exactly.

SPENCER: You killed Ben!

ETTA: What do you want me to say? I'm sorry? I'd like to feel sorry. I'd like to feel something. Relief. Revenge. I don't feel it. Except for this taste of dirt in my mouth, I could be dead. I'm not sorry, Spencer.

A loud knock, Max enters.

MAX: I read all the magazines. *(He moves to sit down.)* Hi Spencer.

SPENCER: Get him out of here.

ETTA: Wait outside.

MAX: What's so top secret?

ETTA: It's business.

He nuzzles her.

MAX: We've got a train to catch.

ETTA: Wait outside.

MAX: *(Stands, moves off, looks back at Spencer.)* You ever been to Miami, Spencer? They got a hell of an ocean park down there. Dolphins? They're more than a fish. *(Max exits.)*

SPENCER: Don't you ever get sick of hanging out with scum?

ETTA: There's nothing wrong with Max that a lobotomy can't cure, but you on the other hand will have to wait for evolution.

SPENCER: I suppose if it's funny it's not a problem.

ETTA: It's not funny and I wasn't joking.

SPENCER: *(Beat.)* Are you threatening me?

ETTA: I don't know, am I?

SPENCER: Evolution, you think I don't know what that means? I know what that means Etta. Dodo birds. Bald eagles. Endangered species . . . extinction.

ETTA: Fly home, Spencer, your nest is on fire.

SPENCER: I'm not the only one, Etta. *(Spencer exits. Etta stands, puts on her shoes.)*

A loud knock, Shelly enters with an enormous suitcase.

SHELLY: Are you Emma Jenkins?

ETTA: I might be.

SHELLY: A friend said I could pick up some film work here.

ETTA: A friend.

SHELLY: She thought if I could do one or maybe two movies I could pay for my headshots and get an agent and put a few bucks by . . .

ETTA: We're closed.

SHELLY: She said that you'd be very upfront and not screw me over. I went to these OTHER agencies run by these PERSIAN assholes . . . ?

ETTA: Are you deaf or what?

SHELLY: She said she's a good friend of yours. She does these seminars on out-of-the-body experience. I saw her do it in front of a bunch of people, she got real light, like you could see through her and then . . . poof. It teaches you how meaningless the body is and how it's never the thing you remember about people? *(Beat.)* Their bodies? Hello? Hey.

ETTA: You know, I took this test when I was a kid.

SHELLY: You mean like a screen test?

ETTA: It was a perception test. 'Cause I was quiet my teacher thought there was something wrong with me. They show you a bunch of pictures, scenes of daily life, and they ask you what's happening to see if you know. And I can remember this one picture, of a woman, floating in the air, and this magician was pointing at her with his wand. And they asked me what was happening. And I said the woman is dead, she's floating to heaven, but my teacher shook her head and said, no Etta, this is magic, this is a trick. But what if we were both wrong?

SHELLY: I once read a book about a man who could bend a spoon with his brain.

ETTA: You know what kind of movies we make here?

SHELLY: Look. I think it's kind of a turn-on to be naked in front of men, I mean . . . they like me and I can make them think I like them, I do it all the time. Not that it's really possible to like them 'cause they're, you know, maggots. But they don't know what I'm thinking, how I laugh at their sick needs. I'm already a great actress, you know what I mean? I bet you trip on this business.

ETTA: How old are you?

SHELLY: Eighteen, but like my stepdad "took me" when I was twelve so you know, I'm not shy. How much do you think I could make anyway?

ETTA: We'd have to see.

SHELLY: Right. *(She begins to undress.)* My boyfriend used to cry when I'd take my blouse off. He would just stare at my tits and cry. He was really screwed up. Don't get shocked 'cause I'm wearin' this leather shit underneath . . . I just came from my other job, I'm a dominant. Listen, do you ever do whip movies? 'Cause I can really use a whip. I just about killed this guy the other night. I start wailin' and forget it's just action. Sometimes I think, how it would be to just . . . well, you know? *(Laughs.)* Sometimes it won't go out of my head. It could be a public service, I bet the city would pay me. *(Beat.)* What do you think?

Etta hands her back her clothes; she dresses.

ETTA: I think you'll be able to make upwards of a thousand dollars a day. I think you could do a couple of films with no problem but any more than that and it will hurt your chances of straight film work. I think you have to be very honest with yourself. *(Etta pulls a card out of her briefcase, writes on it.)* You have to see where you fit in the marketplace. Acting is hard work, not for every-body, it's a very tough business. However, in *this* business, with your looks and your attitude, you could make a small fortune in two or three years, and with good investments, retire.

SHELLY: And do what?

ETTA: Drift. *(Etta hands the card to Shelly.)*

SHELLY: That doesn't sound like much of a life.

ETTA: Think about it, the business I mean, it's not for everybody.

SHELLY: Right.

Shelly picks up her bag, exits. Lights fade out around Etta but as she speaks she gets very bright; the suggestion of a train approaching can be heard faintly building.

ETTA: You have to like to travel. That's the trick to drifting. People you call friends become strangers, one day familiar, the next day better forgotten. You can't want anything, you can't keep anything, because everything . . . disappears.

The sound of the train roars by. Etta vanishes as the lights go black. The train whistle sounds in the distance.

THE END

Bethel Leslie, Frances Sternhagen, and Marge Redmond in *The Exact Center of the Universe* by Joan Vail Thorne, 1999. Photo © by Martha Holmes.

Author's Note

I confess, I find it difficult to write *about* plays. As a teacher whom I much admire once said, "A play isn't *about* something; it *is* something." Rather like an accident, I might add—and even witnessed differently by every member of every audience! Therefore, I'll leave the audiences of *The Exact Center of the Universe* to experience the play in any way they will, and I'll turn my attention to the creative soil out of which it grew.

That soil was unmistakably southern. My birthplace was the Deep South, and my birthright, the anecdotal tradition that every southerner lives and breathes. It's actually difficult to determine whether your average sentient southerner lives life to savor it or to tell stories about it. Storytelling was a fact of life in the South of my childhood. What's more, I had an Irish grandmother! There was no want of blarney or of fiction in my little hometown. I wonder why it is that we so often picture southern towns as small? Are they any smaller than elsewhere? Or do the stories that are told there make them appear a little closer to the campfire or the hearth or the other cozy seats of storytelling?

In addition to being living libraries of history and fiction, the women who raised me—I speak of them in the plural, because I do honestly feel that I had many mothers—were remarkable, by any measure. They were imperious but not tyrannical. They were eccentric but not neurotic. They were certain—to a fault!—and very unlikely to suffer from self-doubt. They loved fiercely—especially their children. They strove for the good life—and they shared what they found. They were not ashamed of their faith—in faith. And yes, if truth be told, they were proud—but with a poignant irony, they knew *and* kept their place. In short, they were *unliberated* women, who were *liberating* to those they loved and cared for. Theirs was a silent power, just off-center of the exact center of the universe. My play is an homage to those women. If any of them has harmed you, you may still laugh. If any has enriched your life, you will remember them with me—as powerful, funny, and just a little bit sad.

To have seen such characters come alive for the first time in the hands of master actors was a privilege for which any playwright would be grateful. Frances Sternhagen, Bethel Leslie, and Marge Redmond brought their collective lifetimes of acting experience to bear on these unusual beings, and found the perfect balance between their arrogance and their innocence, their outrageousness and their wit. The younger actors who were pitted against them were obliged to "rise" to the "occasion." The stage was always peopled with proud creatures who *were* just a little bit off-center of the exact center of the universe.

—Joan Vail Thorne

The Exact Center of the Universe received its world premiere at the Women's Project & Productions (Julia Miles, Artistic Director; Patricia Taylor, Managing Director) in New York City on April 7, 1999. It was directed by John Tillinger; the set design was by Michael Brown; the lighting design was by Philip Widmer; the sound design was by Laura Grace Brown; the costume design was by Carrie Robbins; the production manager was Pamela J. Traynor; and the production stage manager was Christine Catti. The cast was as follows:

VADA LOVE POWELL	Frances Sternhagen
APPLETON POWELL, JR./	
MR. POWELL	Reed Birney
MARY LOU/MARY ANN	Tracy Thorne
ENID	Bethel Leslie
MARYBELL	Marge Redmond

The Exact Center of the Universe was produced by Elsa Daspin Haft, Martin Markinson, Judith Resnick, Sheilah Goldman, Jerome Rosenfeld, and Allen M. Shore at the Century Center for the Performing Arts in New York City on September 8, 1999. It was directed by John Tillinger; the set design was by Michael Brown; the lighting design was by Brian MacDevitt; the sound design was by Laura Grace Brown; the costume design was by Carrie Robbins; the production manager was Joseph L. Robinson; and the production stage manager was Christine Catti. The cast was as follows:

VADA LOVE POWELL	Frances Sternhagen
APPLETON POWELL, JR./	
MR. POWELL	Reed Birney
MARY LOU/MARY ANN	Tracy Thorne
ENID	Sloane Shelton
MARYBELL	Marge Redmond

CHARACTERS

APPLETON POWELL, JR., Vada's beloved son, a definitely unusual, one might even say eccentric man; in his mid-thirties in Act One; in his mid-forties in Act Two.

VADA LOVE POWELL, a charming autocrat of a woman, who has never suffered from self-doubt, and never will; in her late sixties in Act One; in her late seventies in Act Two.

MARY LOU MELE, a perfect match for Vada, even at age twenty in Act One; thirty in Act Two.

ENID SYMONDS, a retired second-grade schoolteacher, with starch and wit, over seventy in Act One; over eighty in Act Two.

MARYBELL BAXTER, the Southern belle par excellence, because she really isn't one, almost seventy in Act One; eighty in Act Two.

MARY ANN MELE POWELL, Mary Lou's much more benign twin sister; played by the same actor who plays Mary Lou.

MR. POWELL, Vada's husband as a young man; played by the same actor who plays Appleton.

SETTING

Vada's sitting room and Enid's tree house in a small town in the deep South.

TIME

Act One takes place in the nineteen-fifties; Act Two takes place in the nineteen-sixties.

ACT ONE

Scene One

The sitting room of Vada Love Powell, an imposing, if not imperious, woman in her late sixties, somewhere in the deep South. The room is overstuffed and overdone, but not overwhelming. On the contrary, it is most inviting. "A surfeit of honey" describes the surroundings perfectly. A small table has been set for tea, and, as tea tables go, it looks sublime. There are photographs in ornate frames—of a male at all ages, from naked infant on satin throw to mature man in white linen suit—overrunning the room. They are all of Appleton Powell, Jr., Vada's only child—except for one formal portrait of Appleton Powell, Sr., wearing fine gentleman's attire of the twenties. The two men look very much alike.

The late fifties. A promise-of-spring afternoon in late February.

The stage is empty. When the lights come up, a warm sun fills the room. After several beats of silence, a definitely unusual, one might almost say eccentric, but distinctive man in his mid-thirties enters. He wears steel-rimmed spectacles and a white linen suit with a camellia in his lapel. He is Appleton Powell, Jr., and he speaks directly to the audience, with a not off-putting southern accent.

APPLE: My mother's sitting room! Used almost daily for some of the most remarkable social exchanges in the entire South—sometimes as an outpost, sometimes as a shrine, but more often as a battlefield. She has an army of friends! They march in and out in their armor—bosoms buttressed, waists corseted, to play bridge, plan bridal teas, conduct Church Guilds, steer Garden Clubs . . . or just "visit." That's what this room is meant for *(He says the word with a pleasant buzzing sound.)* "visiting." But today it's all set up to serve a more . . . predatory purpose. *(The doorbell chimes, and Vada enters one side of the stage, and crosses off the other. As she crosses.)* There's the predator! My indomitable mother! Or is the "visitor" the predator? . . . You be the judge. *(The two women enter now, in a kind feminine flutter. Mary Lou is a vision of loveliness in a pushing-the-season pastel suit.)*

VADA: So *you're* Mary Ann . . . I'm Vada Love.

MARY LOU: I've heard so much about you, Miz Powell.

VADA: You young people! You mean to tell me you didn't wear a coat in this weather?

MARY LOU: But the sun's so kind.

VADA: It's still the middle of February.

MARY LOU: But it's up to sixty-eight degrees.

VADA: Mind you, I wouldn't want to cover up that pretty dress you're wearing. But I wouldn't want to take cold—not in the middle of the Mardi Gras season!

MARY LOU: I won't. I'm the warm-blooded one in the family.

VADA: Do you enjoy Mardi Gras as much as I do? I just dance right through it!

MARY LOU: You still go to the balls?

VADA: Oh, no, no, I only read about them in the paper—*every* adjective describing *every* debutante . . . Why don't you sit right here by me, so we don't have to shout at each other across the room.

MARY LOU: *(Looking around.)* What a lovely room!

VADA: My son says I should take half of what's in here out.

MARY LOU: Yes, he told me . . .

VADA: *(Quick as a cat.)* Told you what?

MARY LOU: About all the beautiful things you have.

VADA: Well, I don't know about beautiful, but every one of them has a history, and deep, deep sentimental value. It must all look a little "random" to a young person like you . . . no feeling for the past.

MARY LOU: Oh, I *love* the past! As a matter of fact, I intend to furnish my house with all antiques. I absolutely love antiques!

VADA: Your family's house doesn't look like it would have antiques.

MARY LOU: You know our house?

VADA: I know most every house in this town. Lived here long enough to watch it go . . . well, "down," if you ask me. People don't take pride in their property anymore.

MARY LOU: Not if they don't own it!

VADA: Now I don't mean you, dear. Your little house looks as neat as can be. I bet it's decorated very nicely. What kind of furniture do you have?

MARY LOU: Just furniture furniture. Sears, so to speak.

VADA: Then where do you intend to get all your antiques? I don't know if you've been to an antique store lately, but the prices are something criminal! *(Indicating the chair across from where they're sitting.)* I saw that very chair in a shop down in the French Quarter. Do you know what they wanted for it? Five hundred dollars! Highway robbery! Don't let that happen to you, dear!

MARY LOU: No ma'am.

VADA: Now! What would you like—tea or coffee? *(With a condescending sigh.)* I have both. Some people insist on coffee—some of my own friends, mind you! But I think that just goes to show how everybody's losing all sense of the finer things, don't you?

MARY LOU: Yes ma'am.

VADA: Now, what would you like?

MARY LOU: *(After a beat.)* I'll have tea, please.

VADA: You have what you want, dear. Don't pay any attention to me. Apple says I'm old fashioned.

MARY LOU: No, I really like tea. I think it's elegant. My sister and I used to have tea parties for our dolls when we were little.

VADA: How sweet! I have an exquisite little Royal Doulton tea set packed away up in the attic. Never had any use for it. No little girls.

MARY LOU: You miss having a little girl?

VADA: I most certainly do not! Apple has given me all the joy a mother could possibly want . . . Now, Mary Ann . . . Beautiful name . . . *(Rolling it off her tongue.)* Mary Ann . . . Just give me a minute in the kitchen, and I'll return with the most exotic tea you've ever touched your pretty tongue to.

MARY LOU: Can I help?

VADA: I should hope not! You're the guest!

Vada gets up and goes out to the kitchen. Mary Lou looks in the direction of her exit, then gets out of the chair, and begins to canvass the photographs of Apple that are crowding the crowded room. She smiles and shakes her head as she goes from one to another, and Apple again addresses the audience.

APPLE: I'd have to give that round to Vada. That's my mother's name— Vada Love Powell—and she wears it like a tiara. Of course, she has the territorial advantage, but don't underestimate the invader. It's much too soon to tell.

VADA: *(Entering with an exquisite tea tray.)* I guess you're saying to yourself she's lost her famous touch. But you can't rush these things, you know . . . A good biscuit can't be coaxed. And I for one *refuse* to bake them beforehand. I wouldn't serve my worst *enemy* reheated biscuits in time of famine! *(She sets the tray down on the tea table, which is now replete with an exotic spread of homemade sweets, and begins to pour the tea.)* Help yourself to one of everything, my dear . . . And don't tell me you're on some kind of diet! I've never been on a diet in my life, and I've never been stout. Ample at times, but never stout! *(Offering her the biscuits.)* These are definitely *la specialité de la maison*—Vada's Bacon Biscuits! They're irresistible with my homemade fig preserves. *(Offering these.)* Here are my very own Not-So-Petit Petit-fours. And my luscious Lemon Squares. Bourbon Balls, and I do mean *bourbon!* I don't know why people are so stingy with the whisky. And Vada's Praline Parfaits! Help yourself, dear . . . Do you cook, Mary Ann?

MARY LOU: I'm a whiz with fudge.

VADA: Milk, lemon, sugar?

MARY LOU: Milk, please. My sister and I won first prize for our peanut butter fudge in the eighth grade.

VADA: I certainly hope you haven't resigned yourself to an eighth-grade palate. I'm absolutely amazed at the number of otherwise intelligent people who remain children in two areas—their prayers and their palates! The very same people who never say anything but "Gimme" to God are the ones who put ketchup on their steak *au poivre!* You sure you have everything you want?

MARY LOU: And more! Everything's delicious!

VADA: Oh, I'm a good cook! I take no false pride in that! You should come for dinner!

MARY LOU: I'd love to.

VADA: I'm sure you would! Well, now that the food's on the table, let's put our cards there too, so to speak . . . Is it true you wish to marry my son, Apple?

MARY LOU: *(Without a moment's hesitation.)* I think it's true your son, Apple, wishes to marry.

VADA: Well, if you don't wish to marry him, what are we doing here?

MARY LOU: I believe you invited me to tea.

VADA: *(Deciding to take a more oblique approach.)* Yes, I did. I most certainly did. And you haven't told me a thing about yourself.

MARY LOU: What would you like to know?

VADA: Tell me about your family. You mentioned one sister. Are there any other siblings?

MARY LOU: No ma'am.

VADA: Do I know your mother? I know most everybody in this town, but I don't think we move in the same circles.

MARY LOU: I don't think you do. Mama works.

VADA: Out of necessity?

MARY LOU: Yes ma'am. She drives a school bus.

VADA: I saw a lady school bus driver! I couldn't believe my eyes! That was your mother?

MARY LOU: Yes ma'am.

VADA: Well, I can only admire people who dedicate themselves to the young.

MARY LOU: You should see her. She's terrific with the kids!

VADA: *Children*, dear. *Kids* are baby goats . . . How nice to hear a child speak well of her mother. I thought Apple was alone in that. And your father? . . . What does he do?

MARY LOU: *(Deftly avoiding the question.)* They both work very hard to send us to college.

VADA: What are you studying?

MARY LOU: Anthropology.

VADA: Whatever for?!

MARY LOU: I love people, and I love travel! I want to do my fieldwork on the tribes of New Guinea!

VADA: That's ridiculous! You can't go off with a bunch of savages, if you plan to get married.

MARY LOU: That's what anthropologists do.

VADA: Not in my family! Anyway, you're much too young for Apple!

MARY LOU: He doesn't seem to think so.

VADA: My son is an incurable romantic. That's why he must have a realist for a wife.

MARY LOU: My twin sister is the realist in our family.

VADA: You didn't tell me you were twins. Identical twins?

MARY LOU: Yes ma'am.

VADA: Oh, I'm so sorry . . . I've always thought there was something unnatural about identical twins. Nature never repeats herself, you know.

MARY LOU: It seems to me Nature does pretty much what she likes.

VADA: Well, Nature or no Nature, we must all put our trust in the Lord.

MARY LOU: *(With an edge.)* Which doesn't always work, does it?

VADA: Oh dear! Don't tell me you're an atheist! I have no patience with laziness!

MARY LOU: Laziness?

VADA: That's all it is! People who don't want to get up and go to church on Sunday mornings!

MARY LOU: What about Nietzsche? You've heard of Nietzsche?

VADA: Of course, I've heard of Nietzsche! He couldn't sleep a wink at night—God was already punishing him! Don't get me started on Nietzsche and his friend Hitler! I pray to God you're not an atheist.

MARY LOU: *(Not apologetic, but expecting the worst.)* Oh, no ma'am, I'm a Catholic.

VADA: *(After a moment of silence, making the best of a bad thing.)* Well, one or two of my friends are Catholics . . . I'm an Episcopalian, thank God.

MARY LOU: *(Under her breath.)* Thank God . . .

VADA: *(Not hearing.)* I'm sorry, what did you say? That's the only thing bothers me about my age. My hearing's not as sharp as it used to be. Mind you, I once had ears like a bird dog's. From the moment he had his first heart attack, I could hear Mr. Powell's breathing from any part of the house. A human heart monitor!

MARY LOU: Apple doesn't often mention his father. Except for his illness.

VADA: Well, all those years he was sick Apple was wonderful to him! And to me! Apple was . . . *(Deeply moved.)* well, I've already said it . . . everything I could ever hope for! Oh, dear Lord! Do you smell that? I just hope I haven't ruined them! *(Vada gets up abruptly, and starts for the kitchen.)*

MARY LOU: It's a miracle he survived! *(Mary Lou ponders, as Apple continues.)*

APPLE: No! No miracle! I was loved! You don't know what it's like to be loved like I was. It was hard—hard on both of us, but I didn't have to prove anything! To her or for her! I was the center of her universe. Therefore, given Vada, I was perfect! Oh, she had to hone me round the edges, point me toward the rainbow, but I was destined to touch it! . . . I know what people say about me . . . *(Mimicking the very people who make fun of him.)* "He's peculiar!" "That Apple's eccentric!" "Sissy!"—I got called that enough in my life! Why not?! A woman raised me! By herself! But that woman's one in a million! So . . . so am I! *(Vada returns with a silver salver with doily and macaroons.)*

VADA: Macaroons! Apple's favorite! *(Presenting them.)* Have one. I think they cooled off on the way from the kitchen.

MARY LOU: These really are exquisite! My daddy loves them. I don't suppose you give away the recipe.

VADA: I most certainly do! I'll give anybody who asks me any one of my recipes. I consider them part of the public domain! . . . Now, we were just coming to something intriguing when I had to leave for the kitchen. What was it?

MARY LOU: Why I'm here.

VADA: Well, we both know that deep down, don't we?

MARY LOU: Actually, I've never been invited to tea before in all my life. I come from very simple people, Miz Powell. When we stop for a cup of something in the afternoon, it's instant coffee!—with a Twinkie!—to go! Or if my grandmother's visiting, we might have a Stella d'Oro cookie! She's Italian!

VADA: Italian?

MARY LOU: And if that's not bad enough for you, my mother's Irish!

VADA: I have to say that's the first thing I haven't liked about you, Mary Ann Mele. You're ashamed of your ancestors!

MARY LOU: I'm not ashamed of my ancestors. I just know they're not allowed in your circle.

VADA: They're not the ones trying to enter my circle.

MARY LOU: But I am?!

VADA: *Are* you? *Do* you wish to marry my son?

MARY LOU: (*Really attacking for the first time, but still in control.*) Are you proposing for him, Miz Powell?! . . . How many girls have you frightened off? Apple's thirty-five years old! He wants to get married and have a family. Are there any young ladies you would find eligible?

VADA: (*Fighting back.*) There are a great many young ladies I would find eligible!

MARY LOU: But do they find Apple eligible? That's the question! He's a most unusual man! Not your garden-variety Gary Cooper! Some people think he's downright peculiar! Did you know that? Have you looked at him lately? Steel-rimmed spectacles, rumpled white linen suit, crooked Panama hat! Have you looked at him?!

VADA: I look at him every day, Miss Mele, and I think he's perfectly beautiful. I'll never understand why women don't adore him. And I think he's one of the smartest men in the world!

MARY LOU: Forgive me, but for once in his life, what *you* think doesn't matter!

VADA: You know how to wound, don't you, young lady? I only want to protect Apple. I couldn't bear it if someone who didn't love him married him for the wrong reason.

MARY LOU: What would be the wrong reason? If it isn't his good looks or his great fortune, what else could it be? What do you fear so much that you'd invite an Irish Italian Catholic girl, whose mother drives a school bus, to afternoon tea? You want to scare me off like the rest of them! You want Appleton Powell all to yourself.

VADA: I most certainly do not!!! Young woman, do you know the parable of the talents? About the man who buried his talent in the ground, he was so afraid he'd lose it. I think that man was the *stupidest* man in the world! . . . Apple is my talent! The Lord gave him to me to nurture and to cherish, and then to let fly and bring his blessing upon his wife and his children and their children.

MARY LOU: Then what are you so afraid of?

VADA: I'm afraid no one will love him as I do.

MARY LOU: No one will! Apple's told me all about you. He's told me how you used to make him sit on the side of his poor daddy's bed when he was nine years old and read the paper to him. How you had him wear his necktie whenever there were ladies in the house, and made him work cheek-by-jowl with the yard boy, and stand up whenever the cook came into the room. I even know what you told him about the birds and the bees!

VADA: Why are you telling me all this?

MARY LOU: To prove to you that nobody will love him like that. And nobody needs to! Apple is already safe and sound because of what you've given him. It wouldn't matter if he didn't marry, but it'd be a pity. The talent ought not be buried! Not after all that!

VADA: I don't know what I told Apple about the birds and the bees.

MARY LOU: You couldn't get away with it nowadays.

VADA: Oh, I know. So much mystery and romance gone out of life. I feel sorry for you young people. You think love just happens. Well, let me tell you, you have to work long and hard to make it last. If you've got to stop to *think*, you've sure got to stop to *love*. *(The telephone rings.)* I can't believe it's let us alone this long. That telephone usually rings itself right off the hook this time of afternoon. *(Vada crosses to the telephone, as Apple appears on the other side of the stage with a phone in his hand.)* Hello . . .

APPLE: *(Playing the game they always play.)* Hello, Mother, this is . . .

VADA: Don't tell me! Is it . . . the butcher?

APPLE: Nooo . . .

VADA: Is it . . . the baker?

APPLE: Nooo . . .

VADA: Is it . . . the Apple of my eye?!

APPLE: Yes ma'am.

VADA: You'll never guess who's sitting right here in the room with me.

APPLE: I might.

VADA: I bet you won't.

APPLE: I bet I will. How about Mary Lou Mele?

VADA: Mary *Ann* Mele.

APPLE: Mary *Lou*, Mother.

VADA: You mean you want to marry her, and you don't even know her name.

APPLE: *(Teasing.)* Who says I'm going to marry her?

VADA: I know the signs. You give me longer kisses on the cheek. You bring me blossoms from the yard. You *hum*—God help us! I know when you're in love.

APPLE: And you always manage to get me out of it.

VADA: And you always agree it was the right thing to do.

VADA:	APPLE:
And I did it for you . . .	Not this time . . . I beg your
What did you say?	pardon. What, Mother?

APPLE: You go first.

VADA: Of course, I go first!

APPLE: Mother, I'm calling long distance.

VADA: Long distance?! Where in the world are you?

APPLE: I'm at the airport.

VADA: The airport. How did you know Mary Ann Mele was here?

APPLE: It's Mary Lou. Ask her!

VADA: Is your name Mary Ann or Mary Lou?

MARY LOU: It's Mary Lou.

VADA: Why did you let me go on calling you Mary Ann?

APPLE: *(Raising his voice.)* Mother, will you listen to me?!

VADA: Appleton Powell, are you shouting at me?

APPLE: Yes ma'am.

VADA: Well, you best have good reason.

APPLE: *(Very gently.)* Mother, I got married today . . . *(He waits to see what's going to happen.)*

VADA: Go on. You don't think I'm going to get hysterical, do you?

APPLE: I married Mary Ann Mele—Mary Lou's twin sister—at noon today—in the rectory of the Catholic Church—with the Catholic and the Episcopal priests *both* presiding. I thought it'd be better this way, Mother, for you . . . and for us . . . Father Marshall's going to come by to see you at five o'clock this afternoon . . . He'll explain.

VADA: *(Very taut.)* Explain?!

APPLE: Please, Mother! We're about to go off on our honeymoon. Father Marshall's bringing our itinerary, so you'll know where to find me if you need me. And he's standing by ready to help you, if you need him.

VADA: Why should I need someone who betrayed me?

APPLE: He didn't betray you, Mother, I did. I begged him to do it this way. It seemed easier for us all.

VADA: I wouldn't call this easy. Not easy for me! Not easy to see my only son married . . . in the rectory of the Catholic Church! Oh, Apple!

APPLE: I really appreciate what you're doing for me, Mother.

VADA: What am I doing for you, Apple?

APPLE: Trying to forgive me. All those other girls were wrong for me. I knew that. I was glad you scared them off. But Mary Ann's different! You'll see. Mary Ann's very different! I have to go now. I love you, Mother. Wish me happiness.

VADA: I wish you all the happiness you've given me, and there isn't anymore than that this side of Paradise.

APPLE: Goodbye, Mother. God bless you.

Apple exits, and Vada slowly hangs up the phone. After a moment Mary Lou stands.

MARY LOU: I'm sure you'd like me to leave.

VADA: No! I'd like you to stand right there and tell me how—I'm going to say it—the *hell* you had the gall to come here and deceive me . . . You knew all along, didn't you?

MARY LOU: Yes ma'am.

VADA: Were you at the rectory?

MARY LOU: *I* was, but my parents weren't.

VADA: I didn't for one minute think they were. I know my son!

MARY LOU: Do you?

VADA: *(Deliberately ignoring the question.)* Why did you lie to me?

MARY LOU: I didn't exactly lie to you.

VADA: You deceived me. Why?

MARY LOU: Twins are very close, Miz Powell. I love my sister as much as you love your son, and she loves Apple as much as I love her. And since neither one of us thinks anyone can love them like we do, I thought I'd make a good guinea pig for you to punish her, and you'd make a good guinea pig for me to punish him. And we'd get all that hurt over with. And you and she and Apple and I could start out without any scars. You said some things to me I wouldn't want you to say to Mary Ann. And I said some things to you, you wouldn't want me to say to Apple. And I don't think we'll ever have to say those things again, do you?

VADA: Are you quite finished, young woman?

MARY LOU: Yes ma'am. Are you finished with me?

VADA: No! There's one thing more. What does your father do for a living?

MARY LOU: Take a deep breath . . . He's a cook.

VADA: A cook?

MARY LOU: At the hotel.

VADA: Well, it's the one place in town you can get a decent meal, except here, of course, and one or two of my friends.

MARY LOU: He runs the restaurant.

VADA: He runs it?

MARY LOU: Yes ma'am.

VADA: Then, for mercy's sake, tell him to call himself a chef! I see absolutely no reason to celebrate ignominity. From now on it must be clearly understood that the father of my daughter-in-law is a chef!

MARY LOU: Look, Miz Powell, about my folks . . . I'm sorry there wasn't any wedding, but they couldn't afford one—not the kind you'd want. It's not Apple's fault.

VADA: Oh, I bet Apple's glad.

MARY LOU: Why would he be glad?

VADA: He's proved to the world—for better or worse—he's not tied to his mother's apron strings. *(The doorbell chimes.)*

MARY LOU: I guess that's your minister.

VADA: Father Marshall is a priest, dear. Priest—just like you have.

MARY LOU: I'll let him in when I go out.

VADA: No you won't! I want Father Marshall to see how well I'm getting on with my in-laws. And then I want *you* to watch *me* take on the entire Episcopal Church! *(The doorbell chimes again, and she starts off, shouting.)* Coming!!! I didn't shoot myself if that's what you think!

She exits as the lights go out on the scene.

Scene Two

The same. But the room is now swallowed in shadows, which evoke a different reality—the internal workings of Vada's mind. Music underscores the scene to suggest that other reality. There is a glow on the photograph of Apple's father, Appleton Powell, Sr.

Twilight following the previous scene.

The tea things are still on the table. Vada paces back and forth for a few moments in silence, taking in the photograph, and a dim light comes up on the figure of a man in deep shadow. He's dressed in a high stiff collar and twenties attire. He is Apple's father, Appleton Powell, Sr., at about the time he and Vada first met.

VADA: I don't understand it, Mr. Powell! I just don't understand it! What did I do?!

MR. POWELL: *(Quietly.)* Everything a mother could.

VADA: *(Not in the least startled by the voice but expecting it.)* And I did it alone, Mr. Powell!

MR. POWELL: I know. I was sick for so long. It was hard on you.

VADA: Hard on me and hard on Apple . . . but that doesn't excuse what he did to me this afternoon.

MR. POWELL: No, but it'll be all right, you'll see.

VADA: All right for you! You don't have to endure it! You never had to endure any of it! Walking up and down, talking to myself till his fever broke. Waiting up at night to hear his key in the door. *(After a beat.)* And now, if I've lost him, I don't have anyone to blame but myself!

MR. POWELL: I must say I'm surprised at you, dear. You're not one to feel sorry for yourself.

VADA: I just don't visit my feelings on anybody else.

MR. POWELL: No, you never did.

VADA: And tomorrow and the next day and the day after that, I have to go out of this house with my head held high and pretend to the world that my own son has not broken his mother's heart. That's what I have to do, Mr. Powell, and do it I will!

MR. POWELL: I admire you for it.

VADA: Thank you, sir.

MR. POWELL: You're most welcome, my dear . . . most welcome . . .

He retreats into the shadows, and she begins to clear the tea things, as the lights go out on the scene.

Scene Three

A tree house in Enid Symons' backyard. It is little more than a platform with side rails and a ladder that reaches down to the ground; the tree branches form the roof. But there is ample room for a bridge table, four chairs, and a small serving table with a tray of lemonade and a beautiful home-baked strawberry cake. The sun streams through the leaves to produce a speckled light, and suggest the movement of a gentle breeze.

The following day—so warm it could be April.

Enid Symons and Marybell Baxter sit on opposite sides of the table. They are counting, shuffling, and dealing cards impatiently. The lemonade pitcher is sweating, and there is an air of anxiety, even in this idyllic setting. A canasta game was scheduled for 2:00 P.M. It is 2:10, and Vada, one of the regulars in the Wednesday Canasta Club, has yet to arrive. The fourth member of the group is permanently absent. Her name is Kitty Carter, but she died at the end of last summer, so one of her friends plays her hand. As the cards ripple and snap, Apple speaks again to the audience.

APPLE: I'm the one who dubbed them—"The Tree-House Gang!" Of course, Mother doesn't approve. "Appleton," she says. "We're not a nest of criminals!" Then she looks at me, and she twitters, "A nest of *rare birds* maybe, fluttering their cards and flirting with God!" I wouldn't put it past that crew to flirt with God! Seventyish—every one of them—and they climb up to that tree house every Wednesday in nice weather to play canasta and consume sweets! Of course, canasta's *way* beneath their dignity! They're wicked bridge players! Canasta's just a good excuse for gossip! Today I'm bound to be the subject of discussion!

ENID: It's ten past two. You think she had car trouble?

MARYBELL: I do not.

ENID: Vada's never late, if God's in His heaven!

MARYBELL: Well, I'm sure God's *not*, far as she's concerned!

ENID: Marybell, why would you say a thing like that?!

MARYBELL: *(Chiding.)* I know that *you* know *exactly* what I know. So don't make such a big fuss about being "above" gossip!

ENID: If something's happened to Vada, it's not gossip. It's tragic!

MARYBELL: Depends on what happened.

ENID: Well, what did?!

MARYBELL: You mean to tell me you were home all morning long, and you haven't heard! I thought my phone would ring off the hook!

ENID: You know I go to the foot doctor on Wednesday mornings.

MARYBELL: Well, that explains it.

ENID: But I didn't go today.

MARYBELL: Why not?

ENID: I was too upset about what happened.

MARYBELL: Wait a minute! I thought you didn't know.

ENID: *(Devilishly.)* I'm holding out to see if you know more.

MARYBELL: Enid Symons! You're acting like a nosy old lady!

ENID: Chicken clucking over the crow!

MARYBELL: Every time my phone rang, I said to myself, "Now that's Enid! She wouldn't leave me in the dark any longer."

ENID: Your line was always busy! Just burning up the wires, weren't you, at our dear friend's expense!

MARYBELL: I resent that, Enid. I really do! I deeply resent the implication of what you just said. I would never do anything at Vada's expense. She's my right arm, and I'm hers! But I tell you right now, I really think she had this one coming.

ENID: So do I.

MARYBELL: Poor Vada's not used to being crossed.

ENID: Crossed?! I love Apple, he's my godson, but I'd say what he did to his mother yesterday wasn't "crossed," it was downright cruel.

MARYBELL: First you say she had it coming, then you say it's cruel. Make up your mind, Enid!

ENID: *(Getting very upset.)* I'd appreciate it very much, Marybell, if you didn't order me around in my own tree house. Where's the rule I have to make up my mind?! I'll do what I please with my mind! I just hope I can hang on to it longer than my poor Bud did.

MARYBELL: I'm sorry, Enid, I really am. This business with Vada has gotten us both *so* upset. The whole town's in shock . . . What exactly did you mean by "cruel?"

ENID: First off, that child's much too young for Apple. Second thing, she's not even an Episcopalian. And third, Marybell—you of all people should know—she's an Italian! What do you think that does to poor Vada?

MARYBELL: Why me of all people?

ENID: You nearly had a fit when Dr. Angelo put up that shrine with the blue Madonna in his front yard, right on your street.

MARYBELL: It had nothing to do with him being Italian!

ENID: Now, Marybell, be honest. I'm not blaming you. I know exactly how you feel.

MARYBELL: *(Suddenly lashing out.)* No, you don't! You don't have the least idea how I feel!

ENID: My goodness! Where in the world did that tongue of fire come from?

MARYBELL: You don't know, you just don't know . . . *(A car honks from the driveway below.)* Oooh . . . There she is! I'd recognize that honk anywhere! Oh, dear! What do we say to her?

ENID: Not a word till she does.

VADA: *(Off. Calling from below.)* Yoo-hoo!

MARYBELL: *(Feebly.)* Yoo-hoo!

VADA: *(Off.)* You two up there already? I'm right on time.

ENID: You are not!!!

Vada hoists herself up the last steps of the ladder and onto the platform of the tree house. She seems totally together, and is beautifully turned out. She's wearing white gloves and carrying her purse and a bottle of sherry.

VADA: *(Without a moment's hesitation.)* You two know what today is?

ENID: My goodness! You're all dressed up.

MARYBELL: 'Course she is, Enid! It's only natural. When I feel *down*, I always dress *up*.

VADA: *(Triumphantly.)* It's Kitty's birthday! I dressed up for Kitty. I remembered her favorite sherry on the way out here, and I drove all the way back to the Piggly Wiggly to get it. I brought a little libation to toast her. And we'll sing "Happy Birthday."

MARYBELL: Isn't that kind of maudlin? You think Kitty would like that?

VADA: All right, we *won't* sing "Happy Birthday." We'll just sit here deaf as mutes!

ENID: *(Laughing along with Marybell.)* Deaf as mutes?!

VADA: Well then, let's just forget about Kitty. I guess she's beyond caring one way or another.

MARYBELL: Oh, I don't think so, Vada. Death isn't the end of life. It's the beginning of . . .

VADA: Please, Marybell, don't get started on your sermons! I'm not in the mood for . . .

MARYBELL: I can still see her in that hospital, thin as a toothpick. A fine stout woman like that! Shrunk to a string bean!

VADA: Oh, it's all right to be morbid about her, but it's not all right to give her a little birthday party.

ENID: I'm the hostess, and I say it's perfectly all right!

VADA: (Sacrificing herself.) No, no! Let's get on with our canasta! Who's going to be Kitty's partner today?!

ENID: Why don't you be?

VADA: I was last week.

MARYBELL: Not last week. *I* was last week.

ENID: Here we go again! If you all don't want to be Kitty's partner, why don't we get a replacement for her. It's not as if people weren't dying to play with us.

VADA: Which people?

ENID: Mildred Huey asked me . . .

VADA: You really want to play canasta once a week with Mildred Huey?! That whiney voice! I don't know how her husband stands it.

ENID: He's deaf as a post!

VADA: (Sweeping all the dealt cards up into her hands.) Time to play, ladies! Let's draw for the deal.

ENID: Vada, we already dealt!

VADA: You can't deal without drawing.

ENID: We had to do something while we were waiting.

VADA: You two are *really* trying to make it hard for me today.

MARYBELL: That's not true! Enid and I were just saying we'd like to be your "right arm." That was one of Mama's favorite expressions. It meant being her strength in time of woe.

VADA: I know what it means, Marybell.

MARYBELL: (Under her breath.) You know just about everything, don't you, Vada?

VADA: You're mumbling again, Marybell. My hearing's sharp as a bird dog's, and I didn't hear a word you just said.

MARYBELL: I said my mama was from Mississippi.

VADA: You never told me that! Enid, did she ever tell you that? Where in Mississippi?

MARYBELL: Vicksburg.

VADA: *(Excited.)* My family's from Vicksburg—both sides. What's your folks' name?

MARYBELL: Oh, I doubt you'd know us, Vada.

VADA: We knew everybody!

MARYBELL: Where did you buy your shoes?

VADA: What does that have to do with . . .

MARYBELL: In Vicksburg—where did you buy your shoes?

VADA: You think I don't remember? I certainly do! The Imperial Shoe Store. Best in town!

MARYBELL: My daddy owned the Imperial Shoe Store.

VADA: I thought those people were Italians.

MARYBELL: They were!

VADA: Fardella, Farrara, something like that . . . *(Suddenly.)* What did you say?

MARYBELL: I said I'm Italian.

VADA: Enid, is this some kind of joke you two are playing, because I don't think it's funny.

ENID: It's all news to me, Vada.

MARYBELL: I just thought, in view of what's happened, this might be a good time to let the cat out of the bag. I, Marybell Baxter used to be Marybell Farrara! What do you think of that?!

ENID: *(Stopping her cold.)* All these years you never said a word!

MARYBELL: Not a word, or I wouldn't be here, would I? Wouldn't be allowed to contaminate your pure Anglo-Saxon blood.

ENID: I think that's disgusting.

MARYBELL: Answer me, Enid, if you'd known when I came here forty years ago that George Baxter had brought home an Italian bride, would you have invited me to your Christmas tea? And Vada, would you have taken me under your wing in the Guild if George's mama hadn't called you up and lied! That's how important it was to the Baxters that nobody knew.

ENID: How in this world could you deceive us like that? All these years!

MARYBELL: I'd almost forgotten I did . . . *(Looking at Vada.)* till all this came up. You live a lie long enough, you turn into it.

ENID: You're awful quiet, Vada. Cat got your tongue?

MARYBELL: You all want me to leave?

VADA: Oh, Marybell! It's ancient history, far as we're concerned. A lot of nice people are Italian.

MARYBELL: You're just going to forget about it?

ENID: We're not living in the Dark Ages!

MARYBELL: Some people are.

ENID: Not us! Right, Vada?

VADA: We're your best friends. What we don't know won't hurt us.

MARYBELL: *(Exasperated.)* But you do know. I just told you. I'm Italian!

ENID: So was Michelangelo! . . . Now, are we here to play canasta or not? It's almost two-thirty!

VADA: Cut for the deal. *(They cut the cards for the deal; Vada cuts for Kitty. Nodding to Kitty's chair.)* Happy Birthday, dear Kitty. *(The other two look at each other with raised eyebrows. They all show their cards, and the one Vada drew for Kitty is an ace.)* Oooh, Kitty has an ace! As her partner, I deal for her, of course. *(Vada begins to deal—eleven cards to each of the four places. She handles the cards exquisitely, like a cross between a riverboat gambler and a concert pianist, as Apple speaks to the audience again.)*

APPLE: You'd never know today was hard for her, would you? Under that corset there's *real* grit! Lived all those years with an invalid. Not a word of complaint! After his heart attack I doubt they ever had sex! But she went right on living her life up to the hilt! Bringing him back news of the battle, puffing his pillows, brushing his hair. He called her his Florence Nightingale, she called him her wounded soldier. When Papa died, she went to work in the bank, and pretty soon she was "puffing their pillows." Wasn't long before the bank became the social center of the town! *(Vada has finished dealing. They all look at their cards, and arrange them according to the rules of the game.)*

ENID: No red treys, I suppose.

MARYBELL: If I had any red treys, Enid, I'd declare them.

VADA: *(Picking up Kitty's hand from across the table.)* Well, Kitty has one. *(She puts a red trey face up on the table, and then draws from the stack.)*

MARYBELL: My Lord! Do you realize we forgot to put up our money! How much will it be today?

VADA: A dollar a game!

MARYBELL: You must feel lucky!

VADA: In honor of Kitty's birthday.

ENID: You'll be mad as hog-*hell* if you don't win.

VADA: *(Sweet as molasses.)* Enid, you don't use that kind of coarse language. Something the matter?

ENID: *(Disgusted.)* I'd *like* to play cards, if you don't mind!!!

VADA: *(To Marybell.)* I don't know when I've seen her so testy. *(To Enid.)* Maybe you should go back on your Metamucil.

ENID: I'm regular as clockwork, thank you! Go on, Marybell!

MARYBELL: Go on what?

ENID: *It's your turn!!!*

MARYBELL: *(Throwing down her hand.)* I'm sorry. I can't continue with this charade! Here we are aggravating one another when Enid and I are worried sick about you, Vada. And you just go on pretending nothing's happened.

VADA: I'm not going to let a silly card game spoil my day.

ENID: We're not talking about cards! We're talking about Apple! *(There is a terrible silence.)*

VADA: What about Apple?

ENID: It's all over town.

MARYBELL: *(To Enid.)* You sure you're doing the right thing? I thought we were going to let her bring it up.

VADA: *"Her!" "Her!"* Now ladies, you know I don't enjoy being talked about in the third person.

ENID: *(Angry and hurt.)* It may come as a shock to you, but you're not perfect, Vada. And neither is your son! You're keeping us out. We're your dearest friends, and you're not willing to trust us with a crumb of your feelings!

MARYBELL: Now, now, Enid, don't get yourself all worked up! Everybody has trouble with their children. Look at poor Kitty! What Little Kit did to that family was a scandal, and they all stood by her. And we stood by them.

VADA: I just want to say one thing, and that's all! There is absolutely nothing scandalous about what Apple did.

MARYBELL: I didn't say that . . .

VADA: Oh, I'm sure it's on yours and everybody else in this town's slippery lips! People just love to talk about me and my son! We're some kind of freaks, because we have our standards, and we hold them high! There's a right way to do things, and that's the way *I* do them! Apple too!

ENID: Oh, not Apple, Vada! Apple does things his way. Always has. Didn't he go as far away to college as he could get? And then when he graduated, didn't he move into those awful see-through apartments they put up, God knows why, right next to the cemetery. Even as a little boy, Apple used to ride his bike out here on a Saturday, to be with Bud and me, when you thought he'd gone on a hayride. Bud built this tree house for Apple!

VADA: *(Defensive.)* He missed having a daddy who could do things with him.

ENID: No. I think he felt sorry we didn't have any children of our own. So he came around once in a while to keep us company. That's why I love him like he was my own. But, Vada, I don't think what he did to you yesterday was decent one bit!

VADA: Now wait just a minute!

ENID: No! I wouldn't want a son who did that!!!

VADA: *(Hitting back—hard.)* Well, you don't have one, do you?!

MARYBELL: Now, Vada . . . Enid . . . Apple just knew deep down in his heart that his mother wouldn't approve, so he had to do it behind her back.

VADA: Apple never did anything behind my back!

ENID: *(Hostile.)* Did you go to the wedding?

VADA: There *was* no wedding!

ENID: All right! Did you go to the Catholic rectory for the *non*-wedding?!

MARYBELL: *(Trying to mollify.)* Doesn't matter, Vada dear. You never did like Catholics very much anyway.

VADA: You don't know what you're talking about! So will you please just shut up! *(After a terrible moment of shock.)* I apologize. I do.

ENID: No, I'm sorry, Vada . . .

VADA: Well, that makes two of us . . . Enid, do you think we could have a piece of that perfectly beautiful strawberry cake? I always find a sweet settling to the stomach in times of stress.

Enid begins to cut and serve four slices of cake, even one to Kitty's empty place. Then she pours the lemonade, as Apple speaks.

APPLE: You see, with Vada, you've got to present her with an inevitable and then she'll adjust. Anything less, and she'll just squash it. I think that's why she gets along so well with God! *She's* got a gift for dealing with the inevitable. *He's* got a gift for doling it out. Neither one of them's much good with give and take! In the hierarchy of command she'd rank somewhere between an empress dowager and a Marine Corps drill sergeant.

ENID: Aren't we ever going to talk about what we need to?

MARYBELL: You know, Vada, I know those Mele girls. They're junior candy stripers at the hospital on my day. So sweet and pretty! They're real nice girls, and *so* polite!

VADA: *I've* met them! One of them. She's very attractive. Blondish. The mother's Irish. I've never seen the father.

MARYBELL: *(Sarcastic.)* Oh, he's *very* Italian!

ENID: What does he do?

VADA: *(Very carefully.)* He's the . . . chef at the hotel.

ENID: I didn't know that. He's a very good cook!

VADA: Italians usually *are* good cooks, Enid.

MARYBELL: I wish you two could hear yourselves.

ENID: What do you mean?

MARYBELL: You're such snobs! Both of you!

ENID: We're no different from anybody else in this town!

MARYBELL: Yes, you are! You're different from me.

ENID: After forty years of hiding from us, now you think you're better than us!

MARYBELL: I'm the same as I always was.

VADA: No, you're not! Now you're honest.

MARYBELL: Vada, I'm trying to teach you something. I'm ashamed of myself, and I don't want you to be.

VADA: Don't you worry about me, Marybell.

MARYBELL: *(Exasperated.)* Dammit, Vada! Now you listen to me! If an Italian wanted to join our church, would you let him?

VADA: An Italian wouldn't want to join the Episcopal church. They have their own church.

MARYBELL: Suppose your new daughter-in-law wanted to join our church.

VADA: She can join, if Apple wants her to!

MARYBELL: Suppose Apple wants to join the Catholic church?

VADA: That's impossible! Apple's a lay reader in *our* church. He's not about to join another church.

ENID: Oh, dear God! Suppose he brings his children up Catholic.

VADA: Apple would never do a thing like that!

MARYBELL: Vada, when are you going to learn? Before yesterday you'd have said Apple wasn't about to marry Mary Ann Mele! But he did, didn't he?

ENID: Why are you being so hard on her, Marybell?

MARYBELL: I hate it when people think they're better than other people. Look what it made me do.

ENID: Nobody cares what you did right now, Marybell. *(Sweetly.)* Vada, you know what I've been thinking? Maybe it won't last.

VADA: *(Not believing her ears.)* What?!

ENID: You never know. Divorces are a dime a dozen these days.

VADA: Dear God!!!

ENID: What?

VADA: How can you say that?

ENID: Well, if you don't like it, you don't want it to last, do you?

VADA: Of course, I want it to last!

ENID: Don't look at me like I'm some kind of criminal. I'm just saying what you're thinking.

VADA: You are not! I not only want it to last. I have every intention of making it last!

ENID: I thought you didn't like her.

VADA: I never said that. If Apple married her, she must be marvelous.

MARYBELL: Even if she's Italian!

VADA: Marybell, you're beginning to get on my nerves.

ENID: My goodness! Such a fuss over a little secret. Everybody has her secrets!

VADA: Not I!!! There's not one skeleton in my closet, and I intend to keep it that way! Enid, it pains me to say it, but your strawberry cake begins to rival my own. *(Looking over to Kitty's place.)* Who ate Kitty's?

ENID: I served her one.

VADA: I know, and I was going to suggest we share it.

ENID: Too late now. Come on, own up. Who ate Kitty's cake?

MARYBELL: *(With guilt written all over her face.)* I didn't touch it.

There's the sound of a car in the driveway, then a honk.

ENID: Now, who's that? We'll never get to play canasta!

APPLE: *(Off. Calling from the bottom of the tree house.)* Mother! We're back!

VADA: Apple?!

APPLE: *(Off.)* Our flight was cancelled—some damn hurricane! And Mary Ann thought we ought to come back and check on you.

VADA: Well, you tell Mary Ann I don't need to be checked on! I'm doing just fine, thank you!

APPLE: *(Off.)* May we come up?

VADA: Why not? I'd like to meet the mother of my grandchildren.

ENID: *(Hating the thought of it.)* You want us to leave?

VADA: No indeed! We might need referees!

MARYBELL: Merciful heavens, Vada, what do you want us to do?

VADA: Watch me meet my Waterloo.

At this moment Apple's head appears above the tree-house floor.

APPLE: Mother, I'd like you to meet my wife.

Now Mary Ann's head appears, and Apple helps her onto the platform. She's dressed in a lovely "going-away" suit and hat. There is a strained silence. The "referees" look sheepishly at each other, and Vada stares straight at Mary Ann.

MARY ANN: I'm sorry it had to be . . . *(She can't finish the sentence.)*

APPLE: What Mary Ann means . . .

VADA: Let her finish, Apple! Had to be what?!

MARY ANN: I'm sorry it had to be . . . this way.

APPLE: *(Filling another gap in the conversation.)* Aunt Enid, Miss Marybell . . .

MARYBELL: I know this pretty little girl, Apple. She's the best junior candy striper at the hospital. Hi, honey. I know what you're going through.

APPLE: . . . this is my wife.

ENID: Hello, dear.

MARY ANN: Hello . . . Miz Powell, I know how much you love your son.

VADA: No, you don't!!!

MARYBELL: Vada, the whole town knows that.

VADA: Keep out of it, Marybell.

ENID: You asked us to stay!

APPLE: Mother, maybe we should go home, and continue this there.

VADA: Maybe you should have thought of that before you came barging in here.

APPLE: *(Angry.)* Come on, Mary Ann, I'm not going to subject you to . . .

VADA: *(Hitting back.)* No indeed! Don't subject *her!* Just your mother! Make her the laughing stock of the universe!

MARYBELL: There's not a soul laughing, Vada. We all feel terribly sorry for you.

ENID: You're not helping things, Marybell.

VADA: You present me with an earthquake, and ask me to accept it. Well, I can't! I can endure it, but I can't accept it, *or* condone it!

APPLE: But yesterday . . . on the telephone . . .

VADA: I've had twenty-four hours to think about what's been done to me!

MARY ANN: We shouldn't have come back so soon. It's my fault. But after sitting around that airport all night, I couldn't spend another minute not facing you.

VADA: *(Attacking.)* Aren't you a little late? Why weren't you willing to face me *before* the wedding?

APPLE: She was! Mary Ann always wanted to tell you about us.

VADA: Then why didn't she?

APPLE: I wouldn't let her. If we told you, you'd forbid it, and then we'd have to disobey you.

VADA: You wouldn't "subject" her to me, is that right?

APPLE: Mother, my wife's young . . .

VADA: *(Very sarcastic.)* Oh, I can see that! And *very* pretty!

APPLE: You're a powerful force. I might have lost her. I couldn't take that chance!

VADA: Enid, do I look like a tornado? Do I sweep you off your feet?

ENID: Vada, I think we should go.

VADA: No indeed! You're the hostess. This is your little nest . . . And Marybell? Do I strike you as a cannibal who gobbles up little girls?

MARYBELL: You better hold on to your tongue now, Vada. It'll run away with you, if you're not careful.

VADA: Picture that! My silver tongue running down the road pulling me behind it . . . *(Hitting hard.)* And you, Mary Ann, do I really frighten you?

MARY ANN: *(Respectfully.)* Yes ma'am. But I think I frighten you much more.

VADA: And I'm *sure* you want to tell me why!!!

APPLE: Mother, please, don't be so hard!

ENID: She's hurting, Apple.

VADA: Your Aunt Enid's right as always. I *am* hurting, Apple. I'm ashamed to go out on the street. The earth has shifted under my feet.

MARY ANN: You're afraid.

VADA: Why? Because a girl from the wrong side of the tracks has stolen my treasure? Don't underestimate me, Mary Ann. Everybody's on the wrong side of somebody's tracks!

MARY ANN: I know that's not why I frighten you. That's just an excuse other people can understand.

VADA: *(Only slightly snide.)* Then do tell me why, dear!

MARY ANN: *(With absolute certainty.)* You're afraid of me because I love your son, and you think nobody in the world deserves to do that besides you!

VADA: How do you know anything about loving, at your age?

MARY ANN: I don't know anything about loving, Miz Powell. I just do it! I just *love* Apple!

VADA: Why should I believe you?

MARY ANN: You won't, because you don't want to.

VADA: It may come as a shock to you, young woman, but I've never done just what I *want* to. Why don't you try me?

APPLE: Try her, Mary Ann.

MARY ANN: I didn't want to marry Apple. I know what people will say—"Gold digger! Social climber!" I have a good family—they don't deserve that. I didn't even want to get married right now. I'd just gotten my degree—had lots of job choices. I gave up ever having the kind of wedding "a girl like me" always wanted. I gave up gaining your respect. I gave up my good name! I gave up all this to marry your son before you could frighten me away from him. And I'd do it again, and more, because I love him!

ENID: Out of the mouths of babes!

Apple kisses Mary Ann impulsively in front of the ladies, and Vada takes it all in. Then she turns, in a different mood, on her friends.

VADA: Well, have you two seen enough?

MARYBELL: Forgive me, but I just have to ask Apple what *her* parents think of *him*.

APPLE: They wish I were young and handsome . . . and rich!

MARYBELL: Well, I don't want to be a traitor to my friend here, but I just think you're the sweetest couple . . . And, Vada, they're going to have the most gorgeous children.

VADA: *(To Mary Ann.)* What *about* children?

MARY ANN: I love children.

VADA: Apple's not getting any younger.

APPLE: Mother, please, do you mind?!

VADA: All you young women are so skinny, I can't tell a thing about your childbearing potential. No pelvis to speak of!

ENID: Everybody's so sure they'll have children any time they want. Such arrogance! As if God had nothing to do with it anymore.

MARY ANN: It *is* arrogant, isn't it, Miss Enid? My poor cousin's been trying so hard to have a baby for three years now.

MARYBELL: Is she Italian too, dear?

MARY ANN: Yes ma'am.

MARYBELL: So am I.

VADA: Marybell, what does that have to do with anything?

MARYBELL: Just want the child to feel comfortable, Vada.

ENID: Well now, how about some strawberry cake? And there's lemonade. We even have sherry. We'll have a little wedding reception right up here in God's heaven.

MARYBELL: *(Always the peacemaker.)* And we'll ask his blessing on these young people. All right with you, Vada?

VADA: The question is, Marybell, is it all right with God?

APPLE: Mother, please forgive us. I do believe God does.

VADA: God's a lot quicker to forgive than I am. *(To Enid and Marybell.)* But I dare anybody in this town to say so! Mary Ann is my family!

MARY ANN: Thank you, Miz Powell.

ENID: You better not let her go on calling you "Miz Powell," if you care anything about what this little ole town says.

MARYBELL: George Jr.'s wife calls me "Mom."

VADA: That's so common.

MARYBELL: I resent that, Vada. I really do.

VADA: I meant "frequently used," Marybell.

ENID: Mildred Huey's daughter-in-law calls her "Dearie," and she thinks it's sweet.

VADA: She would!

By this time Enid has cut more slices of cake, and Apple has poured the sherry.

ENID: *(Lifting her glass.)* God bless!

MARYBELL: *(Lifting hers.)* God bless!

VADA: *(After a beat, lifting hers.)* Well . . . *that* remains to be seen.

The three of them drink to the bride and groom, as the lights go out on the scene.

END OF ACT ONE

ACT TWO

Scene One

Vada's sitting room, as described in Act One, with the following exceptions: a rather large and prominent picture of Mary Ann and several smaller ones of babies and children are crowded into one corner; and the table is set for coffee, not tea—a silver coffeepot, two cups, and a silver salver of beignets drowned in powdered sugar.

A decade after Act One; very early in the morning.

Vada is sitting in her chair, quite still, and oblivious of all around her. She looks much older. Apple enters and addresses the audience. He looks older too, and more distinguished.

APPLE: There's been a lot of tea poured in this room over the years. But not without purpose! My mother never does anything without purpose! . . . Well, never *did* . . . until a while ago . . . about a year ago . . . Sometimes now, if I come in and she doesn't hear me, I find her just sitting there . . . "still." Can you imagine Vada "still?!" It's like this lapse in the Life Force . . . But it's only momentary, and then she's off again on her latest "mission." *(The doorbell rings.)* My sister-in-law, Mary Lou's home on a visit, and she's been summoned to stop by before she leaves town—for coffee, *not tea!* That's significant. It's amazing after what happened in this very room ten years ago, but those two are as thick as thieves.

Vada and Mary Lou enter. Mary Lou has her car keys in her hand and her purse over her shoulder. She's dressed in jeans and a jacket.

VADA: We'll have a quick cup of coffee.
MARY LOU: Very quick! My plane leaves at eight twenty-five . . . *(Not so sure.)* I think . . . *(Opening her purse to look at her ticket.)* I should check.
VADA: Wasn't that a *nice* good-bye party they gave you last night? All your family there—having so much fun—
MARY LOU: Loud!—as usual. Miss Vada, I want to thank you for being so sweet to my parents. They really appreciate it.
VADA: They're fine people! Wonderful grandparents. And your father's osso bucco is *"bellisimo!"* *(Suddenly remembering the tray of beignets.)* Have one of my little beignets. I know you love them.
MARY LOU: If I ate all that sugar this early in the morning, I could fly *myself* to the North Pole.
VADA: I was up at the crack of dawn to make these fresh for you this morning.
MARY LOU: Are you baiting a trap?
VADA: Oh, Mary Lou!

MARY LOU: *(Taking a beignet, eating, and loving it.)* Mmmm!

VADA: *(Pleased that she likes the beignet.)* When are you going to stop running around the world and stay home . . .

MARY LOU: *(Teasing.)* . . . where I belong?

VADA: *(Teasing back.)* That wasn't what I was going to say.

MARY LOU: Oh no?

VADA: No! Stay home and . . .

MARY LOU: . . . settle down?

VADA: *(With feigned exasperation.)* No! Stay home . . . and keep me abreast of the times. You're the only one does that.

MARY LOU: Picture that —Vada Love Powell "abreast of the times."

VADA: You just love to tease me, don't you?

MARY LOU: Yes ma'am. Now go on and tell me . . . What's up?

VADA: I need your help.

MARY LOU: Uh-oh!

VADA: I talked to Mary Ann at the party last night, about the pictures you took of those . . . I know you don't want me to call them "savages."

MARY LOU: *(Enjoying her.)* No, I'd prefer "indigenous peoples."

VADA: You can call them all the fancy names in the world, I still don't see how a nice girl like you ever gets used to living right alongside all those naked bodies . . . breasts swinging . . . privates dangling . . . If there's one thing in God's creation that always seemed to me a sad mistake, it's private parts! *(Mary Lou laughs out loud.)* It's not a laughing matter. In those pictures you sent home, everything's showing! Now, you're the godmother to my grandchildren, and it's my duty to tell you I've seen those innocent little girls "poring" over those pictures!

MARY LOU: *(Teasing again.)* "Poring?"!!!

VADA: Marybell Baxter says her grandson, Georgie, came home and told his mother the Powell girls were showing "dirty" pictures all around the school!

MARY LOU: Oooh, so that's what this is all about.

VADA: I tried to explain to Mary Ann that between those pictures and that poor excuse for "sex" education they get in school, those sweet things are so confused! I know because sometimes they ask me things they won't ask their mother.

MARY LOU: What do you tell them?

VADA: Oh, I'm very modern. Much as I hate it, I bought myself this little book about how babies are made. It's chock-full of all those distressing anatomy terms like . . . *(She finds it distasteful to say the word.)* "vagina." *(Mary Lou bursts out laughing.)* Are you making fun of me?

MARY LOU: No ma'am, I'm not crazy about the word either.

VADA: If there's one word women ought to keep to themselves if they care anything about mystery and romance . . .

MARY LOU: *(Getting her back on track.)* And what did Mary Ann say?

VADA: I don't believe she realizes the consequences of all this. So, Mary Lou, if you could call her before you leave and just explain to her that *we* think . . .

MARY LOU: No, we don't!

VADA: What?

MARY LOU: Miss Vada, those people *exist*, that's the way they dress!

VADA: *Dress?!* That's an overstatement if I ever heard one.

MARY LOU: Do you really think it hurts our little girls to look at pictures of the human body?

VADA: If they look for the wrong reason, I do! . . . You may be an anthropologist, but those children are just normal! They don't have their doctorates in anything but curiosity. And we have to be careful they aren't curious about things they can't handle.

MARY LOU: What things?

VADA: Those people in your pictures, I felt ashamed for them.

MARY LOU: *They're* not ashamed. They're the purest people on earth. Looking at pictures of them couldn't hurt anybody.

VADA: Mary Lou, even Adam and Eve covered themselves up! Thank God, or we'd have to ban the Bible.

MARY LOU: Now, come on, Miss Vada, you love the museum. How do you deal with Greek sculpture?

VADA: I stand way back, and remind myself it's only marble . . . and I feel so sorry for them if their "bits" have been broken off.

MARY LOU: *(Teasing unmercifully.)* And what about those cute little Renaissance cupids?

VADA: *(Teasing back.)* I just thank the Lord they're not full-grown! Furthermore, that's art, and art's beautiful. Those pictures of yours are real life!

MARY LOU: Which is *not* beautiful?!

VADA: There you go again!

MARY LOU: Look, Miss Vada, here's my suggestion. Why don't you sit down with Annie and Loulie and look at the pictures together. Talk about them.

VADA: We've already done that.

MARY LOU: Oh! And what did you say?

VADA: I reminded them of Adam and Eve in the Garden of Eden, and how God made their bodies the way they were, male and female, different . . . Then He gave them fig leaves to cover themselves up.

MARY LOU: No he didn't and you know it!

VADA: Mary Lou, those little children aren't ready for the doctrine of original sin.

MARY LOU: Neither am I. Look, much as I love you, I can't help you with this. It's a different world out there, Miss Vada. Think how fast the earth's spinning right under our feet, it's no wonder we're all a little dizzy. I'm so sorry, I've got to go. Mama's home waiting to drive to the airport.

VADA: Aren't you ever going to settle down?

MARY LOU: I'm not finished sowing my wild oats!

VADA: Mary Lou, only men do that!

MARY LOU: Not these days.

VADA: Mary Lou! . . . Why don't you get yourself a nice beau like Apple?

MARY LOU: I have a beau . . . *(Hesitating.)* a . . . friend. We work together.

VADA: Is he going to ask you to marry him?

MARY LOU: I doubt it. He's a great scholar, and he's married to his work.

VADA: I don't care what he is, you can't give him your favors, if he doesn't have the right intentions.

MARY LOU: *(Smiling.)* My "favors?"

VADA: Dear God, don't tell me you believe in free love!

MARY LOU: Is there any other kind? What do you believe in, Miss Vada? "Duty" love? I've got to go! *(She kisses Vada on the cheek, and starts out with Vada following.)*

VADA: Why don't you bring your friend home with you next time . . . Let me talk to him! *(Vada comes back into the room, and starts to clear the coffee and beignets. She suddenly feels weak, and has to sit down. In her stillness, the lights dim, and the room is drowned in shadows, which again evoke a different reality—the internal workings of Vada's mind. And again music underscores the scene. After a moment Mr. Powell emerges from the shadows.)*

MR. POWELL: Miss Love, may I be of some assistance?

VADA: Oh, no thank you, Mr. Powell, I'm just waiting.

MR. POWELL: For someone, Miss Love?

VADA: No sir, just waiting . . .

MR. POWELL: And that makes you anxious?

VADA: No. I just have time on my hands for . . . questions.

MR. POWELL: I don't remember you as someone who cared much for questions.

VADA: I didn't . . . not then. Now there're so much I want to know.

The music changes to a twenties waltz.

MR. POWELL: *(Offering his hand.)* May I have this dance, Miss Love?

VADA: *(Taking his hand and getting up.)* It would be my pleasure. *(They waltz together nicely, obviously enjoying one another.)*

MR. POWELL: I declare, you're as light as air.

VADA: Thank you, sir.

MR. POWELL: You three Love sisters—the loveliest young ladies in Vicksburg. One prettier than the other! I was quite taken with your oldest sister, May, before you came of age.

VADA: Why didn't you marry May?

MR. POWELL: My heart was set on you, Miss Love.

VADA: Why didn't you tell me?

MR. POWELL: *(Avoiding her question.)* And you, my dear, what were your feelings for me?

VADA: Mama said a lady keeps her feelings to herself! A lady cultivates her very own kind of personal charm! And that's what I tried to do, Mr. Powell.

MR. POWELL: That's what you *did*, Miss Love! You were never one to want charm, or . . .

VADA: Or what?

MR. POWELL: Vitality! I was quite taken with your vitality. You just grabbed at life!

VADA: Mama taught us not to "grab" at anything. *(Vada suddenly stops dancing, and has to sit down.)* I'm sorry, you'll have to excuse me, Mr. Powell, I find myself a little indisposed. They told me at the Ochsner Clinic I had this little heart problem, but I'm not going to let it change my life.

MR. POWELL: Did you ever wonder what you could have done if you hadn't had to use up all that life on me?

VADA: I have no regrets about my life, if that's what you mean.

MR. POWELL: A life without regrets is a lie, Miss Love. Is there something you wanted to ask me?

VADA: I can't find the words.

MR. POWELL: Not you! At a loss for words?

VADA: Not yet . . . not now . . .

MR. POWELL: Well, don't wait too long.

VADA: No sir.

MR. POWELL: I'll be here when you need me.

VADA: Thank you. *(Mr. Powell starts to exit. For an instant Vada's lost in thought. Then she calls him back. Urgently.)* Mr. Powell!

MR. POWELL: What is it, dear?

VADA: May I ask you a favor?

MR. POWELL: Yes ma'am.

VADA: Would you say my name?

MR. POWELL: Vada . . . my darling Vada . . .

Mr. Powell exits, the music fades, and Vada remains lost in her reveries. After a moment or two, she gets up and takes the coffee off to the kitchen. When she's gone Apple enters.

APPLE: Mother!

VADA: *(Off.)* Yoohoo . . .

APPLE: Mother, why was Mary Lou over here so early? I saw her car in the driveway. If it's about those damn photographs . . .

VADA: *(Entering.)* Appleton Powell, are you spying on me? Just because you live next door . . .

APPLE: Mother, I need to talk to you.

VADA: Well, why don't we sit down? Or I could make you some pecan waffles.

APPLE: I don't want any pecan waffles.

VADA: Then, have one of these beignets Mary Lou barely touched.

APPLE: No thank you. Mother, it's about Mary Ann.

VADA: Oh, dear God! I was afraid of that. I've been waiting for something to happen between you and Mary Ann.

APPLE: Nothing's happened between me and Mary Ann.

VADA: Now, Apple, you know I'm always on your side. I don't blame you.

APPLE: No, Mother, I blame you!

VADA: *(Not at first taking in what he just said.)* But I do try to see both sides before I choose yours . . . What did you say?

APPLE: *(Clearly angry.)* I blame you!

VADA: Would you care to tell me what I'm accused of? According to Mary Ann!

APPLE: Mary Ann isn't the one who's accusing you. *I* am!

VADA: *(Dismissing it.)* You wouldn't accuse your own mother, and whatever it is, we know Mary Ann doesn't mean it. You're just putty in her hands . . .

APPLE: Goddamit, Mother! Will you please just shut up and listen to me?!

VADA: What did you say?

APPLE: I'm sorry.

VADA: You should be sorry! I've never in my life heard you use that kind of language, and I *always* listen to you.

APPLE: Well, you better listen to me now! I don't know what you said to her last night, but I've never seen her so upset.

VADA: I told her she was wrong to let our little girls take those . . . "suggestive" pictures to school.

APPLE: You had no right to do that!

VADA: She understood.

APPLE: No, she didn't! She just didn't want to cross you, with everybody there for Mary Lou's good-bye dinner. She's always deferring to you, Mother, and you never say anything kind or complimentary to her *ever!*

VADA: That's not . . . that's simply not true! Everybody knows how proud I am of my daughter-in-law.

APPLE: *She* doesn't!

VADA: I'm very fond of Mary Ann. She's a wonderful mother!

APPLE: Then why are you always telling her what do about the children? Mary Ann has a right to raise her children *her* way. And you have no right to interfere.

VADA: I never interfere, Apple, I intervene! I just want to save those sweet things from a lot of gossip and giggles. I only want what's best for them.

APPLE: How do you always know what's best, Mother, for everybody else?!

VADA: Well, I'm sorry, but right is right!

APPLE: No ma'am. Right is what *you* think it is—the rest of the world is wrong! . . . I want to warn you, Mother, if you so much as mention those photographs to the girls . . .

VADA: *(For the first time blazing back at him.)* I would never, never hurt those precious children. They're mine too, you know.

APPLE: No, they're not! They're Mary Ann's children! They're my children!

VADA: I see . . . Well, I should tell you, Apple, I've already . . .

APPLE: No! Don't tell me anything else. I don't want to hear it. *(Starting out.)* I'm late at the courthouse . . .

VADA: But, Apple, I've . . .

APPLE: Not now, Mother! No more!!

He goes, and the lights go out on the scene.

Scene Two

The same. The table is now set for tea, but not quite as elaborately as in Act One.

Afternoon of the same day.

Enid and Marybell have arrived for tea. The tea has been poured, and Enid is reading a letter while the other two remain remarkably silent, and steal glances at one another. All three look a great deal older than they did, but it's Enid who's been hardest hit by the aging process: She has moments of obvious disorientation and distress. This condition is the sad cause of their meeting this afternoon. Apple enters, but they are, of course, oblivious of him.

APPLE: As Vada would say, "Be careful what you pray for, your prayers may be answered!" . . . I finally told my beloved mother off, but I didn't enjoy it one bit . . . Why did I wait till she got so old? *(After a beat.)* Even absolute monarchs age! Absolutely! The whole Tree-House Gang has grown *old*. There's something very sad and very grand about them, sitting there, trying to work out the large problems of their little lives. And, Vada, dear Vada, is still leading the pack. Of course, *she's* the one who called this "summit" about the . . . "unrest" in the Women's Guild of her beloved Episcopal Church.

Enid finishes reading the letter, folds it carefully and puts it on the table.

ENID: Did we say our opening prayer?

MARYBELL: *(Very sweetly.)* Enid dear, remember now, we're not here for a meeting.

VADA: Yes dear, we had the meeting day before yesterday.

ENID: The meeting is now called to order!

Vada and Marybell just look at one another.

VADA: Well, let's get down to business. What about the letter?

ENID: Ignore it! They're obviously rabble-rousers. I think one of them's from New York.

MARYBELL: *(Sticky sweet with compassion.)* They mean well, Enid. They all have little children, some of them work. And poor things, they always look *so tired!*

VADA: *(Disgusted.)* Marybell, that's exactly the kind of talk that drags Western civilization down! Are the Chinese "tired?" Do you hear about the Japanese being "tired?" But our young people, they're all "so tired." It's become a national disease, and I for one refuse to catch it!

MARYBELL: All very well and good for you, Vada, but those young women are going to resign if we don't do something.

ENID: Where *is* everybody? Hattie never misses Guild. And Gladys . . .

VADA: Enid, will you listen to me for a minute? We're *not* having a meeting of the Guild this afternoon.

MARYBELL: You remember, we had one day before yesterday, and the young people walked out. *(She points to the letter.)*

VADA: Marybell, will you let me handle this . . .

ENID: Now don't you two start.

MARYBELL: Go ahead, handle it! Who's stopping you?

ENID: You know, girls, one of the reasons we're losing members is the way you two keep interrupting all the time. If I can't keep my two best friends in line . . .

VADA: Everybody interrupted everybody, in the good old days.

MARYBELL: Well, things have changed, Vada! It's not the same anymore.

VADA: Thank you, Marybell Baxter, for those words of wisdom!

ENID: But we mustn't let the Guild go downhill, just because the rest of the world is! That's why I'm willing to remain on as president. What would have happened if St. Peter had given up! And look what he had to contend with. Every time I think about the twelve apostles, I can just smell the fish! . . . All those unwashed robes stinking of fish!

VADA: *There's* the problem! *Every* meeting—*all* that rambling! *(Enid stands, and starts to leave the room.)* Enid, where are you going?

It's obvious now that Enid's lost complete track of things.

ENID: The meeting's adjourned.

VADA: No, it's not.

ENID: Well, I have to go . . .

VADA: To the bathroom?

Enid is totally confused by the question. Marybell gets up and goes to her.

MARYBELL: *(Whispering.)* You don't need to go potty, do you?

ENID: I don't think so.

MARYBELL: Well, why don't we sit back down? *(Marybell tries to help her back to her chair, but Enid shrugs her off, and seems to come back to herself completely.)*

VADA: Shall we have a sweet to settle the stomach? *(Passing the tray.)* Pennies from heaven? Mille-spice squares? I ground every single spice myself!

MARYBELL: You know, every time I eat sweets these days, I commence to feel dizzy. I guess it'll be diabetes next.

ENID: Oh, don't worry about diabetes. I've lived with mine for fifteen years. I take my little pill every morning, then I eat my sweets—in moderation, of course! Moderation is the seat of wisdom!

VADA: Says who?

ENID: The Greeks.

VADA: I thought they said wisdom came from suffering.

MARYBELL: Then I ought to be an oracle, after all I've been through.

VADA: Don't start, Marybell. We're not here to discuss your multitude of miseries. We all have our problems at this age. Some of us just don't choose to talk about them all the time.

MARYBELL: I'll forgive you for that, Vada, because *(Gloating over it.)* there'll come a day when you'll get good and sick like the rest of us, and then you'll see. *(Sweetly.)* Enid, have you noticed any changes in yourself recently?

ENID: Nothing but changes!

VADA: Maybe they're telling you something.

ENID: They're telling me you're jealous. Always have been. You'd just love to be president.

MARYBELL: *(Trying hard to get through to her.)* Enid, have you seen your doctor lately?

ENID: He's your doctor too.

MARYBELL: Well, he tells me you haven't.

ENID: That's none of his business. Bud spent enough money on doctors. That's what's so terrible! It costs too much to die.

MARYBELL: I know honey, I know . . . But haven't you noticed how forgetful you're getting? Remember how the firemen had to break down your door, and the key was right down your bosom the whole time.

VADA: I telephoned you last week, Enid, and you said you weren't in.

ENID: That's not so stupid.

MARYBELL: Dr. Delmar warned *me* to be on the lookout for things like that. There may not be enough oxygen getting to the brain.

VADA: And ever since Bud died, you don't eat right, we all know that.

ENID: You think I'm getting senile. That's what you think.

VADA: We don't think anything, except you're getting too forgetful to run the Guild anymore. Those young women are not going to come, if a bunch of old ladies ramble on, and forget to call the meeting to order.

ENID: I didn't forget to call any meeting to order!

MARYBELL: Yes, you did. We went right on sipping sherry for well over an hour before Father Marshall had to tell you to begin.

The telephone rings, and Apple comes onto the side of the stage with a phone in his hand. Vada gets up, and goes to answer her phone.

VADA: Now, who's that? *(Talking to the phone as she crosses to it.)* All right . . . all right . . . *(Picking up the receiver.)* Hello.

APPLE: This is Apple.

VADA: I know who it is.

APPLE: Are Annie and Loulie at your house?

VADA: Of course not! They're at school.

APPLE: They're not at school, Mother.

VADA: Then where are they?

APPLE: If I knew, I wouldn't be calling you.

VADA: Did you call the police?

APPLE: Yes ma'am.

VADA: Oh, dear God!

APPLE: Now don't get yourself all upset. Mary Ann's looking for them.

VADA: What happened?

APPLE: I don't know. Mary Ann didn't have time to tell me.

VADA: Poor thing. She must be crazy with worry.

APPLE: Soon as I hear something, I'll call you.

VADA: We'll pray, Apple. Enid and Marybell are here—we'll put our prayers together . . .

APPLE: Then we know it'll be all right, don't we? Bye, Mother. *(Apple exits with his phone, but Vada doesn't hang hers up right away. There's a moment of hushed silence in the room.)*

MARYBELL: What is it, Vada dear?

VADA: The twins have run away from school. That was Apple wanting to know if they were here.

MARYBELL: What happened?

VADA: He didn't know . . . I told him we'd say a little prayer. Enid, as president of the Guild, would you lead us?

ENID: *(With great reverence.)* Let us bow our heads in prayer . . . *(And they do.)* Dear God, please hear us in this, our hour of need. We know Thou wast the One who said, "Suffer the little children to come unto me." But not so soon, dear Lord. Those little girls need to grow up to be workers in Thy vineyard. Wherefore, we pray Thee, send them back to us, Lord, and let us prepare them for Thy Kingdom. We ask this in Christ's name. Amen. *(The other two join in the "Amen.")*

MARYBELL: That was beautiful, Enid. Thank you.

VADA: Yes, it was, Enid . . . *(Distraught.)* Please, dear God, keep them safe from harm.

ENID: Now, Vada, listen to me. In my second grade, not a year went by that somebody didn't run off somewhere, and we never lost a one of them. You hold yourself together now, give everybody a little time, they'll turn up.

VADA: *(Very agitated.)* Who else should we call? Maybe I should go over there.

Mary Ann enters.

MARY ANN: *(Before anybody can ask.)* They're all right!

VADA: Thank God!

ENID: I told you.

MARY ANN: Up in their own room the whole time. Slipped right by Henrietta . . .

VADA: Where were you?

MARY ANN: Grocery shopping. The phone rang just as I was coming in the door, and I panicked. I didn't even think to look for them in the house.

VADA: Does Apple know they're safe?

MARY ANN: Yes ma'am, he's with them now. I'm hoping he's going to drive them to dancing school.

VADA: Dancing school?! After what happened?

ENID: *(Warning.)* Vada!

MARYBELL: That's right! It's Wednesday! Little Marybell dances on Wednesdays. Margery and I went to watch a couple of weeks ago, and they looked like potatoes twirling around in toe shoes. All stomach!

MARY ANN: I wanted to come over and talk to you . . .

VADA: Well, for heaven's sake, tell us what happened. Why did they take a notion to come home from school without telling anyone? I hope you're going to punish them.

MARY ANN: *(Sharply.)* No, ma'am. I'm not!

ENID: Don't keep us in suspense any longer.

MARY ANN: *(To Vada, indicating Enid and Marybell.)* I don't know if I should go into it right now.

MARYBELL: Enid, maybe we should be going.

VADA: Why in the world should you be going? It's just two little girls up to some of their shenanigans. Now, Mary Ann, don't be silly. Tell us what happened.

MARY ANN: I'm going to have to say some things . . .

VADA: Well, go on and say them. These are my friends. They'll understand.

MARY ANN: I'm afraid it's your fault, Mother Powell.

ENID: Vada, if this is a personal matter . . .

MARYBELL: Enid's right, Vada.

VADA: No, I'd like you to hear what I've done that's so terrible. Go on, Mary Ann, spit it out!

MARY ANN: All right! *(To Enid and Marybell.)* My sister took photographs of one of the tribes she's been studying, and the girls brought them to school . . .

MARYBELL: Oh, we know all about that, Mary Ann. Georgie came home and told his mother there were dirty pictures of naked people all over the place.

MARY ANN: Miss Marybell, they weren't dirty pictures . . .

VADA: *(Interrupting.)* Marybell, that's what I've been trying to explain . . .

MARY ANN: Mother Powell, why didn't you . . .

ENID: *(Interrupting.)* I couldn't believe it when Marybell called and told me the people in the pictures were stark naked!

VADA: Now, Enid, that's the way those people *dress.* The point is little children shouldn't be looking at them.

ENID: Stark naked?! I should say not! They might as well go down to the bus station, and buy one of those dirty magazines. Gladys told me they've got filthy pictures right in the middle, fold out like a map, made her sick to her stomach.

MARYBELL: How come Gladys got to see them?

ENID: Now, how would I know that, Marybell?

MARY ANN: Mother Powell, why didn't you tell me last night you talked to Annie and Loulie about the pictures?

VADA: I was too shocked to hear you didn't agree with me.

MARY ANN: And you said nothing to Apple this morning.

VADA: I tried to, but he walked out on me.

MARY ANN: Yesterday, when the teacher heard all the giggling out on the playground, she took the pictures away, but she planned to use them today in her section on Worlds and Peoples.

VADA: Dear God, she was going to show them in class?!

ENID: Who is their teacher, dear?

MARYBELL: Jane Bilderback.

ENID: Hilda Bilderback's child?

VADA: For God's sake, Enid, there's only one Bilderback family in this town!

ENID: Well, I've heard that young woman is a fine teacher.

MARY ANN: Even if she shows "dirty" pictures?!

ENID: Teachers make mistakes, Mary Ann. One little fellow in *my* second grade took out his "dingle," right in the middle of the Pledge of Allegiance—I noticed because he didn't have his hand over his heart—and I just said, at the end of 'liberty and justice for all,' "Young man, that's a very nice thing you have there, but you better put it up, so nobody steals it." Of course, the word got back to the mothers, and there was a big brouhaha, but it eventually blew over.

VADA: Are you quite finished, Enid? Go on, Mary Ann.

MARY ANN: The minute the teacher took out the photos, the giggling started up again, and before she could say a word about them, Annie and Loulie burst into tears. They said *you* told them the pictures were bad, and they should be ashamed to bring them to school. She couldn't get them to stop crying, so she sent them down to the nurse's office. But it seems they never got there—they ran home instead.

VADA: Mary Ann, you know I wouldn't do anything to hurt our little girls.

MARY ANN: But you did hurt them, Mother Powell! They're still crying, and they don't want to go back to school tomorrow.

MARYBELL: Now, Mary Ann, you know how children make a big fuss over nothing, and then forget about it in a minute. Yesterday Little Marybell cried her eyes out when she spilled her cream of wheat, and two minutes later she was dancing the Sugar Plum Fairy all over my couch.

VADA: Marybell, this is not about cream of wheat, this is about right and wrong . . . Mary Ann, I can't conceal my distress that you and I disagree. Disagreement's so bad for the children!

MARY ANN: Why? I think it's good for the children!

VADA: You mean those indecent photographs . . .

MARY ANN: *I* don't think they're indecent. The teacher doesn't think they're indecent . . .

ENID: I don't know about that, dear, she may be trying to make the best . . .

MARY ANN: My sister doesn't think they're indecent . . . or she wouldn't have taken them!

VADA: *(To Enid and Marybell.)* But we think they're indecent, don't we?

MARYBELL: Well, I haven't seen them, but if the people are naked . . .

ENID: And the children are titillated by them . . .

MARY ANN: *(Very upset.)* I don't care! I don't want my children to be ashamed of the bodies God gave them! *(There is a silence.)* Look, Mother Powell, you're entitled to your opinion, but I'm entitled to mine. You got to raise Apple your way. I have to raise my children my way. Can't we disagree on some things, and go on trying to respect one another's opinion?

MARYBELL: Yes, Vada, this is a democracy after all.

VADA: Marybell, you are an oracle of platitudes!

MARYBELL: I resent that, Vada, I really do.

ENID: Now, don't you two start in again. We have enough strife in one room.

VADA: All that uncertainty, Mary Ann, it's not good for children. It breeds moral indifference! Everything relative—no absolutes! That's how it all began.

MARY ANN: What began?

VADA: The Decline of the West.

ENID: *(Almost under her breath.)* Talk about oracles.

VADA: I heard that, Enid . . .

MARY ANN: I don't care about the Decline of the West! I care about my children! I don't want them to be ashamed of their bodies! I don't want them to look down on people who're different from them! I don't want them to be afraid of what they don't know! I want them to be brave and loving!

VADA: *(After a beat.)* Mary Ann, I think this is the first time you've ever stood up to me.

MARY ANN: You did a terrible thing, Mother Powell. You told the girls their mother was wrong, and you told them behind my back.

VADA: I just didn't want to hurt your feelings.

MARY ANN: You hurt more than that. You hurt our little girls!

VADA: *(Meaning it.)* I'm sorry . . . I don't know what else to say except I'm sorry.

ENID: Vada Love Powell, I never thought I'd hear you say that.

MARYBELL: I just have to say, Mary Ann, much as I love you and Apple, we think Vada has a lot of right on her side.

ENID: Wait just a minute, Marybell! Personally, I don't know what to think now after hearing Mary Ann. It was beautiful what she said. I don't want our children to be ashamed of their own bodies either.

MARYBELL: Nor do we, Enid, nor do we. We just want people to keep their privates to themselves.

ENID: I don't know about that . . . maybe our whole generation needs to kind of . . . air out down there.

MARYBELL: Next thing we know, Enid, you'll be streaking down Main Street.

VADA: I don't know what to expect anymore. The world has changed *so* much!

MARYBELL: And not for the better, if you ask me!

VADA: Well, if it's not for the better, Marybell, what have we been doing here all these years?

ENID: *(Once again distracted.)* Is that Lij blowing for me?

VADA: What?

ENID: Lij—come to pick me up. I don't drive anymore, you know.

VADA: Nobody's blowing for you, Enid.

ENID: You don't hear that horn?

MARYBELL: Lij would never honk the horn. He always comes to the door.

VADA: He better not honk any horn at my house!

ENID: I have to go.

MARY ANN: Apple can drive you, Miss Enid.

MARYBELL: I drove you over here, honey. Certainly I can drive you home.

ENID: Where's Little Apple this afternoon?

MARY ANN: Right outside on his tricycle.

VADA: You mean to tell me you let that child play in the yard while you . . .

MARY ANN: Henrietta's with him.

VADA: That good-for-nothing. Someone could whisk that child off before you could say Lindbergh.

ENID: You all just don't know how lucky you are. You have children.

VADA: Now, Enid, you have more children than all the rest of us put together. *(To Marybell and Mary Ann.)* You can't walk down the street with her without some burly truck driver yelling out from behind the wheel, "Hey, Miss Enid! Remember me, Cyrus Cranshaw, from second grade!"

ENID: Not any more . . . I have to go home.

VADA: Well, you go on and get a good night's rest. And tomorrow I'm going to start bringing you dinners that'll do you some good. We've got to get some nutrients in that system.

ENID: I couldn't let you do that, Vada.

VADA: You just try and stop me!

MARYBELL: Good-bye, Mary Ann. And Vada, thank you for a lovely tea. We can always count on you for at least a thousand calories. But we love it, right, Enid!

ENID: Yes indeed.

Marybell and Enid finally exit, and Vada and Mary Ann are left alone. There is a strained silence.

MARY ANN: Do you have anything more you need to say? *(Vada just shakes her head.)* I'm really sorry, Mother Powell.

VADA: Well, as Apple says, they're *your* children . . . and I mustn't interfere.

MARY ANN: I wish Apple wouldn't speak for me.

VADA: Then you'll have to speak up for yourself, dear! We'll make our convictions known—even if they're wrong—and we won't make the children suffer for them.

MARY ANN: Mother Powell, can I ask you a favor?

VADA: "May," dear. *"May"* I ask you a favor? *(Mary Ann just looks at her, and she realizes her mistake.)* I'm sorry.

MARY ANN: Please don't correct me in front of your friends.

VADA: When did I . . .

MARY ANN: Just now. About Little Apple playing outside.

VADA: Oh, well, that wasn't a correction. That was just a piece of good advice.

MARY ANN: *(Looking at her again.)* You see?

VADA: It's hard to teach an old dog new tricks.

MARY ANN: Yes ma'am . . . Can I help you clear the tea things?

VADA: No, you go on. I'm not helpless yet, thank God. *(As Vada crosses the room to clear the tea things, she feels a sudden weakness, catches her side, and sinks down onto the sofa.)*

MARY ANN: *(Rushing over to her.)* What's the matter?!

VADA: I lost my footing for a second.

MARY ANN: You look pale, Mother Powell.

VADA: It's just the light. We lose the sun so early this time of year. Now you go on and pick up the girls.

MARY ANN: Yes, ma'am.

VADA: And could you stop by with them for a minute on your way home. I'd like to talk to them . . . I'd like to . . . explain . . .

MARY ANN: I'll drop them off.

VADA: No, I think it'd be better if we were all together this time.

MARY ANN: Yes ma'am. I'll bring the girls.

Mary Ann exits. Vada sits very still for a moment. The lights dim to shadow, and music suggests that other reality in Vada's mind; it continues to underscore the scene.

VADA: *(Calling.)* Mr. Powell . . . *(There is no answer, so she calls more urgently.)* Mr. Powell . . .

MR. POWELL: Yes, my dear?

VADA: I was afraid you wouldn't come.

MR. POWELL: Why was that?

VADA: I'm so ashamed.

MR. POWELL: What are you ashamed of?

VADA: I was wrong.

MR. POWELL: You're ashamed of being wrong?

VADA: Yes sir.

MR. POWELL: It's only human, Vada dear.

VADA: What did you say?

MR. POWELL: It's only human.

VADA: But now I'm on the outside looking in.

MR. POWELL: That's where we always are, Miss Love.

VADA: No! It's not that way with them. I see them looking at each other sometimes when they don't know I'm watching . . . I must confess, Mr. Powell, I feel a little jealous.

MR. POWELL: Of Apple and his wife?

VADA: Sometimes they go to their bedroom in the middle of the day. They tell the children they're taking a nap, and the little girls giggle. I don't know why, but it makes me angry.

MR. POWELL: You find it disturbing.

VADA: I don't know. They argue and fight, and then they make up, and they seem so happy and loving. In the spring, they sit out on the patio talking way into the night. I lie there in my bed listening to them laughing and talking. And I think of us, Mr. Powell.

MR. POWELL: It was different in our day.

VADA: For a man? Or just for a woman?

MR. POWELL: I don't know . . .

VADA: Or just for me?

MR. POWELL: Oh, no, my dear, surely you weren't alone. It was different in our day . . .

VADA: We missed all that, didn't we? *(He begins backing out of the room.)*

MR. POWELL: I'm sorry . . .
VADA: I missed all that.
MR. POWELL: I'm so sorry . . .

Mr. Powell disappears, and Vada comments to herself.

VADA: I should have asked a lot more questions. *(She gets up to clear the tea things, but has to sit back down. Closing her eyes, she sits motionless for a moment, until Apple enters, sees her "lifeless" in the chair, and goes over to her with great concern.)*
APPLE: Mother . . . Mother! Are you all right? *(She opens her eyes.)* Mother, what's the matter?
VADA: Nothing! I must have dozed off.
APPLE: Are you sure you're all right? You're very pale.
VADA: I'm perfectly all right. I had a nice little dream about your father.
APPLE: Mother, I want to apologize . . .
VADA: *(Interrupting him.)* No need. Mary Ann and the girls and I have it all worked out.
APPLE: Mary Ann and you?
VADA: And the girls. We had a little talk this afternoon. Even if we don't agree, we'll tell one another, and the children won't suffer for our mistakes.
APPLE: Well, good for you!
VADA: Apple, I'm sorry for what happened . . .
APPLE: It's not the end of the world. We can all learn from our mistakes. The children love you, Mother, and they are so lucky to have you. I, of all people, know that.
VADA: How was your day?
APPLE: Good! Another big client from New Orleans.
VADA: That's better than good!
APPLE: Mother, Mary Ann called me. She said you didn't look good to her. She's right! You *don't* look good. They warned you when you went through the clinic.
VADA: Shall we have our glass of sherry?
APPLE: *(Crossing to pour the sherry.)* What happened to you this afternoon?
VADA: I had one of my little spells.
APPLE: What kind of spells?
VADA: I just drop off for a minute or two.
APPLE: Just what?
VADA: Drop off, blackout, the blood drains out of me.
APPLE: Oh, my God!
VADA: Apple, there's something I've been meaning to tell you, and this is a good day to do it . . . *(She takes a swallow of the sherry Apple has just handed her.)* I have an arrangement with Dr. Davis. I'm not ever having a bypass! No pacemakers! And I won't take any of their high-powered pills! I want to die like my mother did, and my grandmother before her. God's way!

APPLE: Well, you can't stay here by yourself in this condition. We'll have to get someone to stay with you! Or you'll have to come stay with us!

VADA: Absolutely not! To both!

APPLE: Suppose some morning I walk in here and find you . . .

VADA: Dead on the floor?

APPLE: I don't think this is a good time to talk about this.

VADA: No time is a good time! So everybody keeps silent . . . Now, let me finish. I also have an arrangement with that new nursing home over in Covington. God forbid it's necessary, but I've put aside the money, just in case.

APPLE: You know how that makes me feel. Left out. Why didn't you tell me about this?

VADA: Same reason you didn't tell me when you got married. Because you wouldn't let me do it, would you?!

APPLE: No ma'am.

VADA: And I can't live with your family. I'd destroy something wonderful.

APPLE: I still won't let you do it!

VADA: You have to, Apple! Dying is the last thing I'm going to do with my life, and I want to do it well. You have to see that my wishes are carried out.

APPLE: What if you change your mind?

VADA: Appleton Powell, I ask you, do I *ever* change my mind?! Furthermore, this is not about my mind, it's about my soul! I *believe* in heaven, Apple, and I don't want to be all worn out when I get there.

APPLE: *(After a beat.)* Mother, about this morning, I feel bad, but Mary Ann . . .

VADA: *(Interrupting him.)* I understand, Apple . . . "Therefore shall a man leave his father and mother, and shall cleave unto his wife . . . "

APPLE: Yes, but whither I go, you'll go with me, Mother, you and all your strength sealed in the marrow of my bones. *(There is a moment of silence.)*

VADA: I'm glad! . . . Oh, and Apple, there's one more thing. I want *you* to plan my funeral! There's something so satisfying about a nice funeral . . . I'd like a blanket of pink camellias on a steel grey casket—which will be *closed*, no matter how good I look. *(She begins again to clear the tea things.)* I don't want any overwrought eulogies, no charming anecdotes. Just any Scripture readings *you* choose *(After just an instant of thought.)* "through a glass darkly" or "unless ye be born again" . . .

APPLE: *(Amused and helping her clear.)* That doesn't leave very much for me to do.

VADA: Well, you be on the look out for a good epitaph . . . something from Shakespeare maybe . . . or *The Lives of the Saints* . . .

APPLE: *(Much amused.)* Oh, Mother . . .

VADA: *(Pressing right on.)* Now that's all settled, I can get on with my life! I picked enough figs this morning to put up my preserves. And I promised Little Apple an angel food cake.

APPLE: Mother, I'm afraid I have a confession to make.
VADA: Oh, dear!
APPLE: I'm not wild about fig preserves.
VADA: Don't be silly, Apple! You *love* fig preserves!

She exits with the tea things, and Apple follows her—with a knowing glance to the audience— as the lights go out on the scene.

END OF PLAY

Bridgette Wimberly

SAINT LUCY'S EYES

A PLAY IN TWO ACTS

Ruby Dee and Willis Burks II in *Saint Lucy's Eyes* by Bridgette Wimberly, 2001.
Photo © by Martha Holmes.

Author's Note

As a girl, the statue of Saint Lucy in the church connected to my elementary school frightened me until I stepped back and reevaluated the pair of eyes lying on her plate. Eyes I once found judging now looked forgiving. I was inspired to do a play exploring judgment; the law and judgment, forgiveness and judgment, sin and judgment, judgment by others and self-judgment. I wanted to explore the process of forgiveness, a woman who had to reevaluate a pair of eyes watching her.

I would like to dedicate this play to Julia Miles and the Women's Project, Billie Allen, and Ruby Dee. They made my first professional experience as a produced playwright a memorable and moving one and taught me what it meant to collaborate on a play, to get in the trenches, and to stick it out. I will never be able to express what this experience has meant to me, nor thank them enough for what they have given me.

—Bridgette Wimberly

Saint Lucy's Eyes was originally developed by The Cherry Lane Alternative under the artistic direction of Angelina Fiordelissi. It received its world premiere at the Women's Project & Productions (Julia Miles, Artistic Director; Patricia Taylor, Managing Director) in New York City on March 28, 2001. It was directed by Billie Allen; the set design was by Beowulf Borritt, lighting design by Jane Reisman, costume design by Alvin B. Perry, original music and sound by Michael Wimberly; the production manager was B.D. White and the production stage manager was Susan D. Lange. The cast was as follows:

OLD WOMAN	Ruby Dee
YOUNG WOMAN	Toks Olagundoye
BAY	Willis Burks II
WOMAN	Sally A. Stewart

CASTING

YOUNG WOMAN, a very fresh, naive young woman of seventeen dressed in modest clothing in the play's beginning who progresses to a sophisticated well-dressed lawyer of about thirty.

OLD WOMAN, a middle-age woman about fifty to sixty who will age to sixty to seventy at play's end.

BAY, a middle-aged man.

WOMAN, a young woman, somewhere in her twenties. She is more sophisticated than the Young Woman (i.e., she may smoke, wear her hair dyed, dress flashy).

SETS

ACT ONE

A small tenement apartment. We see a worn easy chair adjacent an old black-and-white TV with a coat hanger as an antenna on top. There is a large table center stage with a couple of chairs at this table. We see a couple of doors. One leads to a rest room, the other to the hall outside and there is another opening with a curtain covering it that leads to the kitchen, which is just visible through the split in the curtain. There is a sofa bed in the corner of the room. There is a wooden folding table, folded against the wall or the kitchen window can be extended. We see a large window with a fire escape behind it. It is raining very hard. The room is dimly lit by a few lamps. Periodic thunder can be heard and lightning can be seen illuminating the window. There is music in this act. Popular rhythm and blues hits can be heard faintly.

ACT TWO, SCENE ONE

A room in the Lorraine Motel in 1980. The hotel has fallen into disrepair and is used as a transient motel.

ACT TWO, SCENE TWO

A prison interview room. We see a large table with a couple of chairs. Windows with bars on them. Periodic thunder can be heard and lightning can be seen illuminating the window.

ACT ONE

Scene One

The time is April 3, 1968, in Memphis, Tennessee, in a small tenement apartment.

As the curtain rises, we see two women. The younger woman is standing with her overcoat on. The much older woman is at the table stringing string beans.

YOUNG WOMAN: *(Clutching her coat.)* It's been raining all day.

OLD WOMAN: *(Stringing beans, she nods affirmatively.)* All day. Gonna rain all night.

YOUNG WOMAN: I hate it when it rains. It's dark and dreary. Sad and lonely.

OLD WOMAN: I've had some of my best times on a dark rainy night.

YOUNG WOMAN: Not me. There's something spooky about the night and I've always hated thunder and lightning.

OLD WOMAN: I'm not talking about sitting at home with a cat and a good book. Suppose you ain't been with somebody special? Somebody make all that thunder and big old lightning go away. The rain could be pouring down cats, dogs, rats, and roaches . . . you with the right somebody . . . like a sunny day on the beach, yes ma'am. All curled up cozy. I can remember some beautiful rainy nights. *(Stops stringing beans and walks toward kitchen.)* Had myself a ball. So did he.

YOUNG WOMAN: Who? Who are you talking about?

OLD WOMAN: I don't know who child. Can't remember who. Besides I never kiss and tell. I tell you this though, he was something fine. With a pocket full of dollar bills. That's the one thing that can turn a perfect rainy evening ugly . . . a broke man. *(Shaking her head.)* Ain't got two quarters to rub together. Can't spend nothing but the evening. Remember, you heard it here first. Show me the money or you won't see no honey. Speaking of money. Did you bring it?

YOUNG WOMAN: Yes.

OLD WOMAN: The whole fifty?

YOUNG WOMAN: *(Clutching her coat.)* Fifty dollars. That's what you asked for. Fifty dollars.

OLD WOMAN: Well I have to ask honey. Don't take it personal. Some of these girls come up in here think I take credit. Come in here all they got is twenty, twenty-five dollars. *(Stands and crosses around to the Young Woman.)* This ain't Petries. I ain't got no lay-a-way plan. This is cash and carry operation here. You hear what I'm saying?

YOUNG WOMAN: *(Gives an envelope to the Old Woman.)* Yes ma'am. I brought the fifty. The whole fifty. Just like you asked.

OLD WOMAN: *(Takes the envelope from the Young Woman, counts the money, and puts it in her bra.)* You sure have child. The whole fifty. Well take your coat off and hang it up over there. *(She motions to the coat hooks on UR wall. The Young Woman hesitates.)* That is if you plan on staying. Can't nobody accuse me of kidnapping nobody. You free to go anytime you please. But it's still gonna cost you the fifty. My time. You gotta pay for my time. Somebody else could of used it. It's all about economy. That's what's wrong with colored folks today. Why we take two steps forward and fall half a mile backward. Don't know nothing' 'bout no business. *(Moves to the SL side of the table and picks up the bowl and pot of beans; then walks DL toward the kitchen.)* You have to excuse me. You came a little earlier than I planned and I gotta get my old man's supper on. I didn't think you were coming, way it's been raining. *(Exits into the kitchen. The Young Woman looks about the room clutching her coat, then walks to the front door.)* Like in the Bible, forty days and forty nights. *(Reentering from the kitchen and crosses toward the Young Woman.)* You ain't got your coat off yet? What you hidin' under there? *(Grabbing the Young Woman.)* Let me see. Let me see. You ain't hiding no buffalo are you?

Moving away from Old Woman, her coat comes off in Old Woman's hand.

YOUNG WOMAN: No! No! I ain't hiding nothing. I'm just cold that's all. I'm cold.

OLD WOMAN: Well honey, I have to ask. Don't take it personal. *(The Young Woman takes it and hangs it on the wall coat hook.)* Some of these girls come up in here look like they trying to hide a whole herd of buffalo up under there. Think I'm suppose to do a roundup and perform rodeo tricks I guess.

YOUNG WOMAN: *(As she returns to her chair SR of table.)* I'm just cold that's all. And I hate it when it rains. I hate it when it rains. I just hate it.

OLD WOMAN: Well, don't have no tantrum up in here gal. Won't do you no good. Life's a natural born bitch. Seems you get more things you hate than those you like. I know it's been that way for me anyway. *(Thunder rumbles in the distance. The Young Woman jumps and crosses down to the SR chair. The Old Woman crosses US of the table to the Young Woman.)* Woo! We as jumpy as a kitten. Just some thunder. *(Walking over to comfort and to get her to sit down.)* Just some thunder child.

YOUNG WOMAN: When I was younger, on rainy nights like this, I would curl up in mama and papa's bed. *(Wrapping her arms around herself.)* Right between them. I'd feel so safe. Like nothing could ever touch me. It wouldn't matter how loud the thunder got or how much lightning lit up the sky because I knew they wouldn't let anything harm me.

OLD WOMAN: *(Sitting in the chair SL of the table.)* Safe huh?

YOUNG WOMAN: Yes.

OLD WOMAN: I know what you mean. Everybody need to feel safe. That's how my old man makes me feel. He ain't much to look at. Broken down old thing. Hardworking though. Give me his left eye if I couldn't see out my right one. *(Beat as she comforts the Young Woman.)* Sounds like your mama and papa love you.

YOUNG WOMAN: Yes. I thought Tyrone loved me too.

OLD WOMAN: Tyrone? If that ain't a players name, I pray for lying.

YOUNG WOMAN: Guess he didn't. Love me I mean. Told me I was going to hold him back. He had plans all of a sudden. Big plans. He didn't want to be married. Not to me, not to anybody. He wanted to go to college. So he went and joined the army for the GI bill.

OLD WOMAN: Vietnam!

YOUNG WOMAN: *(Nods.)* He sent me a letter with your address and phone number and fifty dollars in it.

OLD WOMAN: Sound like he sent somebody here before?

YOUNG WOMAN: I don't know. I don't think so.

OLD WOMAN: You still love him? *(The Young Woman shrugs her shoulders. Then shakes her head negatively.)* If you want, I can put some hoodoo on him for you. Cost you another twenty-five, but it will be worth it. I'll have him barking at the moon and chasing cars. *(The Young Woman smiles and shakes her head negatively.)* Well at least I got a smile out of you. Hell, maybe he'll get his worthless butt blown up over there in Vietnam. That'll make him wish he stayed here and did right by you. Course don't listen to me. I ain't got no kinda heart for cowards. *(Exits into the kitchen for a stack of newspaper sections.)*

YOUNG WOMAN: This isn't going to hurt is it?

OLD WOMAN: *(Reenters with several newspaper sections.)* Honey, everything hurts, eventually. Eat too much cake, you get a belly ache. *(Laying out the sections to cover the top of the table.)* Spend too much money, you go broke. Drink too much good whiskey, you get a hangover. Love a man when you shouldn't, well.

YOUNG WOMAN: I'm just scared.

OLD WOMAN: Every young gal and some not so young come up in here scared. Some been in here three, four times before. *(Finishes laying down the sections of paper over the tabletop.)* Course I can understand if it's an occupational thing. You can only be so careful 'for the odds catch up with you. But some of these girls ain't working girls and I see them more times than I should. Stupid. And stupid scares me. I can go to jail for what I do. *(Crosses ULC to the front door, opens it, looks out and closes it and locks it; then crosses RC to the window to look out; and crosses to the DL corner of the bed.)* And when you so stupid that the first time don't learn you not to have a second time, I don't want to see you no more. Now I need the money, but stupid people do a lot of stupid things. Like open they big stupid mouth to the wrong stupid people. Get me thrown in jail 'cause of some stupid heffa couldn't keep her stupid legs or her stupid mouth shut. Now while you're here, you're welcome. I ain't gonna force you to do nothing you don't want to do. You can think of me as Grandma. Fact, that's what many call me. But I'm only your grandma while you're here. And when you walk out that door, you a orphan. I don't know you. You don't know me. I ain't never laid a eye on you before. Is that clear?

YOUNG WOMAN: Yes.

OLD WOMAN: Yes what?

YOUNG WOMAN: Yes Grandma. (*A tea kettle can be heard whistling in the distance.*)

OLD WOMAN: Well there goes the kettle. I guess we can get started. (*The Old Woman stands and heads for the kitchen. Reenters and crosses UR of the SL chair.*) Go and remove your underwear and stockings in the bathroom there, and cover yourself with that sheet.

YOUNG WOMAN: (*Standing.*) My underwear?

OLD WOMAN: Yes child. How you expect me to get to it? Go head. This ain't gonna be no day at the beach. But I ain't the bogey man. This a teach you be scared of men bringing flowers and a whole lot of promises and baby I love yous, but no ring. Men want to go to college and got big plans and you ain't got nothing' but a hard way to go. Remember you heard it here first. Show me the ring, or you won't see no thing.

YOUNG WOMAN: (*Upset and confused.*) Go where? Go where?

OLD WOMAN: (*Pointing toward the bathroom.*) The bathroom child. Over there. Over there. (*Young Woman exits DL behind screen.*) And don't take all day. I gotta get my old man's supper on. He's a hardworking man, don't ask for much. Love him some string beans and white potatoes. He got high blood, so I try not to use too much fat back. (*Continues talking, as she crosses to DR wall, shifts a picture in order to access a jar of money from a hole in the wall behind the picture; takes the jar DR and sits on the DL corner of the bed. She takes the money from her bra, looks back toward the bathroom, then stuffs the money in the jar, and puts the jar back into the hole in the wall.*) His favorite dish peach cobbler. Man love his some of my cobbler. I'm telling you. Right now he out playing poker. Gambling. That's his contribution to the war on poverty. Um. Least that's what he expect me to believe. He gambles hours. So he'll be late tonight. But I still gotta get you out of here, 'for I have to listen to his mouth. Make tonight's storm sound like a pea drop in a bucket. Lord knows I got all the headache I need for a lifetime. (*The lights flicker and thunder is heard in the distance. The Young Woman comes out from the bathroom behind the folding screen. She is wrapped in a sheet and tip toes DR of the recliner.*) Oh! You startled me. I thought you were still in the bathroom there. (*Crosses DL of the table.*) You like some little cat sneakin' around here. What you sneaking around for?

YOUNG WOMAN: I thought somebody was out here. I heard music.

OLD WOMAN: Oh Lord. That's that woman upstairs. She play her music loud enough for everybody and I can't stand a lot of noise. She get her electricity from off the lights in the hall. Always blowing the fuse. 'Specially on nights like this when it's raining. (*Gets a knife from the drawer on the SR side of the table.*) She know this old raggedy building can't take this overload. Stupid.

Stupid people scares me. *(Crosses UC to the water/steam pipes in the corner US of the front door.)* Seem to me if you gonna boot-leg you some electricity, you do it on the Q-T and not play all that boogie-woogie loud ass music. *(Shouting toward the ceiling and banging on the pipe with the knife.)* Hey, hey! Some people ain't got the brains they was born with. I swear I got to move out of here. Tomorrow wouldn't be too soon. *(Walks back to kitchen table and puts the knife back into the table drawer. The Young Woman watches her looking scared to death.)* Get me some place peaceful and nice. Somewhere that's mine. Somewhere I own. Paper got my name on it. That ain't too much to ask nobody for. Don't wanna be one of those people, whole life ain't owned neither pot to piss or window to throw. *(Points upward, then to the Young Woman.)* You understand what I'm sayin'? *(Crossing toward the Young Woman.)* Well lets hope we don't have no trouble tonight. You want a drink of whiskey 'for we start?

YOUNG WOMAN: No. Thank you.

OLD WOMAN: It's covered in the fifty honey. As bug-eyed as you are, I'll throw in an extra shot on the house. Like I said, this ain't gonna be no day at the beach. But it ain't gonna blow you mind neither. You ain't the first, you won't be the last. I ain't trying to scare you none. But I have to tell you. You gonna wish you found something better to do with your night then visit with old Grandma here. A drink or two always makes things a little easier.

YOUNG WOMAN: My papa always said whiskey was the way of the devil.

OLD WOMAN: Your papa said? Well listen to old grandma here. *(Crossing LC to the shelves and picks up a bottle of whiskey and two shot glasses and crosses US of table and puts the whiskey bottle and shot glasses down on the table.)* Ain't nothing wrong with a little help when you need it. Besides, I know you don't always listen to dear papa or we wouldn't be making our acquaintance here tonight. Would we, miss do-everything-her-papa-say?

YOUNG WOMAN: *(Shyly.)* No.

OLD WOMAN: Say what?

YOUNG WOMAN: *(Louder.)* No.

OLD WOMAN: Um hummm. Whiskey is the way of the devil. Well, I ain't the only one with horns and a tail in here. Are you drinking or not?

YOUNG WOMAN: I'll have just a little whiskey. Thank you.

OLD WOMAN: That's better. I'll pour us both a drink. *(Pours two drinks.)* I work better after a taste or two. There we go. *(Puts a glass in front of the Young Woman, who sits in the SL chair at the table.)* Now drink it . . . slow. *(Shifts the SR chair to the US side of the table and sits.)* You don't want to choke yourself. *(Pours and sips her drink.)*

YOUNG WOMAN: *(Takes glass and swallows all of the whiskey at once.)* Oh, this stuff's like fire! *(Coughs.)*

OLD WOMAN: Listen to yourself. I told you to sip it. You throwing it back like a pro. My mama always said a hard head make a sore ass. And I can amen that.

There is a sudden burst of lightning seen in the window followed by a loud thunderbolt. The Young Woman drops to the floor screaming and crawls under the table.

YOUNG WOMAN: Ahhhhh! It's the Lord. It's the Lord. It's the Lord.

OLD WOMAN: What's wrong with you? You gonna get me thrown out of here. Will you calm yourself down. *(Lightning is seen again in the window followed by another thunder bolt.)*

YOUNG WOMAN: It's the Lord. It's the Lord.

OLD WOMAN: What's the Lord?

YOUNG WOMAN: Ahhhh! The Lord. Oh Jesus. Oh Jesus.

OLD WOMAN: The lightning? Are you talking about the lightning?

YOUNG WOMAN: Yes. Yes. I hear his voice in the thunder. His power is in the lightning. Oh! Oh!

OLD WOMAN: Child I told you to sip that whiskey. Now that whisky's done gone to your head. Now you acting stupid. Ain't the Lord, it's the storm. It's just the storm. Don't turn stupid on me. You know how stupid people scares me.

YOUNG WOMAN: I don't want to be stupid Grandma. I don't. But how do you know it's not Him? How do you know? I can hear Him talking to me. I hear Him.

OLD WOMAN: Everybody drink more whiskey than they can handle hear the Lord. They think they hear somebody. How old are you?

YOUNG WOMAN: Seventeen.

OLD WOMAN: Um. Seventeen. That's younger than I can remember. What's the Lord saying?

YOUNG WOMAN: That I'm bad. That I'm going to hell and burn for all eternity.

OLD WOMAN: Why? Why would the Lord say that?

YOUNG WOMAN: Because, I didn't keep His Ten Commandments. I lied and I cheated and now I'm going to kill. I'm going to kill.

OLD WOMAN: Going to kill? Who you gonna kill? I'm the one going to kill. Me. *(Crossing DR of the table and turning to the Young Woman who is still under the table.)* I'm going to do it for fifty dollars. Me. And I don't have no shame in it. I help people. People in trouble. People come to my house and pay me to help them. They come to Grandma's house for help. Yes ma'am. *(Crosses UL of table and shifts SL chair at the table so she can look at the Young Woman.)* I've done so many, what's one more. *(Helps Young Woman crawl out and sits her in chair.)* See child, the Lord ain't gonna punish you. *(Crosses UL of table.)* If there's any punishing to be done, He gonna punish Grandma. Me. Grandma ain't worried. So don't you worry your little seventeen-year-old head off. Grandma do for people what the Lord won't do. I know the Lord gonna forgive me. He forgives everybody. *(Crosses around the the UL side of the table.)* He's gonna forgive you too. So wipe those tears from off your face. Ain't no point of it raining in here too.

YOUNG WOMAN: But how do you know? How do you know? I can't keep it. It will kill mama and papa if I had a baby without a husband. I'm suppose to graduate in June. They got such high hopes for me. I want to go to college. I don't want it. I don't want it. OK now I said it. *(Beating her stomach.)* I don't want it. There I said it. I don't want it.

OLD WOMAN: *(Pours a drink.)* Ok. Ok. You got some fight in you after all. *(Hands her the glass; then sits at table.)* Sip it this time. This ain't KoolAid. You take your time and sip it. Ten years ago I would of told you what's the difference. Have the baby. All most colored women could do is have babies. But you can do something special now. Not that having babies ain't special. I had a couple myself. But be somebody else too besides somebody's mama. Graduate from high school and go to college. Matter of fact, I think it's a sin if you don't. A bigger sin than killin'. *(Finishes drink then shifts her chair around to the SR side of the table and sits.)* I learned how to set women straight working for this white woman. I helped her by keeping house most days. Every now and then though some women would come to her house, stay a while, and then leave. Sometimes they come by theyself. Sometimes they come with another woman. They never looked happy, coming or going. Always looked serious. But grateful. Serious, but grateful. I thought she was a voodoo white woman at first putting spells and roots on somebody for these women. 'Cause women were always coming in, paying her, and going home. Serious.

YOUNG WOMAN: But grateful. A voodoo white woman?

OLD WOMAN: Well turn out, she was helping these girls, like I'm going help you. She taught me how. I was scared first time I see what she was doing. But I didn't say nothing. I almost wet my pants standing right there. But I kept my eyes open. She gave me a drink of whiskey. I swore I heard the Lord talking. Just like you. Afterwards she would go to this Catholic Church around the corner and pray. I don't know who for, 'cause I was too scared to ask. But as much as she was in there, the preacher thought she was some kind of holy woman. *(Takes a sip of whiskey, encourages the Young Woman to take a drink by nudging her glass.)* You ever been in a Catholic Church before?

YOUNG WOMAN: No.

OLD WOMAN: Well it's no day at the beach, let me tell you. It's real dark in there. Candles and the light from the stained-glass windows are the only source of light. They had all these statues around in life-size marble painted to make them look real. There was this one statue named Lucy. Saint Lucy. She was a pleasant enough looking woman, but she had a plate in her hand with somebody's eyeballs on it. These eyeballs would follow you around the church if you looked at them. Worse than them pictures of Jesus. I mean they would actually move. Roll real slow when you moved slow and real fast when you moved fast. One day, I dozed off and she left me in that church all by myself. I tried to find my way out, but got lost and found myself right in front of St. Lucy. Her with those eyes laying in that plate, staring at me. Judging me. Following me everywhere I went.

YOUNG WOMAN: What did you do?

OLD WOMAN: I closed my eyes and I started running like I had some sense. Up one row and down the other. I was too scared to turn around. I knew St. Lucy was behind me with those judging eyes. I tripped and fell between the benches. I felt a hand on my shoulder and I screamed. Loud. The door to the outside just opened and the sunlight came in. I walked out. When I got outside, I got enough courage to turn around and look to see if I saw St. Lucy with her plate of eyes, but there was nobody there. Just the benches. Just the benches.

YOUNG WOMAN: Who was it that touched your shoulder? Who opened the door?

OLD WOMAN: I don't know child. But I tell you this, ever since that day, I could see more clear. Now I'm going to help you see. I'm going to help you face this fear, walk out that door, and see a whole new life. Walk out that door and shine. You hear me girl? Shine like a new silver dollar. Can you do that?

YOUNG WOMAN: Yes.

OLD WOMAN: Now finish your drink. We gotta get started 'for my old man get home expecting his supper. OK? *(Extends her hand to the Young Woman.)*

YOUNG WOMAN: *(Taking the Old Woman's hand and shakes it.)* OK.

OLD WOMAN: It ain't gonna rain no more. You hear me child. It ain't gonna rain no more.

FADE TO BLACK

Scene Two

April 4, 1968. As the lights come up, Bay is seated in his recliner in front of an old black-and-white television set with a coat hanger for an antenna. The volume is on very low. Bay is attempting to get the television to work better. He is aggravated and begins hollering and beating on the TV.

BAY: Come on. Come on now. Oh man! Oh man! This piece of shit.

OLD WOMAN: *(Entering apartment carrying a shopping bag.)* Bay? Bay?

BAY: *(Does not look at her as he fidgets with coat hanger.)* Yeah, yeah baby in here.

OLD WOMAN: *(Walking into apartment closing door behind her.)* I know where you are. I could hear you clear downstairs. Who are you fussing at?

BAY: This damn old TV. Ain't worth the electricity it takes to turn it on.

OLD WOMAN: *(Walking toward table, putting her bags on it.)* Well, it'll have to do for now. Ain't like it's nothin' on there worth watching anyway.

BAY: *(Mumbling and beating on TV.)* Awwww! Come on. Damn it. Come on.

OLD WOMAN: *(Walking over to Bay.)* Move Bay. Let me see if I can fix it.

BAY: Yeah baby, work your magic. Thing's giving me a bad headache.

OLD WOMAN: Umm hmm. I got the magic fingers. *(Begins to fidget with TV.)*

BAY: *(Watching her.)* That may be true, but what we need is a new TV or at least a new used one. This one's had it.

OLD WOMAN: *(Fidgeting with coat hanger.)* Don't start Bay, hear. This TV will have to do. We agreed.

BAY: You agreed. As usual, I got to go along with it.

OLD WOMAN: Ummm hmmm.

BAY: *(Mimicking her in a woman's voice.)* Ummm hmmm.

OLD WOMAN: Look! Look! Here we go. Here we go. There's the picture. We cookin' now Bay. We cookin' with gas.

BAY: OK! OK! Magic fingers. Yes! Yes! My baby got magic fingers. *(Kisses her.)*

OLD WOMAN: *(Walking away.)* Now don't touch it. Hear Bay? Don't touch it and it'll play.

BAY: *(Sitting in front of TV.)* Don't touch it. Don't talk loud around it. Don't even breathe hard on it. You hear me Bay? You hear me Bay? *(The Old Woman unpacks bags, picks up some of her groceries and walks through curtain into kitchen ignoring Bay.)* We need a new TV. A new TV. *(Shouting toward kitchen.)* Nothing that ain't breathing and paying rent should be this ornery.

OLD WOMAN: *(Off Stage Left, in kitchen.)* Oh Bay! Please don't start with me, hear. I had a long day.

BAY: Well am I right? *(Looks back at TV, raising his hands.)* Awwww man! Look at this worthless piece of shit.

OLD WOMAN: *(Reenters from kitchen.)* What? Did you touch it?

BAY: Naw, I didn't touch it.

OLD WOMAN: *(Walking over to Bay.)* Well what's wrong?

BAY: I can hardly hear the damn thing. And I sho' can't read no colored folks lips.

OLD WOMAN: *(Crosses US of his recliner.)* Colored folks? On television? What you watching? *(Leans over the back of the recliner, rubs his shoulders.)*

BAY: King. They talking about the march Monday. Young suppose to go to court and get that injunction removed so we can march and end this damn strike. How long it's been?

OLD WOMAN: *(Picks up paper bag and exits into kitchen.)* Eight weeks.

BAY: Eight weeks. No money. I know I'm tired of trying to convince white folks I'm just as much man, got just as much bills, babies, and want just as much life he do. I'm screaming, I am a man, eight weeks.

OLD WOMAN: *(Reenters with cloth to wipe table and table cloth.)* And four hundred years.

BAY: He don't want to hear it. And this lifting job I got part time is harder and nastier then emptyin' garbage ever been. And don't pay squat. I'm too old for this baby.

OLD WOMAN: *(Wiping off the top of the table.)* It's gonna be all right Bay.

BAY: I'm beginning to wonder.

OLD WOMAN: King's gonna fix it. He's like a bulldog. Put his teeth in your tail . . . *(Spreading table cloth over top of table.)* won't turn loose 'til you cry justice.

BAY: You think so? He ain't got Johnson in his pocket no more. Johnson worried 'bout making that war look good. And now that King done spoke out against it, last thing he wanna hear about is King and a of bunch of garbage emptyin' Negroes in Memphis.

OLD WOMAN: *(Adjusting the table cloth.)* We lucky he came here. You got to have some patience Bay.

BAY: Need the patience of Job and then some to live through this shit.

OLD WOMAN: *(Exiting into kitchen to stir pot and get bowl of peaches.)* And praying don't hurt.

BAY: Ummm.

He continues to adjust TV with a piece of tin foil as the Old Woman comes out of the kitchen carrying a bowl of peaches and a hand towel.

OLD WOMAN: Look at these peaches Bay. Ain't they the prettiest peaches you ever see?

BAY: *(Continues fussing with the TV.)* Peaches. This time of year?

OLD WOMAN: I got them from Mr. Ralph's Market out there by Ms. Allen.

BAY: Way out there? Is that where you been all day?

OLD WOMAN: *(Sitting SR side of table, wiping peaches with a cloth.)* Mmmm hmmm. She needed me to do some washin'. I always stop at the market when I'm out there. Mr. Ralph thinks I'm buying stuff for Ms. Allen. Only reason he sell to me. I swear they sell white folks the prettiest fruit. And cheap. Peaches they sell in colored neighborhoods look like they gone fifteen rounds with Casius Clay. And cost the price of the ticket take to see him do it.

BAY: Mohammed Ali. Man name Mohammed Ali.

OLD WOMAN: Well whatever. Should be against God's law to change the name your mama give you.

BAY: Man got a right to call himself whatever he want to.

OLD WOMAN: That's all most colored mothers can give freely, a name, without begging, scheming, praying, and saving for it.

BAY: The man got a right to change his name. His! Ms. Allen call you every name in the book 'cept the one your mama give you. You answer to ever one of 'em. I don't hear you complaining 'bout that. *(The Old Woman stares at Bay as she arranges peaches in the bowl on the table. Bay calling in a 'woman's voice'.)*

Suzy, Sarah, Sandra, colored girl. *(In his own voice.)* I doubt she know what your real name is. Don't bother you none.

OLD WOMAN: *(Singing.)* Long as I know I'm gonna get my freedom, it's all right. Oh, it's all right.

BAY: And as often as you over there, she must be taken in all the white folks laundry in the entire city.

OLD WOMAN: You miss me that bad?

BAY: I always do. *(Stares at her.)*

OLD WOMAN: We need the money Bay.

BAY: *(Defiant.)* I know we need money. *(They stare at one another until the Old Woman smiles.)*

OLD WOMAN: You know what? I'm goin' to make you a peach cobbler.

BAY: With what? Not with these peaches. *(Picks up a peach and holds it out toward the Old Woman.)*

OLD WOMAN: What's the matter with these peaches?

BAY: These peaches too fresh. Every colored man know rotten peaches make the best cobbler. They must. 'Cause whenever you buy fresh, pretty peaches from waaay way out there Ms. Allen way, you put them in a pretty bowl on display 'til they turn rotten . . . *(The Old Woman attempts to interrupt him, but he stops her from interrupting by raising his hand.)* Ripe. Then you serve them to me.

OLD WOMAN: I do not.

BAY: Yes you do.

OLD WOMAN: Why you trying to pick a fight with me Bay? *(Beat, as she snatches the peach from Bay.)* I went to Ms. Allen's to do laundry.

BAY: *(Gives her a kiss.)* You know I love you and your cobbler. *(He sits back down and continues to fidget with more tin foil for the TV, paying no attention to her. There is a long pause as she goes about her chores.)*

OLD WOMAN: I don't know what's wrong with you. Like you got up on the wrong side of the bed or somethin'. Ms. Allen pay good money. We need money way these bills come in here. Thank God Ms. Allen got work for me. You want to act like I'm the one crazy. I use rotten peaches to make cobblers. You right, you love rotten peaches way you suck up ever crumb. You a rotten peach eatin' fool the way you don't bring your head up from the plate 'til it shine like new money.

BAY: What's that you say Baby?

OLD WOMAN: I said what they saying?

BAY: *(Never taking his eyes off the TV.)* What's that Baby?

OLD WOMAN: Did they say anything about the injunction yet?

BAY: That's what I'm trying to find out. This damn TV. I can't hear nothin'.

OLD WOMAN: Well you can see. Just don't touch the TV whatever you do.

BAY: I can't follow this.

OLD WOMAN: You ain't got to hear nothin' to know what's up. *(Walking over to Bay, pointing at TV.)* Look at those white folks' faces. If they all frowned up, worried looking, specially Mayor Loeb, King got the injunction stopped. If they grinning like a Cheshire cat sitting pretty on your money, gonna be four hundred years and nine weeks.

BAY: I don't even want to think about that. Please don't say it.

OLD WOMAN: The Lord will make a way, Bay. Just watch they faces. White folks can't play poker worth a damn.

BAY: Specially when it comes to Negroes marching up and down Memphis city streets.

OLD WOMAN: Course they got cause to worry, way colored folks showed they tail last week when King was here the first time.

BAY: *(Chuckling.)* He, he, he, he.

OLD WOMAN: All that running, burnin', and breaking windows, and looting. *(Starts toward kitchen.)*

Bay: We kicked butt.

OLD WOMAN: You mean y'all showed butt. Embarrassed King . . . and yourselves. Police the ones kicked butt. Tanks, dogs, hoses, bloody broken heads. It's a wonder King came back here as colored as y'all acted. It's a testimony to his goodness.

BAY: Y'all?

OLD WOMAN: *(Crossing UL of Bay in his recliner.)* You were right in the middle of it.

BAY: Aw, like its all our fault.

OLD WOMAN: I didn't say that Bay and you know it.

BAY: But you believe it. *(She exits into kitchen to get plates and silverware.)* Two colored boys died dead collecting garbage. Men with families, children. You think Loeb and 'em compensated they families? Naw. Ain't got no money for food, none for clothing, no way to pay rent and didn't pay no decent wage from the get go. But they don't care about that. *(Gets up, crosses around LC toward kitchen doorway.)* You suppose to be happy they let your colored ass pick up maggots and shit in the street. And when you dead, you just dead. Throw all the rest of your raggedy, naked, hungry family on the fire like they do in India. Hell yeah we looted. Time to loot. I shoulda got myself a new TV. Seem like that's the only way to get one. Sure can't buy nothin'.

Coming out of kitchen carrying two plates and silverware.

OLD WOMAN: What you standing here outside my kitchen for? You suppose to be reading white folks faces. *(Putting plates and silverware down on table.)* Find out if there's gonna be a march Monday. Maybe y'all can redeem y'all-selves.

BAY: *(Grabbing her from behind.)* Redeem myself. No ma'am. Monday I'm gonna get myself a brand new television.

OLD WOMAN: You gonna end up like Larry Payne. They just buried him the other day. *(Struggling to get free.)* Turn me loose Bay. You just want to argue.

BAY: *(Kissing her neck.)* No I don't Baby.

OLD WOMAN: Stop now. *(Pulling away.)* Darn. *(Walks over to table and begins to set it.)* I know you Bay. After twenty-five years of you. I know when you mad at me.

BAY: What makes you think I'm mad at you? You haven't done anything to make me mad. Have you?

The lights flicker off and on. The Old Woman and Bay look upward. Bay crosses DL to the television while the Old Woman gets a knife out of the SR side drawer of the kitchen table and crosses UC to bang on the pipes.

OLD WOMAN: Oh Lord! It's that stupid woman upstairs boot-leggin' electricity again. *(Banging on the pipes and shouting toward the ceiling.)* Hey! Hey!

BAY: Aw look Baby. The TV messed up again. You gonna work some of your magic on it? *(Crossing back to the table to put the knife back into the drawer.)*

OLD WOMAN: I'm trying to work some of my magic on getting dinner. Ain't but so many tricks I can do in one evening. You ain't lookin' at it anyway. *(Music can be heard from upstairs.)*

BAY: Well I see she's playing music tonight. *(He stands.)* That's better than one of her loud fights. *(She crosses DR of the table.)* I hope she plays something I like. Something mellow like Aretha . . . or The Supremes . . . or

OLD WOMAN: *(Crossing toward him.)* Or what? You making request now?

BAY: I'm trying to make the most of a bad situation. What's wrong with that? Hell, I'm a expert at it. Story of my life. *(She crosses UR of the table as he screams toward the ceiling.)* Hey, play "Ain't No Mountain High" Shhhh! What's that song? What's that song? *(He begins to dance.)*

OLD WOMAN: Oh no, I know I got to get out of here now. You got the woman upstairs entertaining you. We got to move. We got to move. If I have to spend another month here, I know I'll die. *(She walks over to the SR wall above the bed, shifts the picture on the wall, and removes the jar of money in the hole-in-the-wall; and crosses DR and sits on the DL corner of the bed with the jar and removes money from her bra as Bay watches her.)* I want a quiet place with a little garden where I can plant string beans and roses or something. Some place where nobody's dog go and pee on it. That ain't too much to ask nobody for. Somewhere where I can have a little porch and some quiet. No noise 'cept birds. But please no pigeons. Pigeon only live in the slum and on the top of courthouses. *(Counts money and stuffs it into the jar.)* Twenty, forty, sixty, seventy-five. Yes. Lets see, with that money you won last night, that makes four thousand and five dollars Bay. We got enough. I think we finally got enough.

BAY: Seventy-five dollars? Seventy-five dollars? You didn't get seventy-five dollars washing clothes or I need to quit my job hauling garbage and do laundry myself. *(The Old Woman sits with jar in her lap, clutching the jar as she looks straight ahead.)* You did another abortion. *(Stands and crosses UL of the table.)* You done gone fixed some woman.

OLD WOMAN: *(Attempting to quiet him.)* Will you be quiet Bay. What you wanna do, tell the whole world?

BAY: You promised me you quit. I knew it when you walked in here. You lied to me.

OLD WOMAN: I did quit. I ain't done one in two years. I swear Bay. But we need the money. *(Sits SL chair at table.)* With you on strike, I didn't have no choice.

BAY: Oh go put it on me. You know I had to strike. *(Sits on DR end of the bed.)*

OLD WOMAN: I ain't puttin' it on you. But we got to get some money comin' in from somewhere if we gonna buy a house. Your part-time lifting job and my cleaning and washing clothes barely put food on the table and keep the lights on. Bay we had to do something, bring in more money. Bay we can't stay here no more.

BAY: We?

OLD WOMAN: OK, I can't stay here no more. I just want my own place before I die. And I don't want to die here.

BAY: You gonna die in jail old woman. And I got news for you. Ms. Allen ain't gonna do a day. She gonna put it all on the colored girl. Bet she remember your name then. You gonna lose everything trying to get where? Some greener pastures. Some suburb way, waay out Ms. Allen way where the deer and the Klan play. That light you keep seeing. That bright vision is the KKK in white sheets burning a cross in you string bean and rose garden.

OLD WOMAN: Ain't nothing wrong with wanting something.

BAY: Something wrong with wanting things you can't have.

OLD WOMAN: *(Standing.)* We got four thousand and five dollars Bay.

BAY: And what you gonna do with it?

OLD WOMAN: I'm gonna spend it. It's money.

BAY: When you gonna spend it?

OLD WOMAN: *(Confused.)* When?

BAY: *(Loud.)* When?

OLD WOMAN: *(Looking around confused.)* Now! I can spend it now.

BAY: Naw, you ain't. *(Stands and crosses UL of the table.)* Naw you ain't. That money just like them peaches. Just like everything else you got. You save it, and save it and look at it and admire it. *(In a "woman's voice.")* Isn't it pretty Bay? Isn't is pretty? *(Own voice.)* When it comes down to using it, it's too late. It's rotten or it's gone. *(Grabs jar of money from Old Woman, who crosses DL to recliner and sits on SR arm.)* Ten years. Ten years we been saving. Ten years we sacrificed. Ten years we done without. All the risk you took. Like some crusade. Quit, I told you. Quit 'fore some dizzy woman die or get infected and point at you.

OLD WOMAN: *(Stands and crosses to table.)* I ain't gonna hurt nobody Bay. What you worried about? Ain't nobody gonna point no finger my way.

BAY: Why not? 'Cause you say so. These the same girls, all some man got to say is "Hey Baby," legs fly open like the automatic doors at the A&P. *(Crosses UR of table.)* You put your trust in them?

OLD WOMAN: Why not? They trust me. They put they life in my hands, Bay. These *(Showing her hands to him.)* I help these girls. What you think?

Puts the jar of money down on the table.

BAY: *(Crosses DR to the bed and sits.)* Ah!

OLD WOMAN: Girls come here, ain't got no name, ain't got no life. 'Cause he stole it. She got to pray he marry her and give her his name. Her name don't count. Marry her and make her a decent woman. Marry her so they child ain't labeled a bastard. Never own nothin'. Another generation gone. Girls come here 'cause I will do what her man won't. Give her back her name, her name. Girls come here 'cause it's either the devil or the witch. *(Sits on the SR arm of the recliner.)*

BAY: And which one are you?

OLD WOMAN: Sometimes I'm one. Sometimes I'm the other. *(Stands and crosses DR and sits next to Bay on the bed and takes His arm.)* I went out to Ms. Allen's do the laundry, like I say. But she asked for my help. Meant getting paid seven dollars for washin' or seventy-five dollars for holdin' some girl's hand.

BAY: So you chose to hold hands.

OLD WOMAN: I didn't lie to you Bay. I didn't lie to you.

BAY: I can't figure you out. You accuse me of gambling. Wasting money. If I lose, I lose twenty, twenty-five dollars. If you lose, they gonna put your ass so far in the ground, you gonna swear they buried you. You gonna roll the dice one time too many, woman. Gonna come up snake eyes looking you dead in your face.

Singing as she stands and crosses US of the table, picking up the jar of money and continuing around DL toward the recliner.

OLD WOMAN: "Long as I know I'm gonna get my freedom, it's all right, oh it's all right."

BAY: You don't hear me do you?

OLD WOMAN: We can have the house we always wanted Bay.

BAY: It ain't gonna happen.

OLD WOMAN: Why can't it Bay? We got $4,005.

BAY: You got $4,005. Your money. *(She sits on the SR arm of the recliner.)* I wish I could have given you what you wanted. *(He stands and crosses around UC.)* Status, security, nice home with carpet, sectional couch, long stereo, new console TV. But I make a dollar forty cent a hour. This the best I can do here. And here ain't where you wanna be. I'm just a garbageman.

OLD WOMAN: I know what you are Bay. You my man.

BAY: No. *(Cross around toward her. Points at jar.)* That's your man right there. That money. Only thing you live for.

OLD WOMAN: No, Bay. It's you.

BAY: I can't do what that money do for you. I can't buy you a home. And I ain't the kind of man gonna let no woman, including you, buy me one.

OLD WOMAN: What you talking about? This our money. Yours and mine. We saved it together.

BAY: That's you and Ms. Allen's money. Most of it. Y'all did it. Y'all ain't got no use for men. Kill his children. Man ain't got no say about it. Tell him what to eat, when to eat it. When to shit and what flavor. Where he gonna live and where he gonna die. I've been marching eight weeks up and down Beale and Main Street screaming, I am a man, to every white folk in earshot. Eight weeks wearing a sign so when they see me, they know what I am. I ain't gonna wear no sign in here. Not in here.

OLD WOMAN: I know you a man Bay. And like a man only way I ever treated you. But right now you acting like a fool. It don't matter who make the money. I know you don't think I want this money more than I want you? *(Bay stares at her.)* I thought you wanted what I wanted. *(Shoving money at him.)* Here, take the money. Take it. You the man of the house. Do whatever you want with it. Buy a console TV or a new suit or whatever. Here!

BAY: *(Puts jar on the table.)* I don't want it.

OLD WOMAN: Then I don't want it either.

BAY: *(Holds jar toward her.)* You don't want it! You don't want it! *(Opens jar and begins emptying jar, throwing money all over the room.)* Years and years of saving and saving, sacrificing and now you don't want it!

OLD WOMAN: Bay! Bay! What you doing? What's wrong with you?

BAY: *(Continues emptying the jar.)* We ain't been living. Sacrifice, take chances. Now it don't mean nothing. You don't want it. *(Throwing the money.)*

OLD WOMAN: *(Attempting to stop him.)* Bay, why are you acting this way? What's the matter with you?

BAY: All of a sudden, cold turkey. Just like that. How many times you lied to me just to put some money in that jar? Your jar of dreams. I ain't your man. *(Puts the empty jar on the table. Picks up money and shoves it in her face.)* Here's your man, Washington, Jackson, Hamilton. There's your man.

OLD WOMAN: *(Screaming.)* Stop it Bay! Stop it! Stop!!! *(There is a sudden loud explosion and a flash of light outside illuminating the window. Bay and old woman are startled. Smoke begins seeping under the door.)*

OLD WOMAN: *(Yells.)* Oh!

BAY: *(Turning toward the window.)* What was that?

OLD WOMAN: *(Picking up money, meticulously putting each bill in order.)* It's that damn woman upstairs. Maybe you should just move up there. *(Bay stands, walks over to window opening the curtains. It is dark outside and an orange glow continues to illuminate the window.)* Both of you acting stupid around here.

BAY: *(Leans out of the window. Pandemonium can be heard outside.)* What in the hell? *(Shouting.)* What's going on? What happened? *(Street sounds, anxious voices and police sirens can be heard.)*

OLD WOMAN: You want to act a fool. Ain't nothing wrong with wanting something.

BAY: *(Shouting out of the window)* What? Oh man. You lying. When?

OLD WOMAN: I just wanted us to have a home. That ain't too much to ask for? *(Looks up at Bay then goes back to picking up money. Bay coming back out of window, stands motionless, looking shocked. The Old Woman looks up at Bay.)* What's wrong, Bay?

BAY: They killed King. King's dead, baby. He's dead.

OLD WOMAN: What? What are you talking about? Who told you that?

BAY: Colored folks out there gone crazy. It's all over now, baby. White folks gonna have us right back where they want us.

OLD WOMAN: No. This ain't right. This ain't right.

BAY: *(Walking over to TV.)* Let's see if I can find out what the hell happened. *(Beating on TV.)* Come on. Come on.

OLD WOMAN: *(Confused.)* King's dead? How can this be possible? *(Smoke continues seeping under the door.)*

BAY: I don't know. I don't know nothing. This damn old ass TV. *(Slams fist on TV.)* Goddamn it. Can you fix this thing?

OLD WOMAN: Something's burning. Something's on fire around here.

BAY: Folks gone crazy out there. Come and fix this TV, you swear will have to do, 'cause we don't have no money buy another one.

The Old Woman walks over to window as Bay continues fidgeting with TV.

OLD WOMAN: *(Looks out of window.)* God almighty! *(Looks at Bay, screams.)* Bay! Bay, the building's on fire! *(Running from window.)* The building's on fire!

BAY: Fire? Us?

OLD WOMAN: *(Running to Bay and grabbing him by the arm.)* Come on, we got to get out of here. *(The Old Woman puts a hand full of money in her bra.)*

BAY: *(Looking around.)* Oh my God. There's smoke everywhere. *(Touching door.)* Door's hot. The fire's right behind this door. Come on. We got to go out the window. Now. *(Bay helps her toward and out of the window. Once she's out the window, he starts to follow but steps back into the room, picks up the jar and begins to fill it with the money scattered on the bed and floor.)*

OLD WOMAN: *(Kneeling in the window.)* Come on Bay. We ain't got time. Smokes all in here. *(Begins to cough.)* Come on. Leave it. Leave it.

BAY: I'm right behind you. Go head. Go head. I'm right behind you. Go I told you. Go! Go!

She hesitates and then disappears down the fire escape. Bay continues putting money in the jar as smoke continues to fills the room. He grabs his chest, coughs and gasps for breath as he collapses onto the floor. We can hear the Old Woman calling as the sound of fire continues to build.

OLD WOMAN: *(Off stage calling. Her cries muffled by the sound of the riot)* Bay! Bay! Come on Bay, we ain't got time for that. Come on Bay. Leave it. Leave it. *(Calling.)* Bay! Bay! Bay!

The lights flicker off and on a few times. They then go off. The only light remaining is from the old TV. The Old Woman's voice is heard calling and we hear the last lines from Martin Luther King Jr.'s "Mountain Top" speech, in total or in part, coming from the TV over Bay's gasps for life.

We can hear the sound of fire consuming the building.

The lights go to black.

END OF ACT ONE

ACT TWO

Scene One

Twelve years later in a room at the Lorraine Motel, election day, November 1980. It is about seven o'clock. We see a bed. Flashing red lights can be seen periodically outside the window. The muffled sound of music can be heard in the distance. There are two doors. One leads to a rest room, the other to the outside. There are food containers scattered about the room. A woman, young and sophisticated, sits on the bed wrapped in a blanket rocking nervously back and forth. Although she tries to hide it, she is not feeling well and has a fever. After a brief pause, the Old Woman enters from the bathroom drying her hands on a towel.

OLD WOMAN: Gal, please stop that rocking. Don't know what botherin' me more, these old arthritis feet and hips of mine or that sea-saw back and forth you doing. 'Tween that and all this boogie woogie ass music, 'bout to go stone crazy. *(The Old Woman walks over to SR chair DS of a window, her sweater and coat are over the back of the chair and her large handbag is US of it.)* You got everything you need?

WOMAN: What you mean?

OLD WOMAN: *(Folding the towel and putting it over the back of the chair.)* I'm fixin' to go. It's election day. I'm gonna go vote for that Jimmy Carter. Don't know what we gonna do if that movie man gets in.

YOUNG WOMAN: You can't leave me here. Not like this.

OLD WOMAN: *(Putting on her sweater.)* You waited too long for Grandma to help you. Too long. *(From her handbag she takes out a brown paper bag and puts it down on the SR side table by the bed.)* Got a dog-and-pony show going on up under there. Now I brought you some of my world-famous peach cobbler. Enough so you'll have some for your bus ride home . . . or wherever is you headed . . . out of here.

WOMAN: Grandma, please! I can't go home 'til I'm straight. You hear me. I can't.

OLD WOMAN: You gotta go to one of them clinics. They got clinics now. Best I can do, make sure you get on your way.

WOMAN: I can't go to no clinic. You don't understand. They want to put me in the hospital. I can't have no record of this.

OLD WOMAN: You don't have to use your real name honey. Think!

WOMAN: It don't matter who I say I am. They got all them people standing outside picketing with signs. What if I'm seen?

OLD WOMAN: Gal, please. You ain't who they tryin' keep out. Surprised they don't hand you a lollypop on your way in. Well what you goin' to do? Stay here 'til you have that baby? *(Beat.)* Um Hm, you ain't thought that far, have you? Look at you. Look at this place. How long you been here?

WOMAN: I don't know. Awhile.

The Old Woman begins to pick paperplates/boxes from the floor and puts them into the wastebasket UC.

OLD WOMAN: You can't stay here. *(Beat, as she reacts to a sound unheard by the Woman.* You hear that?
WOMAN: What? *(Beat.)* The music?
OLD WOMAN: Ssssshhhh! No Listen, listen. You can't hear that?
WOMAN: I don't hear nothin'. Old walls, sound just bleeds right through them. This place ain't where you come for peace and quite. Ain't you ever been to the Lorraine Motel before?
OLD WOMAN: *(Crossing to the window.)* I've only seen this place from down there, looking up. Looks so different from up here. Small. Closed in. Dark. Feel like a thousand eyes on me. Place sure give me the creeps.
WOMAN: Don't nobody know we're here. And don't nobody care.
OLD WOMAN: I know this was 'for your time, but this use to be the place. Black folk dressed in beads and fur coats. Miss Lorraine, place named after her you know, she kept this place nice. Now this place ain't no more than a whip shack. Nothing but a whip shack now. *(Beat, as she looks about room)* This the last place Martin Luther King saw before he died. Knew they was going to kill him. Stepped right out on that balcony anyway.
WOMAN: Seem to me, if you know somebody out to get you, you'd stay inside where it's safe. I know I would.
OLD WOMAN: Miss Lorraine dead too. She was here that night. Dropped dead right after she heard the news. There ain't nothing but death here.
WOMAN: My grandma say, right before you die, your whole life flashes before you.
OLD WOMAN: Judgment day.
WOMAN: All the mistakes you made. All the regrets. The sins.
OLD WOMAN: *(Crossing toward the bed, resumes picking up trash.)* Think we goin' be like Judas to Jesus?
WOMAN: Betrayed by a kiss.
OLD WOMAN: *(Realizing the Woman has been talking about herself.)* And some silver. People gonna always remember that King died in Memphis. He died right here. Sweet Lorraine. You from Memphis?
WOMAN: No.
OLD WOMAN: Where you from?
WOMAN: Around.
OLD WOMAN: I see. Good a place as any I reckon. *(Flinches from pain and begins rubbing her legs. Sits in the RC chair.)* Calhoun where I from. Grew up in a little rusty shack no bigger than this room.
WOMAN: I was born in Memphis. We moved away when I was twelve. You OK?

OLD WOMAN: Oh this. This come from standing on my feet all my life.

WOMAN: My grandma's legs use to bother her too. She had sugar. She loved when I'd rub them for her. Took the pain out for a little while.

OLD WOMAN: *(Stands and crosses to bed.)* Your grandma, she here in Memphis? That why you here?

WOMAN: *(Laughs knowing her grandma is dead.)* Naw. She ain't here. Ain't nothing in Memphis for me. Nothing. I got plans. Big plans. I'm on my way to New York City. Do some modeling or get a singing or acting career going.

OLD WOMAN: *(Crosses back to chair and sits.)* I wanted to be a singer too. I use to picture myself sitting on top of Duke Ellington's piano, swinging my big pretty legs.

WOMAN: Well I know I can sing. Act too. Lots of people tell me I got what it takes.

OLD WOMAN: You can't always believe what you hear.

WOMAN: You saying I don't have talent?

OLD WOMAN: *(Walking to the Woman.)* I'm saying all that singing and showboating's cute, gotta get somethin' solid under your belt. *(Touching Woman's forehead as though she is trying to fix her hair. Noticing she has a fever, she continues fixing the Woman's hair, concerned.)* Come a cold night, your fanny ain't naked to the wind. My mama told me, hanging over a rusty tub full of dirty clothes and hot soap, eyes full of sorrow and hands so wrinkled and small they didn't look human no more. She say, "Gal, find a hardworking man with a job first, fall in love with him second."

WOMAN: Typical mama. Do as I say, not as I did.

OLD WOMAN: Say, make sure his shoulders are broad and his hand had calluses so thick, pick ax couldn't make a dint in 'em. I wasn't seventeen 'for I sneaked off and married the prettiest man in town. That man was so pretty, I use to sit there and watch him sleep.

WOMAN: Pretty man, huh!

OLD WOMAN: *(Still fixing the Woman's hair.)* Prettyyy. He was scared of work though. Had a excuse for everything. I had two boys 'for I cracked twenty. Wasn't long 'for I was hanging over a rusty tub full of dirty clothes and hot soap, my eyes full of sorrow and hands so wrinkled and small they didn't look human no more. *(Finds a rubber band to put onto the Woman's hair.)* My mama say, old sheep know the road, young lamb gotta find the way. Lord she ain't never lied. He ain't no pretty man, is he? Man prettier than you? At least I got a smile out of you. Pretty smile too. Is he married?

WOMAN: *(Gets off the bed and crosses RC US of chair.)* No, he ain't married.

OLD WOMAN: Oh, O', I done hit a nerve.

WOMAN: He ain't married. I said he wasn't married.

OLD WOMAN: Don't take it personal, honey. Just that I did this for so long, I can usually tell. What's the matter?

WOMAN: I'm fine. This just ain't the right time.

OLD WOMAN: *(Moves toward her.)* Why you wait so long? 'Cause if you waiting for him to leave his wife and marry you, got better odds winnin' a snowball fight in hell.

WOMAN: *(Moves around to the DS side of the chair.)* I don't need no sermon, OK.

OLD WOMAN: OK, OK.

WOMAN: I know this a girl. My mama had six girls.

OLD WOMAN: Keep your voice down.

WOMAN: She cursed the day she had each of us. Said a girl child only gonna bring you pain.

OLD WOMAN: Things have a way of working out. The Lord'll make a way.

Counter-Cross: As the Woman moves toward the bed; the Old Woman crosses RC US of the chair.

WOMAN: Now you promised you'd help me. All you did was bring me some pie. What the hell you think I need with that and my life is falling apart?

OLD WOMAN: Come on, put your dress on. I'll help you. Come on Child.

WOMAN: *(Lies back down on the bed, exhausted.)* I ain't going nowhere.

OLD WOMAN: Let's get you cleaned up. *(Picks up dress and puts it on the UR end of bed; then crossing DS of the bed and exits UL into the bathroom. Returns with a damp washcloth and sits on the SL side of the bed putting the cloth on the Woman's forehead.)* Here we go, come on now. Don't that feel better. Child you 'bout to jump out of your skin. You ought to let me put some hoodoo on him. I'll fix him. He wake up one morning expectin' to find the long ranger, unzip his pants, little Tonto pop out. *(The Woman does not react. Old Woman continues to rub her forehead.)* I was standin' at the bus stop one night. I wanted that bus to come, but I was afraid I couldn't lift my legs high enough to get me up on that bus I was so tired. I started praying. Along came a man in a truck so loud and raggedy, sound like fireworks on the Fourth of July. He stopped the truck. Say, "Baby you need a ride?"

WOMAN: Baby!! I know you ain't gonna tell me you got in a strange man's truck?

OLD WOMAN: Well, I looked at his shoulders first. They was broad. *(Stands and puts the wet cloth down on the SL side stand then crosses DS around the bed and goes toward RC, stops, remembering she'd put the dress on the bed, turns and goes to the bed, pick up the dress then attempts to help the Woman into it as she tells her story.)* I looked at his hands. He had so much dirt stuck up under his skin, lye soap wouldn't wash it off. He told me he was a garbageman. A sanitation worker, way he put it. Picked up all of Memphis' garbage. Heavy, rotten garbage. Hauled it all away with his bare hands. *(Extends her hands.)* These. Dead dogs, maggots, spoiled food, used Kotex. All of yesterdays forgotten dreams, bad news, secrets, lies, regrets, sins. Stuff folks want to forget. He carried it all away. Made folks feel clean again. *(Fussing with and buttoning the dress.)* Got paid only pennies for what they pay preachers good money for. All that filth gets under your skin. Gets in your pores, your blood, eats up your soul. Makes you believe you don't deserve nothin'. Makes you believe you no better then the garbage you haul. He smelled like the dump.

WOMAN: And he stunk too? Does this get any better?

OLD WOMAN: He came to see me every weekend for a year. Saved and gave me the money for my divorce. We got married that summer. *(Still fussing with the dress.)* Raised my boys like they was his own. He wasn't no stranger. He was a answer to a prayer. And the prettiest man I ever knew. Mama said, "Pretty is as pretty does." Lord, she ain't never lied. It's gonna be all right, gal. I know you don't believe it, but it's gonna be all right.

WOMAN: I don't want to be nobody's housewife with no whole lot of kids. I got plans for myself. I don't want to have to wait for some big man with broad shoulders that snore all night to rescue me. I'd rather be dead. I rather be dead.

OLD WOMAN: Come on child. Let me take you to your grandma. *(Stands, picks up an article of clothing, folds and packs it into suitcase.)*

WOMAN: My grandma can't help me. *(Turning her face into the covers on the bed.)*

After packing another article of clothing, the Old Woman stares at the Woman, and picks up her coat she has left on the chair, and begins to gather her things.

WOMAN: *(Noticing her.)* What are you doing? You ain't going nowhere. You can't leave me here.

OLD WOMAN: I don't want to leave you, gal. But I got to get over to the polls for they close. My old man didn't believe in voting. *(The Woman stands and snatches the handbag from the Old Woman and sits back on bed, clutching it. The Old Woman is startled, but tries not to react. Putting her coat over her.)* Said the minute you register they put your name on this hit list. Next thing you know, you dead in a pine box. This will be the first time I voted. First time. Put my best dress on for the occasion. So if they kill me, I'll die respectable, goddamn it.

WOMAN: Ain't nobody gonna kill you for voting. You a crazy old woman.

OLD WOMAN: *(Puts coat down on chair.)* You laugh, but one day you gotta stop running. Stop, turn around and look the monkey in the face. SOB ugly. But his bark worse than his bite. You can't stay indoors, Gal. One day, you gonna have to walk out on that balcony.

WOMAN: I ain't got to walk nowhere, except where I please.

OLD WOMAN: You can't stay here gal. You gone done something to yourself. You sick. You burnin' with fever. Now I'm going to go vote for that Jimmy Carter. I got to do this. You hear me. I didn't know how much 'til I stood in this room. *(Mindlessly picking up and folding an article of clothing.)* Some little ol' white man sitting somewhere got three strands of hair he comb from one his ears t'other. Glasses hangin' way down his nose, britches way down his tail. Don't have no face, but I knowed what he look like. Same little ol' white man call me girl or auntee, all my life. Not allowed to look him in the eye. Say, "Show me your money girl." Take it. Give me the change he wanna give me. Tell me, "These fresh peaches ain't they girl?" I say, "Yes sir, fresh peaches." Smell the rot from the next block. But they fresh 'cause he say they fresh. That's the white man gonna count my vote. My vote equal to his vote. I'm equal to him. He ain't never see my face, but he knowed what I look like. He know I'm lookin' him right in the eye. That's power. Power a scary thing. Power dangerous. Somebody die give me that power. Somebody die right here. *(Points toward window. Puts article in the suitcase. Starts to picks up handbag and coat.)*

WOMAN: Don't go. I can't do this. You been listening to me? I can't do this.

OLD WOMAN: Eat that cobbler and get yourself on that bus.

WOMAN: No! *(Runs to the window and opens curtains, screaming.)* I'll jump. I'll jump.

OLD WOMAN: Gal will you close them curtains! *(Walks over to window and sits Woman in chair.)*

WOMAN: I want to die. I want to die.

OLD WOMAN: Somebody already died here. Died so you could live. Walked out on that balcony for you. You spit on his memory if you die too.

WOMAN: Grandma please! I can't bring another baby home. My mama ain't gonna keep this one. I can't do this. Grandma please!

OLD WOMAN: Keep your voice down I tell you. *(Crosses around bed and begins clearing a place for Woman to lie down.)* How you gonna kill yourself? This a two-story motel. Most you gonna do is break a heel or a nail. If you get lucky, hit your fool head on the concrete, knock some sense in yourself.

WOMAN: I'll do whatever it takes to get myself out of this mess. *(Stands and crosses to bed and sits on it.)* I'll give you more money Grandma. I got more money. You'll do it for more money? *(Digging into purse.)*

Reacting to sounds she can only hear, she turns away from Woman searching for the source of sounds.

OLD WOMAN: Shhh!

WOMAN: He's waiting for me in New York. Told me as soon as I got myself straight, I can join him there. We gonna build a whole new life there. Shake this dull, slow-ass place. We gonna be somebody. He's there now scouting out some acting jobs for me. He's gonna find a place for us. He said I got what it takes. He believes in me. I bet he got me a agent already. I'm gonna make you proud of me Grandma. *(Puts money in the old woman's hand.)* Here, we got time. This can't take that long.

OLD WOMAN: Gal, what difference would it make. You be back here six months tops singing the same song.

WOMAN: You don't know me. You don't know nothin' about me.

OLD WOMAN: Oh I know you. Ain't no job in New York. Ain't no place. Ain't no man. Just you and your pain.

WOMAN: Shut up you hear me. You shut up. *(Grabs the money back from the Old Woman.)* You think you're the only person in the world can do this? I don't need you. For your information, I don't want to end up like you. Crazy, old and poor and can't do nothing but make cobblers. *(The Old Woman crosses around the bed to RC and picks up her handbag and coat then turns and closes the Woman's small suitcase US of the window.)*

WOMAN: You want to pretend like you care about somebody. You ain't nothin' like my grandma. You couldn't hold a candle to her.

OLD WOMAN: Gal, ain't nobody studyin' you.

WOMAN: *(Stands and intimidates the Old Woman by pushing at her and blocking her from leaving the room.)* You're unimportant . . . small . . . old . . . little. Somebody, somebody done thrown away. You think they care if you vote? You think your vote even counts? You think you count? You got power? Please! Nobody needs you. *(The Old Woman crosses LC.)* I don't need you. And you can take your cobbler and your best wishes. *(Slamming the brown bag with the cobbler in it down on the floor in the Old Woman's direction.)*

OLD WOMAN: Gal, I know we shoulda said our good-byes yesterday.

WOMAN: *(Screams and throws money at the Old Woman.)* Grandma!!!

OLD WOMAN: Pick it up. *(The Woman gets down on floor to pick up money.)* Think I ain't got feelings. Think I ain't scared of nothin'. I'm scared when I get to the polls, my name won't be on that list. I'm scared to be left in a corner, legs gone, only thing to look forward to, death. Think I ain't human. *(Beat.)* Yes, I wish I had your youth, 'cause I'd do somethin' with it. Yes, I wish I had your opportunities, 'cause I'd do somethin' with 'em. Yes, I wish I had your money. I need the money. I wouldn't throw it at nobody's feet. The only reason I'm even here, because I want you to do better than me. Better than what your mama did. I wanted that for all of you. All my girls. I pray one of you do somethin'.

WOMAN: If I have her, I'm gonna drown her in the river. Here's all the money I have. *(Putting the money in the Old Woman's hand.)* Three hundred dollars. Three hundred presidents do more for you then that one you want to vote for. Just please don't leave me. I don't have no place else to go.

OLD WOMAN: I have to leave you child. There's death in here. *(Throws money on bed.)* Lord, I know that we should have said our good-byes yesterday.

FADE TO BLACK

During the transition into the jail scene, the following radio announcement is heard.)

"GOOD MORNING MEMPHIS. IT'S OFFICIAL. RONALD WILSON REAGAN HAS BECOME THE FORTIETH PRESIDENT OF THE UNITED STATES, THIS NOVEMER MORNING, BEATING PRESIDENT JIMMY CARTER IN A LANDSLIDE VISTORY. HE'S PROMISING WELFARE REFORM AND A TURN AROUND TO THIS SLUMPING ECONOMY. IN OTHER NEWS TODAY THE AMERICAN HOSTAGES ARE STILL BEING HELD IN IRAN. AND THE WEATHER FORECAST IS, RAIN, AND MORE RAIN . . . "

Scene Two

A prison interview room a short time later. There is a large wooden table with two chairs around it. The window has bars on it. It is raining very hard and periodic thunder can be heard and lightning can be seen illuminating the window. The lights come up with the sound of a metal door sliding shut. The Young Woman, now a sophisticated attorney, enters, wearing glasses, smartly dressed and carrying an attaché and crosses C to the table where the Old Woman is seated but stands when she sees the Young Woman.

YOUNG WOMAN: Hello. *(The Old Woman looks up at the Young Woman.)* I'm . . . *(Puts her attaché down on the floor and sits in the SR chair.)*

OLD WOMAN: *(Interrupting her.)* What's the matter? You look like you just saw a ghost. I ain't dead yet. I think they trying to put me in the electric chair though. You the woman I talked to on the phone yesterday?

YOUNG WOMAN: Yes.

OLD WOMAN: You my lawyer, right?

YOUNG WOMAN: Yes.

OLD WOMAN: You ain't got much to say for a mouthpiece do you?

YOUNG WOMAN: Well. It's not that. It's just that . . .

OLD WOMAN: *(Interrupting her.)* You didn't expect to see a old black woman like me standing here charged with murder?

YOUNG WOMAN: I just pictured you a little different. That's all.

OLD WOMAN: You don't read the papers do you? They had my picture plastered all over 'em. Wouldn't a been a bad picture neither if the words "arrested for murder" weren't under it. I always wanted to make the social page, but not like this. Mind if I sit down. My feet are bothering me something terrible.

YOUNG WOMAN: Please. Are you OK? I can ask the guard to bring you some water and aspirin or . . .

OLD WOMAN: No. No. *(Smiles admirably at the Young Woman.)*

YOUNG WOMAN: I know this isn't exactly the Sheraton, but if you need something let me know.

OLD WOMAN: *(Rubbing her knees and legs.)* No. no, honey. I'm fine. I'm fine. Just old and tired and wanna get out of here s'all.

YOUNG WOMAN: This hasn't been no day at the beach huh?

OLD WOMAN: Took the words right out of my mouth. They got me in one of those holding cells with a bunch of young women. Keep a whole lot of noise going. They 'bout to drive me crazy. *(Continues to smile at the Young Woman.)*

YOUNG WOMAN: *(Smiles at her, then opens briefcase.)* I've gone over what evidence and information the district attorney has on your case so . . .

OLD WOMAN: *(Interrupting her.)* I knew you was black.

YOUNG WOMAN: Pardon me?

OLD WOMAN: Even though you didn't sound like it on the phone. When they arrested me, I called my son Thomas. Smart boy. Work for the post office twenty-three years. I told him to find me a good lawyer. Get me out of this mess. You can do that. Can't you?

YOUNG WOMAN: *(Touching her hand.)* I can try my best. Like I told you on the phone, I've only been out of law school a few years. I'm what you call an associate . . . like a junior attorney. But my law firm has a long history of successes and a lot of very good seasoned senior attorneys who will help me on this case. You'll get the best representation. I promise.

OLD WOMAN: Forgive me for staring. I ain't never seen a black woman lawyer befor'. Not in the flesh.

YOUNG WOMAN: Well, there're more and more of us every year.

OLD WOMAN: A black girl, young . . . and a lawyer. My, my. And work for a firm. Got a suit and a briefcase. I ain't scared to have you represent me neither.

YOUNG WOMAN: What?

OLD WOMAN: Some people think 'cause you female and black . . . don't know your dooky hole from your elbow. Excuse my colorful tongue, but you know what I mean.

YOUNG WOMAN: Yes. Unfortunately I do. But we're not going to let that stop us.

OLD WOMAN: Ain't stopped us befor'. Ain't gonna stop us now.

YOUNG WOMAN: Yes ma'am.

OLD WOMAN: I didn't kill that girl you know. Ain't never laid a eye on her before in my life.

YOUNG WOMAN: *(Reaching in her briefcase, picks up papers.)* Well, all the evidence they have against you is purely circumstantial. Meaning evidence not bearing directly on the fact. In this case, her death or the botched abortion that led to it. *(Picks up another paper.)* The Coroner lists the cause of death as septicemia. *(Looks up at the Old Woman.)* Infection. She died of an infection. She never stated where she got the abortion or who performed it. All they found on her person that links her to you is a card with your address and phone number. *(Putting papers back on table.)* Circumstantial. Purely circumstantial.

OLD WOMAN: But what does all that mean though? 'Cause she dead and she got my phone number and address in her pocketbook mean I killed her?

YOUNG WOMAN: It boils down to that. They may have some evidence or some reason to suspect that you performed abortions. But they don't have to. She was found in a motel in a black neighborhood she didn't live in. Speculating, she went there to have the abortion or to recuperate and never recovered.

OLD WOMAN: They ain't got no reason to believe I did nothing like that to that girl. I'm just a old woman who minds her business. Don't want no business to mind me. They got somebody say I did it?

YOUNG WOMAN: I don't know. This is all the information I have right here. But if this is it, tomorrow at your arraignment, I will ask the judge to dismiss the charges against you for lack of evidence.

OLD WOMAN: You make it sound so easy.

YOUNG WOMAN: That is the easy part. Hard part starts if the judge denies my request.

OLD WOMAN: Um! Funny how things can affect you. Here it is some young girl come to my neighborhood and die. They want to put me in jail for the rest of my life for it. Why didn't she just go to the hospital when she saw she was feeling poorly. The papers say that girl was more than four months gone. Um! Stupid. Stupid. Stupid. Stupid.

YOUNG WOMAN: Or scared. Or confused. Or just ashamed.

OLD WOMAN: Same thing. If they cause you to lose your life, they all lead to stupid.

YOUNG WOMAN: And abortions are legal now. She didn't have to go to the quote unquote back alley.

OLD WOMAN: Um! Yeah, they legal. But only a hand full of doctors do 'em here. Cost so much. Three, four hundred dollars. At least that's what I hear. Some people ain't got money like that.

YOUNG WOMAN: Guess all she had was fifty dollars.

OLD WOMAN: Honey it cost more than fifty dollars, get yourself set straight waaay back when I was young. Fifty dollars got to be the rate for family and friends. Hundred, hundred fifty at least what it cost ten years ago. Befor' they made all this legal. So I hear. Ain't never been none of my business.

YOUNG WOMAN: *(Shocked.)* Yes. I suppose you're right. You can't get yourself nothing for fifty dollars. *(Long pause as she gets up from table and walks center stage away from the Old Woman, stops, her back to the Old Woman.)* Your son Thomas . . . you say he referred me to you?

OLD WOMAN: That's right. He's a supervisor at the post office. Know a lot of people and a regular walking encyclopedia of information. But he got your name from his son Tyrone.

YOUNG WOMAN: Tyrone! If that ain't a players name, I pray for lying.

OLD WOMAN: Um. Player since the day he was born. Always running to his grandma get him out the trouble. Cold in here. Place sho gives me a chill. Looks like it's never gonna stop raining. Like in the Bible, forty days and forty nights. I hate it when it rains like this. Dark and dreary. Sad and lonely.

YOUNG WOMAN: I don't know. I've had some of my most memorable times on a dark, rainy night.

OLD WOMAN: Um. It's funny you would say that. I use to love a rainy night myself. The harder the better. Give me a reason to get all cozy. You know what I mean? Me and Bay. Together twenty-five years. We had a fight, day he died. Never got to say I was sorry.

YOUNG WOMAN: I'm sorry to hear that. I didn't know you lost your husband. I was hoping he could give you an alibi.

OLD WOMAN: No ma'am. He can't help me no more. And all the water in the Mississippi can't put out this fire burning in my heart. You married?

YOUNG WOMAN: Yes. Two years now.

OLD WOMAN: Umm. You still on your honeymoon. No wonder you like a rainy evening. Pardon me for asking, but if you the lawyer, who wear the pants in the house?

YOUNG WOMAN: My husband's a lawyer too. So I guess we both do. How long has your husband been gone?

OLD WOMAN: Um. It's been more than a dozen years. Died on the same day as Dr. Martin Luther King. Hope he went to heaven with him. I hope he had the chance to tell King thank you for everything. Thank you for coming all the way to Memphis. If they acted right in the first place . . . King wouldn't a been shot in Memphis. Wouldn't a died in Memphis. Black folks wouldn't a be so mad they burn down they own buildings where they had to live. Bay and King might be alive today. And I wouldn't be here. 'Cause I'd be in my own home. Maybe have my picture in the paper for grandma of the year. And I'd be with Bay. I'd be with Bay.

YOUNG WOMAN: If only we could see into the future in the first place, we wouldn't get into trouble . . . make bad choices. We wouldn't get on the plane that was going to crash or turn head-on into oncoming traffic or stay in a burning building with no way out. We wouldn't love, because the people we love may die. We wouldn't have children, they may disappoint us. We wouldn't love a man that was going to leave us or die trying to get rid of babies we don't want 'cause he's gone, and can't afford, even if he stayed. We wouldn't live, because there's pain in living. Everything hurts . . . eventually. We can only pray for wisdom and make the best choices at that time.

OLD WOMAN: (Stands.) I don't need no young woman give me no lecture on life. What you know about it? What you know about anything?

YOUNG WOMAN: I know I'm standing on the shoulders of many people. Hope one day somebody will stand on my shoulders. Bay won. I'm proof of that.

OLD WOMAN: Bay's dead. He's gone. And I'm old and alone. What you know about it? What do you care?

YOUNG WOMAN: I know. I know. And I care.

OLD WOMAN: Care? About what?

YOUNG WOMAN: *(Stands, takes off glasses.)* About you. I'm here to help you. Look at me. Please look at me. *(Beat.)* Grandma!! *(Beat, as the Old Woman turns and looks hard at her.)* The name Lucy means light.

OLD WOMAN: Lucy?

YOUNG WOMAN: It took a long time to find her, but I finally did . . . in a little church in New York.

OLD WOMAN: What you talking about? Found who?

YOUNG WOMAN: I went to law school in New York. New York has a whole lot of churches. Hundreds of them. I must have called fifty before I finally found her . . . Saint Lucy with her plate of eyes.

OLD WOMAN: *(Crossing DR.)* Who told you about Saint Lucy?

YOUNG WOMAN: According to tradition, she was born to noble parents in Sicily. *(Crosses DL of table.)* Her mother arranged for her to marry a pagan gentleman. *(The Old Woman turns to the Young Woman.)* But she refused. She had decided to offer herself and her virginity to God. And so, because she rejected him, he exposed her as a Christian. Seems in 300 AD you were persecuted for being Christian. Ironically, the governor sentenced her to life in a brothel. But when the guards tried to take her, they were unable to move her. They tried to burn her to death, but the flames make no impression on her. Finally, they stabbed her and cut her throat. She died in prison. One tradition has her eyes torn out by her judge. In another, she tore them out herself to present them to the man who condemned her. In both cases, they were miraculously restored. Seems whatever blinds you, faith can help you see again.

OLD WOMAN: *(Crosses to the UR corner of table.)* During the strike, you put your cans out if you were against the strike and the city picked up your trash.

YOUNG WOMAN: The police report states that the woman had the abortion about four to five days before she died.

OLD WOMAN: If you were for the strike, you didn't put your cans out. Almost ten weeks of garbage.

YOUNG WOMAN: Somebody had been taking care of her. The room was clean, the bedding, the floor. She was clean. And she could not have had the strength to take care of herself. Somebody brought her food everyday. Somebody took loving care of her.

OLD WOMAN: White folks wondered where black folks was hidin' all that garbage. Course, we wasn't makin' no money. Common sense tell you . . . no money, no groceries, no garbage.

YOUNG WOMAN: Somebody, the desk clerk, the housekeeper . . . somebody had to notice someone coming and going out of that room every day. Somebody saw something!

OLD WOMAN: I took the garbage out to where I worked. Put it in white folks trash out there in North Memphis, including a empty chitterlings bucket. Nobody questioned a thing.

YOUNG WOMAN: We have to be able to show that the person wasn't you. That you were nowhere near that motel. That it couldn't of been you.

OLD WOMAN: In all that time, Bay never asked where the garbage went. All he knew was it was gone. Poof! Like magic. People want you to get rid of they garbage. They just don't want to know how. *(Counter-cross: She crosses to DL corner of table as the Young Woman crosses to the UR corner of the table. She has her back to the Young Woman. Long pause.)* I didn't kill that girl.

YOUNG WOMAN: I know you didn't. Stupidity killed her.

OLD WOMAN: Or maybe she did die trying to get from where it's dark, up somewhere where it's brighter. *(Beat.)* You must think I'm a monster.

YOUNG WOMAN: A monster?

OLD WOMAN: How long have you known I was Tyrone's grandmother?

YOUNG WOMAN: *(Regaining her composure.)* I don't know anyone named Tyrone. And before you walked through that door, I ain't never laid an eye on you before.

The Old Woman smiles acknowledging her response. Thunder can be heard rumbling in the distance. She turns slightly toward window.

OLD WOMAN: Does the Lord still talk to you?

YOUNG WOMAN: All the time.

OLD WOMAN: What He say?

YOUNG WOMAN: That He loves you. That He forgives you. That He's going to stand by you.

A louder burst of thunder is heard.

OLD WOMAN: What's He saying now?

YOUNG WOMAN: That you have to love and forgive yourself. But that ain't the Lord. That's just the storm. Just the storm.

OLD WOMAN: I swear I didn't kill that girl.

YOUNG WOMAN: I'm going to help you prove it.

OLD WOMAN: What's this gonna cost me?

YOUNG WOMAN: Fifty dollars. That's my price for relatives and friends. But you're going to need a little more than that to make bail.

OLD WOMAN: I ain't never seen it this dark.

YOUNG WOMAN: Who was it that said, only when it's darkest, can you see the stars? *(Moves toward the Old Woman.)*

OLD WOMAN: *(Looking at the Young Woman.)* Only somebody who stood in the dark and wasn't afraid to open they eyes and see. *(Beat.)* Forgive me for staring, but I'm looking at a lawyer, got a suit on and a briefcase and work for a firm. My my!

YOUNG WOMAN: Somebody told me to go out there and shine.

OLD WOMAN: Shine like a new silver dollar.

YOUNG WOMAN: Yes ma'am. Now, we have to get to work on what to do if the Judge denies my request for dismissal. It's going to be a battle. But we're going to fight it together. *(Extends her hand to the Old Woman.)* OK!

OLD WOMAN: *(Taking her hand, shaking it.)* OK!

YOUNG WOMAN: *(Hugs the Old Woman.)* It ain't gonna rain no more. You hear me Grandma. It ain't gonna rain no more.

Lights fade to black.

END OF ACT TWO

Appendix:
WPP Production Chronology

Thanks to our co-producers: The Acting Company, American Music Theater Festival, Classic Stage Company, Houston Grand Opera, INTAR, Los Angeles Theatre Center, Music-Theatre Group, New Federal Theatre, New Georges, Pan Asian Repertory, Playwrights Horizons, Portland Stage Company, P.S. 122, and The Public Theater/New York Shakespeare Festival.

1978–1979

Choices

Conceived by Patricia Bosworth
Adapted by Patricia Bosworth,
    Caymichael Patten, and Lily
    Lodge
Directed by Caymichael Patten
Sets and costumes by A. Christina
    Giannini
Lights by Larry Crimmins
Nov. 30–Dec. 17, 1978
The American Place Theatre*

Signs of Life

By Joan Schenkar
Directed by Esther Herbst
Costumes by Whitney Blausen and
    Walker Hicklin
Lights by Pat Stern
June 1–10, 1979
The American Place Theatre

Warriors From a Long Childhood

By Lavonne Mueller
Directed by Betsy Shevey
Sets by Henry Millman
Costumes by K. L. Fredericks
Lights by Ira Mark Lichtman
May 17–27, 1979
The American Place Theatre

Letters Home

By Rose Leiman Goldemberg
Directed by Dorothy Silver
Sets by Henry Millman
Costumes by Susan Denison
Lights by Kathleen Giebler
Oct. 12–Nov. 4, 1979
The American Place Theatre

---

*Theatre name indicates location of production.

1979–1980

Holy Places
By Gail Kriegel Mallin
Directed by Victoria Rue
Sets and costumes by Kate Edmunds
Lights by Annie Wrightson
Dec. 6-16, 1979
The American Place Theatre

Milk of Paradise
By Sallie Bingham
Directed by Joan Vail Thorne
Sets by William Barclay
Costumes by Mimi Maxmen
Lights by Annie Wrightson
Feb. 28–Mar. 9, 1980
The American Place Theatre

Personals
Directed by Julianne Boyd
Music by Michael Ward
Sets by Patricia Woodbridge
Costumes by Rachel Kurland
Lights by Bill Ballou
May 8–18, 1980
The American Place Theatre

1980–1981

After the Revolution
By Nadja Tesich
Directed by Joyce Aaron
Sets by Christina Weppner
Costumes by Sally Lesser and
    Kathleen Smith
Lights by Frances Aronson
Nov. 11–23, 1980
The American Place Theatre

Still Life
Written and Directed by Emily Mann
Sets and costumes by Tom Lynch
Lights by Annie Wrightson
Feb. 10–22, 1981
The American Place Theatre

Constance and the Musician
Book and lyrics by Caroline Kava
Music by Mel Marvin
Directed by Joan Micklin Silver
Sets by William Barclay
Costumes by Whitney Blausen
Lights by Judy Rasmuson
June 10–21, 1981
The American Place Theatre

1981–1982

The Death of a Miner

By Paula Cizmar
Directed by Barbara Rosoff
Sets by Leslie Taylor
Costumes by Heidi Hollmann
Lights by Arden Fingerhut
Feb. 24–Mar. 14, 1982
The American Place Theatre

The Brothers

By Kathleen Collins
Directed by Billie Allen
Sets by Christina Weppner
Costumes by K. L. Fredericks
Lights by Ann Wrightson
Music by Michael Minard
Mar. 31–Apr. 11, 1982
The American Place Theatre

1982–1983

Little Victories

By Lavonne Mueller
Directed by Bryna Wortman
Sets by William M. Barclay
Costumes by Mimi Maxmen
Lights by Phil Monat
Music by Clay Fullum
Sound by Regina M. Mullen
Jan. 26–Feb. 13, 1983
The American Place Theatre

Heart of a Dog

Written and performed by Terry
    Galloway
Directed by Suzanne Bennett
Sets by Maxine Willi Klein
Costumes by Mimi Maxmen
Lights by Joni Wong
Sound by Jane Pipik
June 1–4, 8–11, 1983
The American Place Theatre

Territorial Rites

By Carol K. Mack
Directed by Josephine Abady
Sets by David Potts
Costumes by Mimi Maxmen
Lights by Frances Aronson
Sound by Gary Harris
June 1–12, 1983
The American Place Theatre

1983–1984

A . . . My Name Is Alice

Conceived and directed by
   Joan Micklin Silver and
   Julianne Boyd
Sets by Adrianne Lobel
Costumes by Mimi Maxmen
Lights by Ann Wrightson
Choreography by Yvonne Adrian
Music direction by Jan Rosenberg
Nov. 2–14, 1983
The American Place Theatre

A Festival of Six One-Act Plays and One Studio Production*

Sets by Johniene Papandreas
Costumes by Mimi Maxmen and
   Judy Dearing
Lights by Jane Reisman
Sound by Bruce Ellman
Mar. 19–April 1, 1984
The American Place Theatre

Special Family Things
By Ara Watson and Mary Gallagher
Directed by Page Burkholder

The Only Woman General
By Lavonne Mueller
Directed by Bryna Wortman

A Festival of Six One-Act Plays and One Studio Production* (continued)

Old Wives Tale
By Julie Jensen
Directed by Alma Becker

Aye Aye Aye I'm Integrated
By Anna Deavere Smith
Directed by Billie Allen

Candy & Shelley Go to the Desert
By Paula Cizmar
Directed by Carey Perloff

The Longest Walk
By Janet Thomas
Directed by Claudia Weill

To Heaven in a Swing
Written and performed by Katharine
   Houghton
Directed by Joan Vail Thorne
Sets by Rosaria Sinisi
Costumes by David Toser
Lights by Anne Militello

---

*Production on tape at the New York Public Library for the Performing Arts.

1984–1985

Four Corners

Conceived, directed, and designed by
Gina Wendkos
Co-written by Gina Wendkos and
Donna Bond
Sets by Gina Wendkos
Costumes by Donna Bond
Lights by Anne Militello
Sound by Tom Gould
Feb. 6–17, 1985
The American Place Theatre

Paducah*

By Sallie Bingham
Directed by Joan Vail Thorne
Sets by Karen Schulz
Costumes by Mimi Maxmen
Lights by Anne Militello
Apr. 8–28, 1985
The American Place Theatre

1985–1986

Breaking the Prairie Wolf Code

By Lavonne Mueller
Directed by Liz Diamond
Sets by Richard Hoover
Costumes by Mimi Maxmen
Lights by Jane Reisman
Composed by Alice Eve Cohen
Nov. 13–Dec. 8, 1985
The American Place Theatre

Women Heroes: in Praise of Exceptional Women*

Sets by Marc D. Malamud and Ina
Mayhew
Costumes by Judy Dearing
Lights by Marc D. Malamud
Sound by Gary Harris
Mar. 21–April 6, 1986
The Samuel Beckett Theatre

Parallax
Written and directed by Denise
Hamilton

Personality
Written by Gina Wendkos and Ellen
Ratner
Co-Directed by Gina Wendkos and
Richard Press

How She Played the Game
By Cynthia L. Cooper
Directed by Bryna Wortman

Colette in Love
By Lavonne Mueller
Directed by Mirra Bank

Millie
By Susan J. Kander
Directed by Carol Tanzman

*Emma Goldman: Love, Anarchy, and
Other Affairs*
By Jessica Litwak
Directed by Anne Bogart

*Production on tape at the New York Public Library for the Performing Arts.

1986–1987

The Snicker Factor: An Evening of Political Satire

Conceived and directed by Suzanne
  Bennett and Liz Diamond
Music composed and directed by
  Adrienne Torf
Written by: Billy Aronson, William
  Boardman, Cynthia Cooper, Holly
  Hughes, Lavonne Mueller,
  Michael Quinn, Jack Shannon,
  Y. York
Lights by Nicole Werner
Feb. 9–20, 1987
The American Place Theatre

Consequence

By Kat Smith
Directed by Alma Becker
Sets by Robert Perdziola
Costumes by Judy Dearing
Lights by Anne Militello
Sound by Aural Fixation
Mar. 18–Apr. 5, 1987
The American Place Theatre

1987–1988

Abingdon Square*

Written and directed by María Irene
  Fornés
Sets by Donald Eastman
Costumes by Sam Fleming
Lights by Anne Militello
Oct. 8–25, 1987
The American Place Theatre

Etta Jenks

By Marlane Gomard Meyer
Directed by Roberta Levitow
Sets by Rosario Provenza
Costumes by Ray C. Naylor
Lights by Robert Wierzel
Sound by Jon Gottlieb
Apr. 6–24, 1988
Apple Corps Theatre

Reverend Jenkins' Almost All-Colored Orphanage Band

By Gail Kriegel
Original music and arrangements by
  Luther Henderson
Directed by Vernel Bagneris
Sets and lights by Max Gorgal
Costumes by Jo Ann Clevenger
Music direction by Walter Payton
Sound by Reginald Toussaint
Nov. 27–Dec. 13, 1987
Le Petit Theatre du Vieux Carre,
New Orleans

---

*Production on tape at the New York Public Library for the Performing Arts.

1988–1989

Ma Rose*

By Cassandra Medley
Directed by Irving Vincent
Sets by Phillip Baldwin
Costumes by Judy Dearing
Lights by Pat Dignan
Sound by Aural Fixation
Oct. 11–30, 1988
Apple Corps Theatre

Ladies

By Eve Ensler
Music by Joshua Schneider
Directed by Paul Walker
Sets by Victoria Petrovich
Costumes by Donna Zakowska
Lights by Debra Dumas
Sound by John Kilgore
Mar.–Apr., 1989
St. Clement's Theater

Niedecker

By Kristine Thatcher
Directed by Julianne Boyd
Sets by James Noone
Costumes by Deborah Shaw
Lights by Frances Aronson
Sound by Bruce Ellman
Mar. 7–26, 1989
Apple Corps Theatre

1989–1990

Mill Fire

By Sally Nemeth
Directed by David Petrarca
Sets by Linda Buchanan
Costumes by Laura Cunningham
Lights by Robert Christen
Sound by Rob Milburn
Oct. 10–29, 1989
Apple Corps Theatre

Violent Peace*

By Lavonne Mueller
Directed by Bryna Wortman
Sets by James Noone
Costumes by Mimi Maxmen
Lights by Victor En Yu Tan
Sound by Bruce Ellman
Feb. 20–Mar. 11, 1990
Apple Corps Theatre

---

*Production on tape at the New York Public Library for the Performing Arts.

1989–1990 *(continued)*

Tales of the Lost Formicans*

By Constance Congdon
Directed by Gordon Edelstein
Sets by James Youmans
Costumes by Danielle Hollywood
Lights by Anne Militello
Composed by Melissa Shiflett
Sound by John Gromada
Apr. 17–May 6, 1990
Apple Corps Theatre

1990–1991

Day Trips

By Jo Carson
Directed by Billie Allen
Sets by James Noone
Costumes by Barbara Beccio
Lights by Anne Militello
Sound by Lia Vollack
Oct. 30–Nov. 25, 1990
The Judith Anderson Theatre

Night Sky*

By Susan Yankowitz
Directed by Joseph Chaikin
Sets by George Xenos
Costumes by Mary Brecht
Lights by Beverly Emmons
Sound by Mark Bennett
May 14–Jun. 9, 1991
The Judith Anderson Theatre

The Encanto File *and Other Short Plays*

Plays by: Rosa Lowinger, Marlane
    Meyer, Sally Nemeth, Mary Sue
    Price, Caridad Svich
Directed by: Melia Bensussen,
    Melanie Joseph, Susana Tubert
Sets by Mark Fitzgibbons
Costumes by Barbara Beccio
Lights by Franklin Meissner, Jr.
Sound by Bruce Ellman
Mar. 19–Apr. 14, 1991
The Judith Anderson Theatre

---

*Production on tape at the New York Public Library for the Performing Arts.

1991–1992

Approximating Mother

By Kathleen Tolan
Directed by Gloria Muzio
Sets by David Jenkins
Costumes by Elsa Ward
Lights by Jackie Manassee
Sound by Mark Bennett
Oct. 29–Nov. 24, 1991
The Judith Anderson Theatre

Lardo Weeping

Written and performed by Terry
    Galloway
Directed by Donna Marie Nudd
Costumes by Teresa Jaynes, Patricia
    Dominguez, and M. L. Baker
Music by Vivian Potts
Jan. 16–19, 1992
PS 122

Chain *and* The Late Bus to Mecca

By Pearl Cleage
Directed by Imani
Sets by George Xenos
Costumes by Ornyece
Lights by Melody Beal
Sound by Bill Toles
Feb. 28–Mar. 22, 1992
The Judith Anderson Theatre

Dream of a Common Language

By Heather McDonald
Directed by Liz Diamond
Sets by Anita Stewart
Costumes by Sally J. Lesser
Lights by Michael Chybowski
Composition and sound by
    Daniel Moses Schreier
May 13–June 7, 1992
The Judith Anderson Theatre

1992–1993

You Could Be Home Now

Written and performed by Ann
    Magnuson
Composed by Tom Judson
Directed by David Schweizer
Choreography by Jerry Mitchell
Sets by Bill Clarke
Costumes by Pilar Limosner
Lights by Heather Carson
Sound by Eric Liljestrand
Oct. 26–Nov. 1, 1992
Joseph Papp Public Theatre/
    Martinson Hall

The Brooklyn Trojan Women

By Carole Braverman
Directed by Margot Breier
Sets by Ted Glass
Costumes by Leslie Yarmo
Lights by Heather Rogan
Sound by Bart Fasbender
June 1–30, 1993
45th Street Theatre

Frida: The Story of Frida Kahlo

By Hilary Blecher
Puppetry by Michael Romanyshyn
Lyrics and monologues by Migdalia
    Cruz
Music by Robert Rodriguez
Oct. 14–25, 1992
Brooklyn Academy of Music

1993–1994

Eating Chicken Feet

By Kitty Chen
Directed by Kati Kuroda
Sets by Robert Klingelhoefer
Costumes by Hugh Hanson
Lights by Michael Chybowski
Sound by Jin van Bergen
Oct. 26–Nov. 20, 1993
Playhouse 46 at St. Clement's

Black

By Joyce Carol Oates
Directed by Tom Palumbo
Sets by David Mitchell
Costumes by Elsa Ward
Lights by Jackie Manassee
Sound by Bruce Ellman
Mar. 7–Apr. 3, 1994
INTAR Hispanic American Arts
    Center

1993–1994 *(continued)*

The Autobiography of Aiken Fiction

By Kate Moira Ryan
Directed by Adrienne Weiss
Sets by Narelle Sissons
Costumes by Angela Wendt
Lights by Rick Martin
Sound by Jennifer Sharpe
Apr. 26–May 15, 1992
The Samuel Beckett Theatre

1994–1995

Why We Have a Body

By Claire Chafee
Directed by Evan Yionoulis
Sets by Peter B. Harrison
Costumes by Teresa Snider-Stein
Lights by Donald Holder
Sound by Janet Kalas
Nov. 1–27, 1994
The Judith Anderson Theatre

The Last Girl Singer

By Deborah Grace Winer
Directed by Charles Maryan
Sets by Atkin Pace
Costumes by Lana Fritz
Lights by John Gleason
Sound by Darren Clark
Musical direction by John
  Wallowitch
May 2–28, 1995
Kampo Cultural Arts Center

1995–1996

Crocodiles in the Potomac

By Wendy Belden
Directed by Suzanne Bennett
Sets and lights by Roger Hanna
Costumes by Elizabeth Fried
Sound by Mark Bruckner
Oct. 19–Nov. 12, 1995
Theatre Row Theatre

1996–1997

Go Go Go

Written and performed by Juliana
    Francis
Directed by Anne Bogart
Oct. 25–Nov. 3, 1996
PS 122

Terra Incognito

Written and directed by María Irene
    Fornés
Music by Roberto Sierra
Sets by Van Santvoord
Costumes by Willa Kim
Lights by Philip Widmer
Musical direction by Stephen Gosling
Mar. 19–Apr. 13, 1997
INTAR Hispanic American Arts
    Center

Under a Western Sky

By Amparo Garcia
Directed by Loretta Greco
Sets by Christine Jones
Costumes by Kaye Voyce
Lights by Kevin Adams
Composer and sound by David van
    Tieghem
Apr. 23–May 18, 1997
INTAR Hispanic American Arts
    Center

1997–1998

The Water Children

By Wendy MacLeod
Directed by David Petrarca
Sets and lights by Michael Philippi
Costumes by Therese Bruck
Sound by Edward Cosla
Oct. 22–Nov. 16, 1997
Playwrights Horizons Studio Theatre

Phaedra in Delirium

By Susan Yankowitz
Directed by Alison Summers
Sets by Christine Jones
Costumes by Teresa Snider-Stein
Lights by Beverly Emmons
Sound by Fabian Obispo
Jan. 20–Feb. 15, 1998
Classic Stage Company

The Summer in Gossensass

Written and directed by María Irene
    Fornés
Sets by Donald Eastman
Costumes by Gabriel Berry
Lights by Philip Widmer
Mar. 31–Apr. 26, 1998
Judith Anderson Theatre

1998–1999

The Knee Desires Dirt

By Julie Hébert
Directed by Susana Tubert
Sets by Peter Harrison
Costumes by Tracy Dorman
Lights by David Higham
Original music and sound by Fabian
    Obispo
Oct. 27–Nov. 22, 1998
Women's Project Theatre

The Chemistry of Change

By Marlane Meyer
Directed by Lisa Peterson
Sets by Zhanna Gurvich and
    Christopher Barreca
Costumes by Katherine Roth
Lights by Kevin Adams
Sound by Laura Grace Brown
Feb. 10–Mar. 7, 1999
Women's Project Theatre

The Exact Center of the Universe

By Joan Vail Thorne
Directed by John Tillinger
Sets by Michael Brown
Costumes by Carrie Robbins
Lights by Philip Widmer
Sound by Laura Grace Brown
Mar. 30–Apr. 25, 1999
Women's Project Theatre

1999–2000

Gum

By Karen Hartman
Directed by Loretta Greco
Songs by Kim D. Sherman
Sets by Myung Hee Cho
Costumes by Elizabeth Hope Clancy
Lights by Frances Aronson
Sound by Obadiah Eaves
Oct. 6–31, 1999
Women's Project Theatre

Our Place in Time

By Clare Coss
Directed by Bryna Wortman
Sets by Narelle Sissons
Costumes by Gail Cooper-Hecht
Lights by Jane Cox
Sound by Stefan Jacobs
Jan. 26–Feb. 20, 2000
Women's Project Theatre

1999–2000 *(continued)*

Two-Headed

By Julie Jensen
Directed by Joan Vail Thorne
Sets by David P. Gordon
Costumes by Carrie Robbins
Lights by Michael Lincoln
Original music and sound by Scott
    Killian
May 3–28, 2000
Women's Project Theatre

2000–2001

Hard Feelings

By Neena Beber
Directed by Maria Mileaf
Sets by Neil Patel
Costumes by Katherine Roth
Lights by Russell Champa
Sound by Eileen Tague
Oct. 11–Nov. 4, 2000
Women's Project Theatre

Saint Lucy's Eyes*

By Bridgette A. Wimberly
Directed by Billie Allen
Sets by Beowulf Borritt
Costumes by Alvin B. Perry
Lights by Jane Reisman
Mar. 28–Apr. 22, 2001
Women's Project Theatre

Leaving Queens

Book and lyrics by Kate Moira Ryan
Music by Kim D. Sherman
Directed by Allison Narver
Musical direction by Paul J. Ascenzo
Sets by Anita Stewart
Costumes by Louisa Thompson
Lights by Jennifer Tipton
Feb. 25–Mar. 18, 2001
Women's Project Theatre

O Pioneers!

Adaptation and lyrics by Darrah
    Cloud
From the novel by Willa Cather
Music by Kim D. Sherman
Directed by Richard Corley
Musical direction by Kimberly
    Grigsby
Sets by Loy Arcenas
Costumes by Murell Dean Horton
Lights by Dennis Parichy
Sound design by David A. Arnold
May 2–13, 2001
Women's Project Theatre

---

*Production on tape at the New York Public Library for the Performing Arts.

2001–2002

Carson McCullers
(Historically Inaccurate)

By Sarah Schulman
Directed by Marion McClinton
Sets by Neil Patel
Costumes by Toni-Leslie James
Lights by Donald Holder
Sound design by Janet Kalas
Jan. 9–Feb. 3, 2002
Women's Project Theatre

Additional Contact and Copyright Information

LITTLE VICTORIES

A . . . MY NAME IS ALICE

Act I

Act II

PRETTY YOUNG MEN lyrics by Susan Birkenhead; music by Lucy Simon: Copyright © 1984 Calougie Music and Algebra. All rights reserved.

DEMIGOD by Richard LaGravanese: Copyright © 1984 Richard LaGravanese. All rights reserved.

THE FRENCH SONG lyrics and music by Don Tucker; monologue by Art Murray: Copyright © 1977 Murray and Tucker. All rights reserved.

PAY THEM NO MIND lyrics and music by Calvin Alexander and James Shorter: Copyright © 1965 Calvin Alexander/Gujim Records. All rights reserved.

HOT LUNCH by Anne Meara: Copyright © 1983 Anne Meara. All rights reserved.

EMILY, THE M.B.A. lyrics by Mark Saltzman; music by Stephen Lawrence: Copyright © 1983 SJL Music Co. All rights reserved.

SISTERS lyrics by Maggie Bloomfield; music by Cheryl Hardwick: Copyright © 1983 Bloomwick Publishing. All rights reserved.

HONEYPOT lyrics by Mark Saltzman; music by Stephen Lawrence: Copyright © 1983 SJL Music Co. All rights reserved.

ABINGDON SQUARE

ETTA JENKS

THE EXACT CENTER OF THE UNIVERSE

rights, motion picture, recitation, lecturing, public reading, radio broadcasting, television, video or sound recording, all other forms of mechanical or electronic reproduction, such as CD-ROM, CD-I, DVD, information storage and retrieval systems and photocopying, and the rights of translation into foreign languages, are strictly reserved. Particular emphasis is laid upon the matter of readings, permission for which must be secured from the author's agent in writing.

The English language stock and amateur stage performance rights in the United States, its territories, possessions, and Canada for *The Exact Center of the Universe* are controlled exclusively by DRAMATISTS PLAY SERVICE, INC., 440 Park Avenue South, New York, NY 10016. No professional or nonprofessional performance of the Play may be given without obtaining in advance the written permission of DRAMATISTS PLAY SERVICE, INC., and paying the requisite fee.

Inquiries concerning all other rights should be addressed to Helen Merrill Ltd., 295 Lafayette Street, Suite 915, New York, NY 10012. Attn: Beth Blickers.

SAINT LUCY'S EYES